第一部分：辨識句意（第 1-3 題）

1. (**C**) (A)　　　　　(B)　　　　　(C)

Jennifer has just finished eating her pizza, and she's very content. 珍妮佛剛吃完她的披薩，而且非常滿足。

* finish〔'fɪnɪʃ〕*v.* 完成　　pizza〔'pitsə〕*n.* 披薩
  content〔kən'tɛnt〕*adj.* 滿足的

2. (**C**) (A)　　　　　(B)　　　　　(C)

It's Valentine's Day. I'd better buy some roses for Mom.
今天是情人節。我最好買些玫瑰花送媽媽。

* Valentine's Day〔'vælən͵taɪnz 'de〕*n.* 情人節
  had better V. 最好～　　rose〔roz〕*n.* 玫瑰

3. (**B**) (A)　　　　　(B)　　　　　(C)

John bought a new pair of shoes and a watch, and he paid four thousand five hundred dollars.

約翰買了一雙新鞋和一支手錶，他付了四千五百元。

* *a pair of* 一雙　　pay〔pe〕*v.* 付（錢）【三態變化：pay-paid-paid】

第二部分：基本問答（第 4-10 題）

4. (**A**) How do you pronounce your last name, James?

詹姆士，你的姓怎麼唸？

(A) Lee-ow. Sounds like meow. 廖。聽起來像喵。

(B) J-A-M-E-S. J-A-M-E-S。

(C) 2655-0991. 2655-0991。

* pronounce〔prəˋnauns〕*v.* 發音
last name 姓【first name 名】
sound〔saund〕*v.* 聽起來　　meow〔mıˋau〕*n.* 喵喵【貓叫聲】

5. (**B**) Is that your friend Thomas sitting by himself?

獨自坐在那裡的，是你朋友湯瑪斯嗎？

(A) Thanks. I'm glad you like it. 謝謝。我很高興你喜歡。

(B) It is. Let's go see if he wants company.

沒錯。我們去看看他要不要人陪。

(C) He didn't say. I'm not sure where he went.

他沒說。我不確定他去哪裡。

* *by* oneself 獨自　　glad〔glæd〕*adj.* 高興的
go see 去看（= *go and see*）　　if〔ıf〕*conj.* 是否
company〔ˋkʌmpənı〕*n.* 同伴；陪伴　　sure〔ʃur〕*adj.* 確定的

6. (**A**) Do you have an extra pencil I could borrow for the class period? 你有多的鉛筆能借我在這堂課用嗎？

(A) I'm afraid I don't. 我恐怕沒有。

(B) You should have told me. 你早該跟我說的。

(C) The class was canceled. 那堂課被取消了。

* extra〔'ɛkstrə〕*adj.* 額外的　　borrow〔'bɑro〕*v.* 借用
period〔'pɪrɪəd〕*n.* 期間　　***I'm afraid (that)***… 恐怕…
should have + pp. 早該…　　cancel〔'kænsḷ〕*v.* 取消

7. (**A**) Have you ever taken a ferry boat to Dolphin Island?
你曾經搭過渡輪到海豚島嗎？

(A) Yes, I have. <u>是的，我有過。</u>

(B) Yes, I was. 是的，我曾經是。

(C) Yes, I am. 是的，我是。

* ever〔'ɛvɚ〕*adv.* 曾經　　ferry〔'fɛrɪ〕*n.* 渡輪
dolphin〔'dɑlfɪn〕*n.* 海豚　　island〔'aɪlənd〕*n.* 島

8. (**C**) What color are your eyes? Are they green or blue?
你的眼睛是什麼顏色的？是綠色還是藍色的？

(A) They are round. 它們是圓的。

(B) They are square. 它們是正方形的。

(C) They are blue. <u>它們是藍色的。</u>

* square〔skwɛr〕*adj.* 正方形的

9. (**A**) Does this bus stop at the World Trade Center?
這輛公車有停在世貿中心嗎？

(A) You had better ask the driver. <u>你最好問司機。</u>

(B) I think the fare is $1.50. 我想車資是一塊五毛。

(C) That's a fair trade. 那是公平的交易。

* trade〔tred〕*n.* 貿易；交易　　***World Trade Center*** 世貿中心
fare〔fɛr〕*n.* 車資　　fair〔fɛr〕*adj.* 公平的

10. (**C**) Do you like my new hairstyle? 你喜歡我的新髮型嗎？

(A) It feels wonderful! 感覺很棒！

(B) It sounds good! 聽起來很好！

(C) It looks great! <u>看起來很好看！</u>

* hairstyle〔'hɛr,staɪl〕*n.* 髮型　　feel〔fil〕*v.* 使人感覺
wonderful〔'wʌndəfəl〕*adj.* 極好的　　　great〔gret〕*adj.* 很棒的

第三部分：言談理解（第 11-21 題）

11. (**A**)　M：Did I miss anything in chemistry class yesterday, Nancy?

　　　　男：昨天化學課我有錯過任何事嗎，南西？

　　　　W：Not really, Joe.　We reviewed the chapter on gases and watched a video.

　　　　女：其實沒有，喬。我們複習關於氣體的章節還有看影片。

　　　　Question：What do we know about the speakers?

　　　　　　　　我們知道關於說話者的什麼事？

　　　　(A) They are classmates.　他們是同學。

　　　　(B) They are co-workers.　他們是同事。

　　　　(C) They are siblings.　他們是兄弟姊妹。

　　　* miss〔mɪs〕*v.* 錯過　　chemistry〔'kɛmɪstrɪ〕*n.* 化學
　　　not really 其實沒有　　review〔rɪ'vju〕*v.* 複習
　　　chapter〔'tʃæptə〕*n.* 章　　on〔ɑn〕*prep.* 關於
　　　gas〔gæs〕*n.* 氣體　　video〔'vɛdɪo〕*n.* 影片
　　　co-worker〔ko'wɜkə〕*n.* 同事
　　　siblings〔'sɪblɪŋz〕*n. pl.* 兄弟姊妹

12. (**B**)　M：Hey, Nina.　I don't know if you've heard, but a bunch of us are going to spend the day at Swanson Beach tomorrow.　You're welcome to join us.

　　　　男：嘿，妮娜，我不知道妳是否有聽到，但我們一夥人明天要去史望森海灘玩一天。歡迎妳加入我們。

　　　　W：No, I didn't hear anything about it, Brad.　Who's going?

女：不，我完全沒聽說這件事，布萊德。有誰要去？

M : Me, Jenny, Vince, Debbie, and the Gracie twins.
　　Tom, Betty, and Jerry might come if their parents say
　　it's OK.

男：我、珍妮、文斯、戴比，和葛雷西雙胞胎。如果父母同意，
　　湯姆、貝蒂，和傑瑞可能會來。

W : It's nice of you to invite me, Brad, but I have to help
　　my mother around the house tomorrow.

女：你人真好還邀請我，布萊德，但我明天必須幫我媽做家事。

M : Too bad, but listen.　If you finish up early, you know
　　where to find us.　We'll be there pretty late, too.
　　Vince and I are going to build a bonfire at sunset.

男：太可惜了，但聽著。如果妳提早做完，妳知道去那裡可以找
　　到我們。我們也會在那裡待到很晚。文斯和我在日落時要架
　　設營火。

W : Gosh, sounds like fun.　Maybe next time.

女：哎呀，聽起來很好玩。也許要下次了。

Question : Why won't Nina spend the day at the beach?
　　　　　　為什麼妮娜不能去海灘玩一天？

(A) She has to study.　她必須唸書。

(B) She has household chores.　<u>她要做家事。</u>

(C) She burns easily.　她很容易曬黑。

* bunch〔bʌntʃ〕*n.* 一群　　join〔dʒɔɪn〕*v.* 參加
　twins〔twɪnz〕*n. pl.* 雙胞胎　　invite〔ɪn'vaɪt〕*v.* 邀請
　help** sb. **around the house 幫忙某人做家事
　finish up 做完　　pretty〔'prɪtɪ〕*adv.* 相當
　build〔bɪld〕*v.* 建造　　bonfire〔'bɑn,faɪr〕*n.* 營火
　sunset〔'sʌn,sɛt〕*n.* 日落　　gosh〔gɑʃ〕*interj.* 哎呀！；糟糕！
　fun〔fʌn〕*n.* 有趣　　maybe〔'mebi〕*adv.* 可能；或許

household〔'haʊs,hold〕*adj.* 家庭的　　chores〔tʃɔrz〕*n. pl.* 雜事
household chores 家事　　burn〔bɜn〕*v.*（皮膚）曬黑

13. (**B**) M：Do you have any specials today?

男：你們今天有什麼特餐嗎？

W：Yes, we're offering fried chicken and cornbread for $7.99.

女：有，我們提供炸雞和玉米麵包，只要七點九九元。

M：That sounds good.　I'll have that.

男：聽起來不錯。我要吃那個。

Question：What did the man order?　男士點了什麼？

(A) Pizza. 披薩。

(B) Fried chicken. 炸雞。

(C) Pasta. 義大利麵。

* special〔'spɛʃəl〕*n.* 特餐　　offer〔'ɔfɚ〕*v.* 提供
fried chicken 炸雞　　cornbread〔'kɔrn,brɛd〕*n.* 玉米麵包
sound〔saʊnd〕*v.* 聽起來　　have〔hæv〕*v.* 吃
order〔'ɔrdɚ〕*v.* 點（餐）　　pasta〔'pɑstə〕*n.* 義大利麵

14. (**C**) W：This has to be the most boring concert I've been to so far.

女：這一定是我到目前為止聽過最無聊的音樂會。

M：Why is that?　Don't you like Mozart?

男：為什麼這麼說？妳不喜歡莫札特嗎？

W：Of course, I love Mozart.　This performance lacks energy.

女：我當然很喜愛莫札特。這個表演缺乏活力。

M：Maybe they're holding back for the second half.

男：也許他們是為了下半場而保留實力。

W：I'm not counting on it.

女：我不指望了。

Question : What does the woman mean by "I'm not
　　　　　counting on it"?

　　　女生說的那句「我不指望了」是什麼意思？

(A) A friend is waiting for her. 有個朋友正在等她。

(B) She has a problem with numbers. 她不喜歡算術。

(C) The performance won't get better. 表演不會變得更好。

* boring〔'borɪŋ〕*adj.* 無聊的　　concert〔'kɑnsɝt〕*n.* 音樂會
have ever been to 曾經去過　　***so far*** 到目前爲止
Mozart〔'mozɑrt〕*n.* 莫札特
performance〔pɚ'fɔrməns〕*n.* 表演　　lack〔læk〕*v.* 缺乏
energy〔'ɛnɚdʒɪ〕*n.* 活力　　***hold back*** 抑制；保留
half〔hæf〕*n.* 一半　　***the second half*** 下半場；後半場
count on 依靠；指望　　***have a problem with*** sth. 不喜歡某事
numbers〔'nʌmbɚz〕*n. pl.* 算術

15. (**A**) M : Yeah, so… Belgium was great. I loved it. So, how
　　　　　　　was your summer abroad, Michelle?

　　　男：是啊，所以…比利時很棒。我愛比利時。那麼，蜜雪兒，妳
　　　　　在國外的暑假如何呢？

　　　W : Amazing! I met so many new people, but the time
　　　　　went by so fast.

　　　女：很棒！我認識了許多新朋友，但時間過得好快。

　　　M : I know what you mean. Eight weeks goes by so fast.
　　　　　It hardly seemed like a vacation at all.

　　　男：我知道妳的意思，八週的時間很快就過去了。幾乎不像是個
　　　　　假期。

　　　W : I can't wait until we're in college and have more
　　　　　time off.

　　　女：我等不及以後我們大學時，能有更多的時間放假。

　　　Question : What do we know about the speakers?

　　　　　　　我們能知道關於說話者的什麼事？

(A) They both traveled abroad during the summer.

  他們兩人都在暑假期間出國旅遊。

(B) They both got accepted to a good school.

  他們兩人都考上好學校。

(C) They both spent time in Belgium.

  他們兩人都在比利時待過一段時間。

* yeah〔jɛ〕*n.* 是的（= *yes*）　　Belgium〔'bɛldʒəm〕*n.* 比利時
  abroad〔ə'brɔd〕*adv.* 在國外
  amazing〔ə'mezɪŋ〕*adj.* 很棒的　　meet〔mit〕*n.* 遇見；認識
  time goes by so fast 時光飛逝　　hardly〔'hɑrdlɪ〕*adv.* 幾乎不
  seem〔sim〕*v.* 似乎　　vacation〔ve'keʃən〕*n.* 假期
  at all 絲毫　　*can't wait* 等不及
  college〔'kɑlɪdʒ〕*n.* 大學　　off〔ɔf〕*adv.* 休息
  during〔'djʊrɪŋ〕*prep.* 在…期間　　accept〔ək'sɛpt〕*v.* 接受

16. (**B**) W : Lunch is on me, Simon.

  女：賽門，午餐我請客。

  M : No, Lori! You paid last time.

  男：洛莉，不行！上次是妳付的。

  W : That's OK. I just got a bonus at work.

  女：沒關係。我剛拿到工作獎金。

  M : Wow, that's good for you! But promise that next time you'll let me pay.

  男：哇，妳真棒！但答應我，下次妳要讓我買單。

  W : It's a deal.

  女：一言為定。

  Question : What does Lori mean by "It's a deal"?

  　　　洛莉說「一言為定」是什麼意思？

  (A) She feels cheated. 她覺得被騙。

  (B) She agrees with the man. 她同意男士的意見。

  (C) She paid last time. 上次是她付錢。

* ***Lunch is on me***. 午餐我請客。　　***last time*** 上次
  That's OK. 沒關係。　　　bonus〔'bonəs〕*n.* 獎金
  wow〔waʊ〕*interj.* 哇　　***good for you*** 眞好；好棒
  promise〔'prɑmɪs〕*v.* 保證　　deal〔dil〕*n.* 交易
  It's a deal. 一言爲定。　　mean〔min〕*v.* 意思是
  cheat〔tʃit〕*v.* 欺騙　　agree〔ə'gri〕*v.* 同意

17. (**C**) W : Do you know if this bus goes to the zoo?
　　　　女： 你知道這班公車是否有到動物園呢？
　　　　M : I think it does, but you should ask the driver.
　　　　男： 我認爲有，但妳應該問司機。
　　　　W : Thanks.
　　　　女： 謝謝。
　　　　Question : Where are the speakers? 說話者在哪裡？
　　　　(A) On a boat. 在船上。
　　　　(B) On a train. 在火車上。
　　　　(C) On a bus. 在公車上。
　　　　* zoo〔zu〕*n.* 動物園

18. (**C**) A good vocabulary will help you throughout life. Being able to express yourself is key to succeeding in your social life, your academic life, and later in the "real world". Reading daily will pay back in volumes. Don't underestimate the value of books on tape, occasionally substituting these for the radio on a longer car trip. Keep a variety of reading materials at home such as magazines, books and newspapers.
　　　　有豐富的字彙量會讓你終生受益。能在社交生活、學術生活，和以後的「眞實世界」中，好好表達自己，是成功的關鍵。每天閱讀會讓你收穫良多。別低估有聲書的價值，長途開車時，偶爾可用這些來取代廣播。要在家裡保存像是書報雜誌之類的，各式各樣的閱讀材料。

Question : What might be valuable on a long car journey?

長途開車時，什麼可能是很有價值的？

(A) An MP3 player. MP3 播放器。

(B) A comfortable pillow. 舒服的枕頭。

(C) A book on tape. 有聲書。

* vocabulary〔vəˈkæbjəˌlɛrɪ〕*n.* 字彙

a good vocabulary 大的字彙量（= *a wide vocabulary*）

throughout〔θruˈaʊt〕*prep.* 在整個期間

throughout life 終生　　***be able to V.*** 能夠…

express〔ɪkˈsprɛs〕*v.* 表達　　key〔ki〕*adj.* 非常重要的

succeed〔səkˈsid〕*v.* 成功　　social〔ˈsoʃəl〕*adj.* 社交的

academic〔ˌækəˈdɛmɪk〕*adj.* 學術的　　later〔ˈletɚ〕*adv.* 後來

daily〔ˈdelɪ〕*adv.* 每天　　***pay back*** 回報

volumes〔ˈvɑljəmz〕*n. pl.* 大量

underestimate〔ˌʌndɚˈɛstəˌmet〕*v.* 低估

value〔ˈvælju〕*n.* 價值　　tape〔tep〕*n.* 錄音帶

books on tape 有聲書（= *audio books*）

occasionally〔əˈkeʒənlɪ〕*adv.* 偶爾

substitute〔ˈsʌbstəˌtjut〕*v.* 用…代替

substitute A for B 用 A 代替 B

variety〔vəˈraɪətɪ〕*n.* 變化；多樣性　　***a variety of*** 各式各樣的

material〔məˈtɪrɪəl〕*n.* 材料　　magazine〔ˌmægəˈzin〕*n.* 雜誌

valuable〔ˈvæljəbl̩〕*adj.* 珍貴的　　journey〔ˈdʒɝnɪ〕*n.* 旅程

player〔ˈpleɚ〕*n.* 播放裝置

comfortable〔ˈkʌmfɚtəbl̩〕*adj.* 舒服的　　pillow〔ˈpɪlo〕*n.* 枕頭

19. (**A**) W : What time is it?

女：現在幾點？

M : I don't know. I guess it's probably after five o'clock by now.

男：我不知道。我猜現在大概已經過了五點。

W : Five o'clock!? Oh, no! You're right. It's five-fifteen.

女：五點!? 噢，不！你說的對。現在五點十五分。

M：What's the problem?

男：有什麼問題嗎？

W：I was supposed to meet Diana in the park at five.

女：我五點應該要跟黛安娜在公園見面。

M：You'd better get moving.

男：妳最好要動身了。

Question：What will the woman most likely do next?

這位女士接下來最可能做什麼？

(A) Take a taxi to the park. 搭計程車去公園。

(B) Ride her bicycle to the store. 騎腳踏車去商店。

(C) Walk to the library. 走路去圖書館。

* guess〔gɛs〕v. 猜　***by now*** 現在已經
be supposed to V. 應該…　***had better*** 最好
move〔muv〕v. 走動；移動　likely〔'laɪklɪ〕adv. 可能
next〔nɛkst〕adv. 接下來　library〔'laɪˌbɛrɪ〕n. 圖書館

20. (**C**) M：Thanks for showing me around, Irene. I had a great time.

男：艾琳，謝謝妳帶我四處走走。我玩得很愉快。

W：You're welcome, James. I remember what it was like the first time I visited the city.

女：不客氣，詹姆士。我記得我第一次到這個城市時的情況。

M：There's so much to see and do. I would have been lost without you.

男：有好多事物要看跟做。如果沒有妳，我就會不知所措。

W：Don't mention it.

女：不客氣。

Question：How did Irene help James?

艾琳如何幫助詹姆士？

(A) By driving him downtown. 開車帶他到市中心。

(B) By finding his missing wallet. 找到他遺失的皮夾。

(C) By acting as his tour guide. 充當他的導遊。

* ***show** sb. **around*** 帶某人四處逛
   have a great time 玩得很愉快   visit〔'vɪzɪt〕*v.* 拜訪；去
   lost〔lɔst〕*adj.* 迷惑的；不知所措的
   mention〔'mɛnʃən〕*v.* 提到   ***Don't mention it.*** 不客氣。
   ***drive** sb.* 開車載某人   downtown〔'daʊn'taʊn〕*adv.* 到市中心
   missing〔'mɪsɪŋ〕*adj.* 失蹤的；找不到的
   wallet〔'wɑlɪt〕*n.* 皮夾   ***act as*** 充當；擔任
   tour〔tʊr〕*n.* 旅行   guide〔gaɪd〕*n.* 導遊

21. (**B**) Now that you've brought your new friend home, it's time for the fun part—and the hard part! This is your chance to really prove to your parents, yourself, and your pet that you're a responsible guardian. It's a lot to live up to, but don't worry—you can do it! All you need to know is what your pet needs, and then give it to it.
既然你已經帶你的新朋友回家了,該是最有趣——也最困難的部份的時候了!這真的是你向父母、你自己,和你的寵物,證明你是個負責任的守護者的機會。有很多要實行的事,但是不用擔心——你做得到!你所必須知道的,就是你的寵物需要什麼,然後滿足牠。

Question：Who would be most interested in this information? 誰會對這個資訊最有興趣?

(A) New parents. 新手父母。

(B) New pet owners. 新手寵物主人。

(C) New employees. 新進員工。

* ***now that*** 既然   fun〔fʌn〕*adj.* 有趣的
   hard〔hɑrd〕*adj.* 困難的   chance〔tʃæns〕*n.* 機會
   prove〔pruv〕*v.* 證明   pet〔pɛt〕*n.* 寵物
   responsible〔rɪ'spɑnsəbļ〕*adj.* 負責任的
   guardian〔'gɑrdɪən〕*n.* 守護者；監護人   ***live up to*** 實行
   be interested in 對…有興趣   owner〔'onɚ〕*n.* 擁有者
   employee〔ˌɛmplɔɪ'i〕*n.* 員工

TEST 2 ▶ 詳解

第一部分：辨識句意（第 1-3 題）

1. (**A**) (A)　　　　　　　(B)　　　　　　　(C)

Julie was thinking about what to eat: pizza or a burger. She chose pizza.

茱莉亞在考慮吃什麼：披薩或漢堡。她選了披薩。

* pizza〔ˈpitsə〕*n.* 披薩　　burger〔ˈbɝgɚ〕*n.* 漢堡
  choose〔tʃuz〕*v.* 選擇【三態變化：choose-chose-chosen】

2. (**A**) (A)　　　　　　　(B)　　　　　　　(C)

Susan is sitting in a chair, reading a magazine and watching television. 蘇珊正坐在椅子上看雜誌和電視。

* magazine〔ˌmægəˈzin〕*n.* 雜誌

3. (**C**) (A)　　　　　　　(B)　　　　　　　(C)

Maryanne is giving a card to her teacher on Teacher's Day. 瑪莉安在教師節時給她的老師一張卡片。

第二部分：基本問答（第 4-10 題）

4. (**A**) Thank you for your help. 謝謝你的幫忙。

   (A) No problem. 不客氣。

   (B) Help yourself to the drinks. 請自行取用飲料。

   (C) You are welcome to join. 歡迎你加入。

   * **help** *yourself to* 自行取用　　join〔 dʒɔɪn 〕*v.* 加入

5. (**B**) I prefer tea to coffee. 我喜歡茶甚於咖啡。

   (A) How about you? 那你呢？

   (B) Me too. 我也是。

   (C) I think so, too. 我也這麼認為。

   * prefer〔 prɪ'fɝ 〕*v.* 比較喜歡　　***prefer** A **to** B* 喜歡 A 甚於 B

6. (**B**) Who made these cupcakes?
這些杯子蛋糕是誰做的？

   (A) They're delicious. 它們很美味。

   (B) Gina did. 吉娜做的。

   (C) I'm full. 我很飽。

   * cupcake〔'kʌp,kek 〕*n.* 杯子蛋糕
     delicious〔 dɪ'lɪʃəs 〕*adj.* 美味的　　full〔 fʊl 〕*adj.* 飽的

7. (**A**) Where is your friend, Tom?
湯姆，你的朋友在哪裡？

   (A) He went home. 他回家了。

   (B) He is from Japan. 他來自日本。

   (C) He was my classmate. 他是我的同學。

8. (**C**) What type of music do you listen to?

你聽什麼類型的音樂？

(A) Action films. 動作片。

(B) Comic books. 漫畫。

(C) Pop music. 流行音樂。

* type〔taɪp〕*n.* 類型　　action〔'ækʃən〕*n.* 行動；動作
comic〔'kɑmɪk〕*adj.* 漫畫的　　pop〔pɑp〕*adj.* 流行的

9. (**C**) Who is your favorite teacher?

你最喜愛的老師是誰？

(A) Blue. 藍色。

(B) Saturday 星期六。

(C) Mr. Chen. 陳老師。

* favorite〔'fevərɪt〕*adj.* 最喜愛的

10. (**B**) What can I do for you today, ma'am?

今天我能為妳做什麼，女士？

(A) I have no information about that.

我沒有關於那件事的資訊。

(B) I bought this computer here last week. It seems to
have many problems.

我上週在這裡買了這台電腦。它似乎有很多問題。

(C) We can exchange your tablet for a new one.

妳的平板電腦我們能換新的給你。

* ma'am〔mæm〕*n.* 夫人；太太；女士
information〔,ɪnfə'meʃən〕*n.* 資訊
computer〔kəm'pjutə〕*n.* 電腦　　seem〔sim〕*v.* 似乎
exchange〔ɪks'tʃenʒ〕*v.* 交換；退換
exchange A for B 將 A 換成 B
tablet〔'tæblɪt〕*n.* 平板電腦 (= *tablet computer*)

第三部分：言談理解（第 11-21 題）

11. (**B**)　W : Is that your second piece of pie, Joe?

女：喬，那是你的第二片派嗎？

M : Yes.　It's just so delicious that I can't help myself!

男：是的，太好吃了，以致於我忍不住想吃！

W : Maybe I should have some.

女：也許我應該吃一些。

Question : What is Joe doing?　喬正在做什麼？

(A) Asking for a second piece of pie.

要求吃第二片派。

(B) Eating a second piece of pie.

正在吃第二片派。

(C) Offering a piece of pie to the woman.

給那位女士一片派。

* ***so…that*** 如此…以致於　　help〔hɛlp〕*v.* 避免；阻止

can't help *oneself* 忍不住　　have〔hæv〕*v.* 吃

ask for 要求　　***a second*** 另一個（= *another*）

offer〔ˈɔfɚ〕*v.* 提供

12. (**B**)　W : What was that noise?

女：那是什麼噪音？

M : I think another bird flew into the window.

男：我想有另一隻鳥飛來撞到窗戶了。

W : Again?　Is it dead?

女：又撞到了嗎？牠死了嗎？

M : I don't know.　Go outside and look.

男：我不知道。去外面看看吧。

Question : Why are the speakers concerned?

說話者在關心什麼？

(A) They smelled smoke. 他們聞到煙味。

(B) They heard a loud noise. <u>他們聽到一個很大的聲音。</u>

(C) They saw a stranger at the door.

他們看到門口有個陌生人。

* noise〔nɔɪz〕*n.* 噪音　　***fly into the window*** 飛撞窗戶

concerned〔kən'sɝnd〕*adj.* 關心的　　smell〔smɛl〕*v.* 聞到

smoke〔smok〕*n.* 煙　　loud〔laʊd〕*adj.* 大聲的

stranger〔'strendʒɚ〕*n.* 陌生人

13. (**C**) W : Did you remember to feed Champ?

女：你記得餵強普嗎？

M : Yes, Mom.

男：是的，媽。

W : Did you take him for his walk?

女：你有帶牠去散步嗎？

M : Not yet. We're leaving now.

男：還沒。我們正要去。

Question : Who is Champ? 誰是強普？

(A) A friend. 一個朋友。

(B) A family member. 一位家庭成員。

(C) A pet. <u>一隻寵物。</u>

* feed〔fid〕*v.* 餵　　***take~for a walk*** 帶～去散步

not yet 還沒　　member〔'mɛmbɚ〕*n.* 成員

pet〔pɛt〕*n.* 寵物

14. (**B**) W : Hi, Mr. Miller. It's Rosie from Dr. Caldwell's office.

I'm calling to confirm your appointment this

afternoon at four-thirty.

女：嗨，米勒先生，我是凱德威爾醫師診所的蘿西。我打電話來

是要跟你確認今天下午四點半的約診。

M : Hi, Rosie. Thanks for the call. I was wondering if you could squeeze me in a little earlier. For instance, around four o'clock?

男：嗨，蘿西。謝謝妳的來電。我正在想是否妳能幫我安插早一點的時間。例如，四點鐘左右？

W : I'm sorry, Mr. Miller. Dr. Caldwell's schedule is booked solid today.

女：很抱歉，米勒先生。凱德威爾醫師今天都被約滿了。

M : OK. No problem. See you at four-thirty.

男：好。沒問題。四點半見。

Question : What will the man most likely do this afternoon?

這位男士今天下午最有可能做什麼？

(A) Visit a lawyer. 去找律師。

(B) Visit a doctor. 去看醫生。

(C) Visit a banker. 去找銀行業者。

* office〔'ɔfɪs〕*n.* 辦公室；診所　　confirm〔kən'fɝm〕*v.* 確認
appointment〔ə'pɔɪntmənt〕*n.* 約會；約診
wonder〔'wʌndɚ〕*v.* 想知道　　squeeze〔skwiz〕*v.* 擠壓
squeeze sb. in 把某人擠入　　schedule〔'skɛdʒul〕*n.* 時間表
book〔buk〕*v.* 預訂　　solid〔'salɪd〕*adv.* 全部地；完全地
lawyer〔'lɔjɚ〕*n.* 律師
banker〔'bæŋkɚ〕*n.* 銀行家；銀行業者

15. (**B**) M : Have you enrolled in your classes for next semester, Michelle?

男：蜜雪兒，妳下學期的課選了嗎？

W : Not yet, Mick. I might take next semester off and do some traveling.

女：還沒，米克。我可能下學期會休學去旅行。

M : When are you going to make that decision?

男： 妳什麼時候會做決定？

W : I'm still talking it over with my parents. There's still plenty of time before school starts again in the fall. For now, I'm just trying to enjoy the summer.

女： 我還在跟我父母討論。現在離秋季開學還有很多時間。我現在只想好好享受這個夏天。

M : Well, I wouldn't wait too long to make up your mind. Classes fill up pretty fast.

男： 嗯，我不會等太久才做決定。課很快就會額滿。

Question : When did the conversation take place?

這個對話發生在何時？

(A)　Winter. 冬天。

(B)　Summer. <u>夏天。</u>

(C)　Fall. 秋天。

* enroll〔 ɪn'rol 〕*v.* 註冊；登記
  semester〔 sə'mɛstɚ 〕*n.* 學期　　***take ~ off*** 休息
  do some traveling 去旅行　　decision〔 dɪ'sɪʒən 〕*n.* 決定
  talk over 討論　　***plenty of*** 許多的
  fall〔 fɔl 〕*n.* 秋天　　***make up*** one's ***mind*** 下定決心
  fill up 變滿　　pretty〔 'prɪtɪ 〕*adv.* 相當
  take place 發生

16. (**A**)　W : There's a film festival in Highland Park this weekend, Brian.

女： 這個週末在高地公園會有電影節，布萊恩。

M : Hmm. Sounds interesting. Are you going?

男： 嗯。聽起來很有趣。妳要去嗎？

W : I want to, but…. Maybe we could go together.

女： 我想去，但⋯。也許我們能一起去。

M : That would be great!

男：那就太棒了！

W : Let's plan on Saturday afternoon.

女：我們預定週六下午去吧。

M : It's a date!

男：這是約會！

Question : What will the speakers most likely do this weekend? 說話者這個週末最有可能做什麼？

(A) See some films. 看一些電影。

(B) Go on a hike. 去健行。

(C) Have dinner together. 一起吃晚餐。

* film〔fɪlm〕*n.* 電影   festival〔'fɛstəvl〕*n.* 節慶
weekend〔'wik'ɛnd〕*n.* 週末   sound〔saʊnd〕*v.* 聽起來
interesting〔'ɪntrɪstɪŋ〕*adj.* 有趣的   date〔det〕*n.* 約會
hike〔haɪk〕*n.* 健行   ***go on a hike*** 去健行

17. (**A**) Every team sport is different. Some let you shine as an individual and benefit the team, such as track and field. Others, like volleyball, rely on all the players working together equally. In many sports, a team means just two people; in others, it means many more. Some of these sports were invented just recently and some date back hundreds, or even thousands, of years.

每個團隊運動都是不同的。有些會讓你個人受注目，同時也讓隊伍受益，像是田徑。有些像是排球，依靠團隊合作。在許多運動中，一隊代表兩個人，有些團隊運動則是指更多人。有些運動是近期才發明的，而有些則是可追溯到數百年，甚至數千年前。

Question : What is true about team sports?

關於團隊運動何者為真？

(A) Teams can be as small as two people.

<u>隊伍可能會小到只有兩個人。</u>

(B) Most were invented recently.

大部份是最近發明的。

(C) Individuals are not allowed to participate.

不允許個人參加。

* team〔tim〕*n.* 隊伍；團隊　　***some…others*** 有些…有些

shine〔ʃaɪn〕*v.* 發光；出色

individual〔ˌɪndə'vɪdʒʊl〕*n.* 個人

benefit〔'bɛnəfɪt〕*v.* 使獲益　　***such as*** 像是

track and field 田徑　　volleyball〔'valɪˌbɔl〕*n.* 排球

rely on 依靠　　player〔'pleə〕*n.* 球員

work together 合作　　equally〔'ikwəlɪ〕*adv.* 相等地；同樣地

mean〔min〕*v.* 意思是　　invent〔ɪn'vɛnt〕*v.* 發明

recently〔'risn̩tlɪ〕*adv.* 最近　　***date back*** 追溯

allow〔ə'laʊ〕*v.* 允許　　participate〔par'tɪsəˌpet〕*v.* 參加

18. (**A**) W：What do you think of this dress?

女：你覺得這件洋裝怎麼樣？

M：It… looks familiar?

男：它…看起來很眼熟？

W：Yes, I wore it to Olivia's party. Do you like it?

女：沒錯，我穿過它去奧莉薇亞的派對。你喜歡嗎？

M：Sure… I like it.

男：當然…我喜歡。

W：What do you think of these shoes?

女：那你覺得這些鞋子怎麼樣？

M：They match perfectly, I guess.

男：我猜它們很搭。

W：What about this handbag?

女：那這個手提包呢？

M：OK, now you're pushing it.

男：好，現在妳是在得寸進尺。

Question：What does the man mean when he says, "OK, now you're pushing it"?

這位男士說：「好，現在妳是在得寸進尺」是什麼意思？

(A) He is tiring of the woman's questions.

他受夠了女士的問題。

(B) He is feeling pressured to buy something.

買東西讓他覺得有壓力。

(C) He is ready to leave for the party now.

他現在準備前往派對。

* familiar〔fə'mɪljɚ〕*adj.* 熟悉的   match〔mætʃ〕*v.* 搭配
perfectly〔'pɝfɪktlɪ〕*adv.* 完美地   *What about~?* ~如何？
handbag〔'hænd,bæg〕*n.* 手提包   *push it* 冒險；得寸進尺
be tired of 對~厭倦   pressured〔'prɛʃɚd〕*adj.* 有壓力的
ready〔'rɛdɪ〕*adj.* 準備好的   *leave for* 動身前往

19. (**B**) W：What time do you have to work, Ron?

女：榮恩，你幾點要工作？

M：Four in the afternoon.

男：下午四點。

W：What time do you get off?

女：你幾點下班？

M：Just after midnight.

男：就在半夜十二點之後。

Question：What time does Ron get off work?

榮恩幾點下班？

(A) Noon. 中午。

(B) 12:01 a.m. 清晨十二點零一分。

(C) 11:00 p.m. 晚上十一點。

* ***get off*** (***work***) 下班　　midnight〔'mɪd,naɪt〕*n.* 半夜十二點

20. (**B**) At some point, it becomes time to choose a special friend, a "best" friend. This should be someone who you can rely on, not someone who is good-looking and popular who will use you for your talents. This person should be loyal to you, and shouldn't be eager to talk behind your back about you. You should be able to trust this person to keep personal secrets, and not tell them. This choice is an important one, so don't underestimate it! And remember, a boy can be a girl's best friend, and vice versa.

在某個時刻，就是你該選個特別朋友的時候，一個「最好的」朋友。這個人應該是你能依靠的人，而不是某個好看又受歡迎，會利用你的才華的人。這個人應該要對你忠誠，而且不應該渴望在背後談論你。你應該能信任他，會保守個人的秘密，不會說出去。這是個重要的選擇，所以不能低估它！而且要記得，男孩可以當女孩最好的朋友，反之亦然。

Question：Which of the following is NOT something to look for in a best friend?

下列何者不是找好朋友的條件？

(A) Can keep a secret. 能保守秘密。

(B) Loves to gossip. 愛說閒話。

(C) Dependable. 很可靠。

* point〔pɔɪnt〕*n.* 時刻　　special〔'spɛʃəl〕*adj.* 特別的
  good-looking〔'gʊd'lʊkɪŋ〕*adj.* 好看的
  popular〔'pɑpjələ〕*adj.* 受歡迎的　　talent〔'tælənt〕*n.* 才能
  loyal〔'lɔɪəl〕*adj.* 忠誠的　　eager〔'igə〕*adj.* 渴望的
  behind *one's* ***back*** 背地裡；背著某人　　trust〔trʌst〕*v.* 信任
  personal〔'pɝsn̩l〕*adj.* 個人的　　secret〔'sikrɪt〕*n.* 祕密

choice〔tʃɔɪs〕*n.* 選擇
underestimate〔'ʌndə'ɛstə,met〕*v.* 低估
vice versa〔'vaɪsɪ 'vɝsə〕*adv.* 反之亦然　　***look for*** 尋找
keep a secret 保密　　gossip〔'gɑsəp〕*v.* 說閒話
dependable〔dɪ'pɛndəbl̩〕*adj.* 可靠的

21.(**A**) M：How long have you been waiting?

男：妳已經等多久了？

W：Only a few minutes.　I was running late, too.

女：只有幾分鐘。我也遲到了。

M：Good.　Sorry about that.　Traffic was awful.

男：好。很抱歉。交通情況很糟。

W：I know!　It must be due to the rain.

女：我知道！一定是因為下雨。

Question：What do we know about the speakers?

我們知道關於說話者的什麼事？

(A) Both were late for the meeting.

兩人見面都遲到。

(B) Both were early for the meeting.

兩人見面都早到。

(C) Both were on time for the meeting.

兩人見面都準時到。

* ***be running late*** 遲到了　　traffic〔'træfɪk〕*n.* 交通
awful〔'ɔful〕*adj.* 糟糕的　　***due to*** 由於
meeting〔'mitɪŋ〕*n.* 會面　　***on time*** 準時

 TEST 3 ▶ 詳解　

第一部分：辨識句意（第 1-3 題）

1. (**A**) (A) 　(B) 　(C)

Some kids are in a theater watching a movie.

有些小孩正在電影院看電影。

* kid〔kɪd〕 *n.* 小孩　　theater〔ˈθiətɚ〕 *n.* 戲院；電影院

2. (**C**) (A) 　(B) 　(C)

There are three bowls of fruit and three bottles of milk on the table.　桌上有三碗水果和三瓶牛奶。

* bowl〔bol〕 *n.* 碗　　bottle〔ˈbatḷ〕 *n.* 瓶子

3. (**B**) (A) 　(B) 　(C)

Leslie is carving a pumpkin to celebrate Halloween.

萊絲莉正在雕刻南瓜，要慶祝萬聖節。

* carve〔karv〕*v.* 雕刻　　pumpkin〔'pʌmpkɪn〕*n.* 南瓜
celebrate〔'sɛlə,bret〕*v.* 慶祝
Halloween〔,hælo'in〕*n.* 萬聖節

第二部分：基本問答（第 4-10 題）

4.(**C**) Who is that kid riding the skateboard?

那個在溜滑板的小孩是誰？

(A) It's pretty cold today. 今天相當冷。

(B) He is going to church. 他正要去教堂。

(C) I don't know. I've never seen him before.
<u>我不知道。我以前從沒見過他。</u>

* skateboard〔'sket,bord〕*n.* 滑板　　pretty〔'prɪtɪ〕*adv.* 相當
church〔tʃɝtʃ〕*n.* 教堂　　***go to church*** 上教堂

5.(**A**) It's too hot to play outside today. What should we do?

今天太熱了，不能在外面玩。我們應該做什麼？

(A) Let's play video games. <u>我們打電動吧。</u>

(B) Open the door. 開門。

(C) Maybe not. 或許不是。

* ***too⋯to*** 太⋯以致於不　　outside〔'aut'said〕*adv.* 在外面
video games 電動遊戲　　maybe〔'mebɪ〕*adv.* 或許

6.(**A**) What time is your appointment to speak with Professor
Smith? 你跟史密斯教授約幾點談話？

(A) Three-thirty. <u>三點半。</u>

(B) Tuesday. 星期二。

(C) April. 四月。

* appointment〔ə'pɔɪntmənt〕*n.* 約會
professor〔prə'fɛsɚ〕*n.* 教授

7. (**B**) How often do the garbage trucks come through the neighborhood? 垃圾車多久會來這附近一次？

   (A) They do a good job. 他們做得很好。

   (B) Several times a night. <u>一晚好幾次。</u>

   (C) They make a lot of noise. 他們製造很多噪音。

* ***How often…?*** …多久一次？　　garbage〔'gɑrbɪdʒ〕*n.* 垃圾
truck〔trʌk〕*n.* 卡車　　through〔θru〕*prep.* 遍及；在…各處
do a good job 做得很好　　several〔'sɛvərəl〕*adj.* 幾個的
time〔taɪm〕*n.* 次數　　***make noise*** 製造噪音

8. (**A**) Vacation is almost over. Are you excited about the new school year? 假期即將結束。你對於新學年感到興奮嗎？

   (A) I can't wait to go back to school!
<u>我迫不及待要回學校！</u>

   (B) Let's leave it here. 我們把它留在這裡吧。

   (C) We don't celebrate the holiday. 我們不慶祝節日。

* vacation〔ve'keʃən〕*n.* 假期
excited〔ɪk'saɪtɪd〕*adj.* 興奮的
school year 學年　　holiday〔'hɑlə,de〕*n.* 節日

9. (**A**) Something is wrong with my car. It wouldn't start this morning. 我的車子有些問題。它今天早上發不動。

   (A) Have you contacted a mechanic? <u>你聯絡技工了嗎？</u>

   (B) Have you called a plumber? 你打電話找水管工人了嗎？

   (C) Have you made an appointment? 你預約了嗎？

* wrong〔rɔŋ〕*adj.* 不對勁的　　start〔stɑrt〕*v.* 發動
contact〔'kɑntækt〕*v.* 聯絡　　mechanic〔mə'kɛnɪk〕*n.* 技工
plumber〔'plʌmɚ〕*n.* 水管工人　　***make an appointment*** 預約

10. (**C**) How far is the shopping mall from here?

購物中心離這裡多遠？

(A) I was shopping. 我正在逛街。

(B) All buses stop here. 所有的公車都停在這裡。

(C) About a five-minute walk. 走路大概五分鐘。

* *shopping mall* 購物中心　　walk〔wɔk〕*n.* 步行距離；路程

第三部分：言談理解（第 11-21 題）

11. (**A**) W : Where is Tommy?

女：湯米在哪裡？

M : He'll be here in a minute.

男：他馬上就會到。

W : Oh, I thought he was coming with you.

女：噢，我以爲他會跟你一起來。

M : No, he had something else going on. I came alone on the bus.

男：不，他有別的事要忙。我自己搭公車來。

W : Do you have the tickets?

女：你有票嗎？

M : Yes, right here. Three seats in the back row, so we'll have a good view of the screen.

男：有，在這裡。三個後排的座位，所以我們看螢幕時會有個好視野。

W : Great! Let's get in line now and Tommy can join us when he arrives.

女：太棒了！我們現在去排隊，等湯米到時，就能加入我們。

Question : What are the speakers most likely going to do? 說話者最有可能會做什麼？

(A) See a movie. <u>看電影。</u>

(B) Take a test. 參加考試。

(C) Go for a swim. 去游泳。

* ***in a minute*** 立刻　　***go on*** 進行
  alone〔ə'lon〕*adv.* 單獨地　　back〔bæk〕*adj.* 後面的
  row〔ro〕*n.* 排　view〔vju〕*n.* 視野
  screen〔skrin〕*n.* 螢幕　　***get in line*** 去排隊

12. (**C**) Whatever their weight, it's important that children eat
properly and get lots of exercise to build a healthy body.
If they're carrying too much fat in their bodies, they are
at a greater risk of heart disease and diabetes in later life.
If they're underweight, it's just as important for them to
eat healthy food and be active.

不論體重多少，小孩子吃得好和做很多運動，以打造一個健康的
身體，是很重要的。如果他們體內有太多脂肪，在往後的人生，
得到心臟疾病和糖尿病的風險較大。如果體重不足，吃健康的食
物還有運動，對他們一樣重要。

Question : Which of the following is NOT something fat
　　　　　kids risk later in life?

　　　　下列哪一個不是胖小孩在以後人生中會有的風險？

(A) Heart disease. 心臟病。

(B) Diabetes. 糖尿病。

(C) Poor balance. <u>平衡感不好。</u>

* whatever〔hwɑt'ɛvɚ〕*conj.* 無論什麼
  weight〔wet〕*n.* 體重　　properly〔'prɑpɚlɪ〕*adv.* 適當地
  exercise〔'ɛksɚˌsaɪz〕*n.* 運動　　build〔bɪld〕*v.* 建造
  healthy〔'hɛlθɪ〕*adj.* 健康的；有益健康的
  carry〔'kærɪ〕*v.* 具有　　fat〔fæt〕*n.* 脂肪
  risk〔rɪsk〕*n.* 風險　*v.* 有…風險　　***at a~risk*** 冒～風險
  heart disease 心臟病　　diabetes〔ˌdaɪə'bitɪz〕*n.* 糖尿病

later〔ˈletɚ〕 *adj.* 以後的
underweight〔ˈʌndɚˌwet〕 *adj.* 體重不足的
active〔ˈæktɪv〕 *adj.* 活躍的；活動的
poor〔pʊr〕 *adj.* 差勁的　　balance〔ˈbæləns〕 *n.* 平衡

13. (**B**)　W : You've never been to Carlo's Pizzeria before?　Really?
　　　　女：你以前從未去過卡蘿披薩店？真的嗎？
　　　　M : I used to come to this spot when it was a Chinese restaurant.　I haven't had a chance to stop by since it became a pizza place.
　　　　男：我以前去這個地點的時候，那是一間中國餐廳。自從它變成披薩店，我就還沒機會去。
　　　　W : Oh, boy, you're in for a treat!　Carlo's makes the best deep-dish pizza on the West Coast.　I'm so glad they moved to Benson City.　The old Carlo's was all the way out in North Park.
　　　　女：喔，天啊，你一定會覺得好吃！卡蘿做的厚片披薩是西岸最好的。我很高興他們搬到班森市。以前的卡蘿披薩店在遙遠的北方公園。
　　　　M : Hmm.　Good to know.　I'm excited.　Let's order a pizza, shall we?
　　　　男：嗯。知道這件事真好。我很興奮。我們點一個披薩，好嗎？
　　　　W : What sort of toppings do you like?
　　　　女：你喜歡在上面放什麼種類的料？
　　　　M : I play it safe when it comes to pizza.　Cheese, sausage, and maybe some pepperoni.
　　　　男：只要一談到披薩，我都打安全牌。起司、香腸，或許再加一些辣味香腸。
　　　　W : How about mushrooms and olives?
　　　　女：蘑菇跟橄欖如何？

Question：What do we know about Carlo's Pizzeria?

我們知道卡羅披薩店的什麼事？

(A) It's located on the East Coast. 它位於東岸。

(B) It used to be located somewhere else.

　　它以前位於別的地方。

(C) It only serves thin crust pizza. 它只供應薄的披薩。

* pizzeria (ˌpitsəˈriə) *n.* 披薩餐館

used to V. 以前… 　　spot (spɑt) *n.* 地點

restaurant (ˈrɛstrənt) *n.* 餐廳　　**stop by** 順道拜訪

place (ples) *n.* 餐館　　boy (bɔɪ) *interj.* 哇；天啊

be in for 肯定會經歷　　treat (trit) *n.* 樂事

You are in for a treat. 你一定會覺得很好吃。

deep-dish (ˈdipˌdɪʃ) *adj.* 用深盤烘製的

west (wɛst) *adj.* 西方的　　coast (kost) *n.* 海岸

glad (glæd) *adj.* 高興的　　move (muv) *n.* 搬家

all the way 一路；大老遠　　out (aut) *adv.* 在遠方

hmm (m) *interj.* 嗯　　excited (ɪkˈsaɪtɪd) *adj.* 興奮的

order (ˈɔrdɚ) *v.* 點（餐）；訂購　　sort (sɔrt) *n.* 種類

topping (ˈtɑpɪŋ) *n.* （食品上面的）配料

play it safe 不冒險　　**when it comes to** 一提到

cheese (tʃiz) *n.* 起司　　sausage (ˈsɔsɪdʒ) *n.* 香腸

pepperoni (ˌpɛpəˈroni) *n.* 辣味香腸

mushroom (ˈmʌʃrum) *n.* 蘑菇　　olive (ˈɑlɪv) *n.* 橄欖

be located on 位於　　east (ist) *adj.* 東方的

serve (sɝv) *v.* 供應　　crust (krʌst) *n.* 餅皮

14. (**C**) W：How do you like your new teacher? Um… is it…
　　　　　 Ms. Frazier?

女：你覺得新老師，嗯…法莉茲兒女士對嗎？

M：Yeah, Frazier. She's OK. Doesn't say much, which
　　 is kind of weird.

男：對呀，法莉茲兒。她還可以。話不多，有點奇怪。

W : Hmm, you're the second person to say that. Boris had the same reaction.

女：嗯，你是第二個這麼說的人。柏里斯的反應也一樣。

M : I don't know. It seems like most teachers are always talking. She writes the assignment on the board, tells us to get started, and that's it.

男：我不知道。似乎大部份的老師總是說個不停。她把作業寫在黑板上，告訴我們開始做，就這樣。

Question : What does Boris think of Ms. Frazier?

柏里斯覺得法莉茲兒老師如何？

(A) She treats the girls better. 她對女生比較好。

(B) She gives easy lessons. 她上的課很簡單。

(C) She doesn't talk much. 她話不多。

* yeah〔jɛ〕*adv.* 是的（= *yes*）　　***kind of*** 有點（= *a little*）
weird〔wɪrd〕*adj.* 奇怪的　　reaction〔rɪˈækʃən〕*n.* 反應
seem〔sim〕*v.* 似乎　　assignment〔əˈsaɪnmənt〕*n.* 作業
board〔bord〕*n.* 黑板（= *blackboard*）　　***that's it*** 就這樣
treat〔trit〕*v.* 對待　　***give a lesson*** 授課

15. (**A**) M : Hey, Lucy! So good to see you.

男：嘿，露西！真高興看到妳。

W : Hi, Steve, you're back. How was your vacation?

女：嗨，史蒂夫，你回來啦。假期如何？

M : Amazing! We did and saw so many incredible things.

男：很棒！我們做了也看了很多令人無法置信的事物。

W : Give me a couple of highlights.

女：告訴我幾個最精采的。

M : Well, riding an elephant was probably the coolest thing I've ever done in my life. And then we spent two days exploring an ancient temple.

男：嗯，騎大象可能是我有生以來做過最酷的事。然後我們花了
　　兩天的時間探索一間古老的寺廟。

Question : What do we know about Steve?
　　　　　我們知道關於史蒂夫的什麼事？

(A) He just returned from a trip. 他剛旅行回來。

(B) He's getting ready to go on a trip.
　　他正準備好要去旅行。

(C) He's still enjoying his trip. 他仍然在享受他的旅行。

* amazing〔ə'mezɪŋ〕*adj.* 很棒的
　incredible〔ɪn'krɛdəbl〕*adj.* 令人難以置信的
　give〔gɪv〕*v.* 說出　　couple〔'kʌpl〕*n.* 兩個；一對
　a couple of 幾個；兩三個
　highlight〔'haɪ,laɪt〕*n.* 最精彩的部份　　cool〔kul〕*adj.* 酷的
　explore〔ɪk'splor〕*v.* 探索　　ancient〔'enʃənt〕*adj.* 古代的
　temple〔'tɛmpl〕*n.* 廟　　*go on a trip* 去旅行

16. (**A**) W : When were you born?
　　　　　女：你在何時出生？

　　M : On July 20th, 1988.
　　　　男：在 1988 年 7 月 20 日。

　　W : Oh, I'm two months older than you.
　　　　女：噢，我比你早 2 個月。

　　Question : In what month was the woman born?
　　　　　　　這個女士在幾月出生？

　　(A) May. 五月。

　　(B) August. 八月。

　　(C) September. 九月。

17. (**B**) M : How about joining me for lunch at the Chop Shop,
　　　　　Laura?

男：跟我一起去巧普商店吃午餐好嗎，蘿拉？

W : I'd love to, Mark, but I have a science presentation this afternoon and I need the extra time to prepare.

女：我很樂意，馬克，但我今天下午要做科學報告，需要額外的時間準備。

M : Gotcha.

男：知道了。

Question : What does the man mean?

男士的意思是什麼？

(A) He caught Laura in a lie. 他發現蘿拉在說謊。

(B) He understands Laura's reply. 他了解蘿拉的回答。

(C) He has what Laura is looking for.

他有蘿拉正在找的東西。

* join〔dʒɔɪn〕v. 加入　　science〔'saɪəns〕n. 科學
presentation〔,prɛzn̩'teʃən〕n. 報告；發表（演說）
extra〔'ɛkstrə〕adj. 額外的　　prepare〔prɪ'pɛr〕v. 準備
gotcha〔'gɑtʃə〕interj. 這下把你抓住了！（= I've got you!）；
　　我明白了！（= I've got it!）
lie〔laɪ〕n. 謊言　　*catch sb. in a lie* 抓到某人在說謊
reply〔rɪ'plaɪ〕v. 回答

18. (**C**) W : Hi, Reese. You look worried this morning. What's going on?

女：嗨，瑞斯。你今天早上看起來很擔心。發生什麼事了？

M : I forgot to study for the math test, Irene.

男：我忘了唸要考的數學，艾琳。

W : Uh-oh. What are you going to do?

女：噢喔。那你要怎麼辦？

M : What can I do? The test is in 15 minutes.

男：我能怎麼辦？再十五分鐘就要考試了。

W : Well, maybe you can cram as much as possible in 15 minutes. I can help if you want. I stayed up half the night studying for this thing. I'm going to ace it.

女： 嗯，也許你能在十五分鐘內盡可能 K 書。如果你想要的話，我可以幫你。我熬了大半夜唸書就是爲了這個考試。我要考高分。

M : Gee, Irene. Really? You'd be willing to help me?

男： 哇，艾琳。眞的嗎？妳願意幫我嗎？

W : Sure! Let's get started. The clock is ticking.

女： 當然！我們開始吧。時間很緊迫。

Question : How does Irene feel about the test?

艾琳覺得這考試如何？

(A) Very worried. 她非常擔心。

(B) A little worried. 她有點擔心。

(C) Confident. <u>她有信心。</u>

* **go on** 發生　　uh-oh〔ˈʌˏo〕*interj.* 喔

in〔ɪn〕*prep.* 再過　　cram〔kræm〕*v.* 塡塞；K 書

as…as possible 盡可能　　**stay up** 熬夜

ace〔es〕*v.* 在…中得好成績　　gee〔dʒi〕*interj.* 哎呀

willing〔ˈwɪlɪŋ〕*adj.* 願意的　　**get started** 開始

tick〔tɪk〕*v.* 發出滴答聲

The clock is ticking. 時間一分一秒地過去。

confident〔ˈkɑnfədənt〕*adj.* 有信心的

19. (**C**) W : I'd like a garden salad and a bowl of soup, but I'm a vegetarian.

女： 我想要一份田園沙拉和一碗湯，但我吃素。

M : In that case, you should try our cream of mushroom soup.

男： 那樣的話，妳應該試試我們的奶油蘑菇濃湯。

W : Is it vegetarian?

女：這是素的嗎？

M : Yes.

男：是的。

Question : Where did this conversation most likely take

place? 這段對話最有可能在哪裡發生？

(A) In a bank. 在銀行。

(B) In a department store. 在百貨公司。

(C) In a cafeteria. <u>在自助餐廳。</u>

* garden〔'gɑrdn̩〕*n.* 花園

salad〔'sæləd〕*n.* 沙拉　　soup〔sup〕*n.* 湯

vegetarian〔ˌvɛdʒə'tɛrɪən〕*n.* 素食者　*adj.* 素食的

case〔kes〕*n.* 情況　　***in that case*** 那樣的話

cream〔krim〕*n.* 奶油

cream of mushroom soup 奶油蘑菇濃湯

take place 發生　　bank〔bæŋk〕*n.* 銀行

department store 百貨公司

cafeteria〔ˌkæfə'tɪrɪə〕*n.* 自助餐廳

20. (**C**) The key to success is a three-step process. First, decide
what you want to achieve. You must have a goal. It
must be clear-cut. Second, start taking action toward
achieving your goal. This includes thinking about proper
methods and expected results. Finally, perhaps the most
important key to success is determination. You must be
single-minded about achieving your goal. Every step you
take must be in the direction of success, even if you
encounter obstacles and setbacks. Just remember that
one step forward, no matter how small, brings you closer
to the goal, and every mistake is a learning experience.

成功的關鍵有三個步驟。首先，決定你想要達成什麼。你必須有一個目標。目標必須很明確。第二，開始採取行動，去達成你的目標。這包含要思考正確的方法和預期的結果。最後，也許成功最主要的關鍵就是決心。你必須心無旁鶩地達成目標。你所採取的每一個步驟，都必須朝著成功的方向，即使你遭遇阻礙和挫折。只要記得，每往前一步，不論是多小的一步，都讓你更靠近目標，而且每一個錯誤都是一種學習的經驗。

Question：What does the speaker urge the listener to
　　　　　 remember? 說話者要聽眾記得什麼？

(A) Time heals all wounds. 時間會療癒所有的傷口。

(B) It is easy to succeed. 很容易就能成功。

(C) Every mistake is a learning experience.
　　 每個錯誤都是一種學習的經驗。

* key〔kɪ〕*n.* 關鍵　　success〔sək'sɛs〕*n.* 成功
　step〔stɛp〕*n.* 步驟　　process〔'prɑsɛs〕*n.* 過程
　decide〔dɪ'saɪd〕*v.* 決定　　achieve〔ə'tʃiv〕*v.* 達成
　goal〔gol〕*n.* 目標　　clear-cut〔'klɪr'kʌt〕*adj.* 明確的
　take action 採取行動　　toward〔tord〕*prep.* 朝向
　include〔ɪn'klud〕*v.* 包括　　proper〔'prɑpɚ〕*adj.* 適當的
　method〔'mɛθəd〕*n.* 方法
　expected〔ɪk'spɛktɪd〕*adj.* 預期的
　result〔rɪ'zʌlt〕*n.* 結果　　finally〔'faɪnl̩ɪ〕*adv.* 最後
　perhaps〔pɚ'hæps〕*adv.* 或許
　determination〔dɪ,tɝmə'neʃən〕*n.* 決心
　single-minded〔'sɪŋgl̩'maɪndɪd〕*adj.* 一心一意的；專心的
　direction〔də'rɛkʃən〕*n.* 方向　　***even if*** 即使
　encounter〔ɪn'kaʊntɚ〕*v.* 遭遇
　obstacle〔'ɑbstəkl̩〕*n.* 阻礙　　setback〔'sɛt,bæk〕*n.* 挫折
　forward〔'fɔrwɚd〕*adv.* 往前　　***no matter*** 無論
　bring〔brɪŋ〕*v.* 使　　mistake〔mə'stek〕*n.* 錯誤
　experience〔ɪk'spɪrɪəns〕*n.* 經驗

urge〔ɜdʒ〕v. 催促；力勸　　heal〔hil〕v. 治癒
wound〔wund〕n. 傷口　　succeed〔səkˋsid〕v. 成功

21. (**B**) M：Hi, Lisa. Where are you going in such a rush?

男：嗨，麗莎。妳這麼急是要去哪裡？

W：Sorry, Ted. I don't have time to chat. If I miss the bus I'm going to be late for choir practice.

女：抱歉，泰德。我沒時間聊天。如果我錯過公車，唱詩班的練習我就會遲到。

M：Oh, OK. But isn't this your umbrella? You better not forget it. It's supposed to rain later this afternoon.

男：喔，好。但這不是妳的雨傘嗎？妳最好別忘了。今天下午稍晚可能會下雨。

W：Thanks, Ted. See you later.

女：謝謝，泰德。待會見。

Question：Where is Lisa going? 麗莎要去哪裡？

(A) Band practice. 樂團練習。

(B) Choir practice. 唱詩班練習。

(C) Basketball practice. 籃球練習。

* rush〔rʌʃ〕n. 匆忙　　***in a rush*** 匆忙
　chat〔tʃæt〕v. 聊天
　choir〔kwaɪr〕n.（教會的）唱詩班
　practice〔ˋpræktɪs〕n. 練習
　You better not… 你最好不要…（ = *You had better not*… ）
　suppose〔səˋpoz〕v. 推測；以為
　be supposed to V. 應該…
　later〔ˋletɚ〕adv. 較晚地；待會　　band〔bænd〕n. 樂團

🎧 TEST 4 ▶ 詳解

第一部分：辨識句意（第 1-3 題）

1. (**B**) (A)　　　　　　(B)　　　　　　(C)

Wanda and Frank are enjoying their coffee but Henry is not. 汪姐和法蘭克正在享用咖啡，但亨利沒有。

＊ enjoy〔ɪn'dʒɔɪ〕v. 享受

2. (**C**) (A)　　　　　　(B)　　　　　　(C)

A famous singer gave a performance on June 7th.
一位知名的歌手在六月七日做了一場表演。

＊ famous〔'feməs〕adj. 有名的　　singer〔'sɪŋɚ〕n. 歌手
performance〔pɚ'fɔrməns〕n. 表演
give a performance 做了一場表演

3. (**C**) (A)　　　　　　(B)　　　　　　(C)

　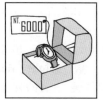

Richard is very fond of a watch that costs one hundred and twenty thousand dollars.

理察非常喜歡一支十二萬美元的手錶。

* *be fond of* 喜歡　　cost〔kɔst〕*v.* 花費；值…

第二部分：基本問答（第 4-10 題）

4. (**B**) Have you ever tried Korean food before?

你以前吃過韓國食物嗎？

(A) I have tried my best. 我已經盡力了。

(B) No, I don't think I have. 沒有，我想我沒吃過。

(C) Yes, it took about an hour. 有，它花了大約一小時。

* try〔traɪ〕*v.* 嘗試　　Korean〔ko'riən〕*adj.* 韓國的
  try one's best 盡力　　take〔tek〕*v.* 花費

5. (**B**) Is Michael Anderson there? 麥克・安德森在嗎？

(A) He is not speaking. 他沒在說話。

(B) This is he speaking. 我就是。

(C) Speaking. He is not here. 我就是。他不在這裡。

* *This is he speaking.* 【電話用語】我就是。(= *Speaking.*)

6. (**A**) Are you ready to order? 你準備好要點餐了嗎？

(A) Yes. I'll have the bacon cheeseburger meal.
    是的。我要培根起司漢堡餐。

(B) Yes. I'll be right there. 是的。我會在那裡。

(C) Yes. I'll try this on first. 是的。我會先試穿這個。

* ready〔'rɛdɪ〕*adj.* 準備好的　　order〔'ɔrdɚ〕*v.* 點（菜）
  bacon〔'bekən〕*n.* 培根
  cheeseburger〔'tʃiz,bɝgɚ〕*n.* 起司漢堡
  meal〔mil〕*n.* 一餐　　right〔raɪt〕*adv.* 恰好；正好；就
  right there 就在那裡　　*try on* 試穿

7. (**B**) Emily, did you have a history test yesterday?
愛蜜莉，妳昨天有歷史考試嗎？

(A) Yes, she did. 是的，她有。

(B) Yes, I did. 是的，我有。

(C) Yes, you did. 是的，你有。

* history (ˈhɪstrɪ) *n.* 歷史　　test (tɛst) *n.* 測驗；考試

8. (**C**) Excuse me. When does the next train to Fulong depart
the station? 對不起。下一班到福隆的火車什麼時候發車？

(A) Seventy-five dollars. 七十五元。

(B) On platform B. 在 B 月台。

(C) Not until five o'clock. 直到五點才會發車。

* depart (dɪˈpart) *v.* 離開　　platform (ˈplætˌform) *n.* 月台
not until 直到～才…

9. (**A**) Would you do me a favor and watch my backpack while I
use the restroom?
你能幫我一個忙，在我上廁所時看管我的後背包嗎？

(A) Sure, no problem. 當然，沒問題。

(B) You should. 你應該。

(C) He can't. 他不能。

* ***do*** *sb.* ***a favor*** 幫某人的忙　　watch (watʃ) *v.* 注意；看守
backpack (ˈbækˌpæk) *n.* 後背包
restroom (ˈrɛstˌrum) *n.* 廁所

10. (**B**) Is there anything I can do to help you get ready for your
trip? 有什麼我能幫忙，讓你做好去旅行的準備？

(A) You're welcome. I'm happy to help.
不客氣。我很高興能幫忙。

(B) Thanks. But I'm just about finished.
謝謝。但我差不多快完成了。

(C) Never mind. I didn't want to go anyway.
沒關係。反正我當時並不想去。

* **ready** (ˈrɛdɪ) *adj.* 準備好的　　**trip** (trɪp) *n.* 旅行
just about 差不多　　**finished** (ˈfɪnɪʃt) *adj.* 完成的
never mind 不客氣；沒關係
anyway (ˈɛnɪˌwe) *adv.* 反正

第三部分：言談理解（第 11-21 題）

11. (**A**) The sun is shining, the ocean waves are rolling in, and your feet are sinking in the warm sand. You and your partner are facing a big net, and two people are on the other side waiting for you to start serving.
陽光閃耀，海浪滾滾而來，你的腳陷入溫暖的沙中。你和你的夥伴正面對一個大網子，在另一邊有兩個人，正等著你們開始發球。

Question : What are you doing? 你正在做什麼？
(A) Playing beach volleyball. 在打沙灘排球。
(B) Watching a film. 在看電影。
(C) Preparing a meal. 在準備餐點。

* **shine** (ʃaɪn) *v.* 照耀　　**ocean** (ˈoʃən) *n.* 海洋
wave (wev) *n.* 海浪　　**roll** (rol) *v.* 滾動
sink (sɪnk) *v.* 下沉；陷入　　**sand** (sænd) *n.* 沙子
partner (ˈpɑrtnɚ) *n.* 夥伴　　**face** (fes) *v.* 面對
net (nɛt) *n.* 網子　　**serve** (sɝv) *v.* (網球、排球) 發球

12. (**B**) M : May I speak with Nancy, please?
男：請問我能跟南西說話嗎？
W : This is Nancy. Who's this?
女：我是南西。你是哪位？

M : Oh, hi, Nancy. I didn't recognize your voice. This is Todd.

男：喔，嗨，南西。我沒認出妳的聲音。我是陶德。

W : Hi, Todd. I have a cold and I'm all stuffed up. That's why I sound like this.

女：嗨，陶德。我感冒了，而且鼻塞。那就是為什麼我的聲音聽起來像這樣的原因。

M : Sorry to hear that. Hope you get well soon.

男：很遺憾聽到這件事。希望妳能儘快康復。

W : So what's up?

女：有什麼事嗎？

M : Actually, I was calling to see if you wanted to see a movie tonight, but I guess you're under the weather.

男：其實我是打來看看妳今晚是否想看電影，但我猜妳身體不舒服。

Question : Why did Todd call Nancy?

陶德為什麼打電話給南西？

(A) To see how she was feeling. 要看看她感覺如何。

(B) To invite her to a movie. <u>要邀請她去看電影。</u>

(C) To tell her about the class she missed.

要告訴她關於她沒上的課的事。

* recognize〔'rɛkəg,naɪz〕*v.* 認出　　voice〔vɔɪs〕*n.* 聲音
  have a cold 感冒　　stuff〔stʌf〕*v.* 填；塞
  be stuffed up 鼻塞　　sound〔saʊnd〕*v.* 聽起來
  What's up? 發生什麼事？　　actually〔'æktʃʊəlɪ〕*adv.* 事實上
  under the weather 不舒服　　invite〔ɪn'vaɪt〕*v.* 邀請
  miss〔mɪs〕*v.* 錯過

13. (**A**) M : Josie, have you finished using my EPad?

男：喬西，我的 EPad 妳用完了嗎？

W : Yes. I put it on the desk in your room, just like you told me.

女：是的。就像你告訴我的，我把它放在你房間的書桌上。

M : Well, it's not there now.

男：嗯，它現在不在那裡。

W : I swear, Jeff, I left it there about an hour ago. Maybe Dad borrowed it.

女：我發誓，傑夫，我大約一小時前把它留在那裡。也許是爸爸借走了。

M : No, Dad doesn't use the EPad, and Mom's at work. It had to have been Jason.

男：不，爸爸不會用 EPad，而且媽媽在上班。一定是傑森。

W : Oh, but I think Jason went to swimming class. He couldn't have taken it... unless....

女：噢，但我想傑森去上游泳課。他不可能帶走它…除非…。

M : Unless he took it with him.

男：除非他帶著它一起去。

Question : Who was the last person to see the EPad?

誰是最後看到 EPad 的人？

(A) Josie. 喬西。

(B) Jeff. 傑夫。

(C) Dad. 爸爸。

* Josie ('dʒozɪ) *n.* 喬西　　finish ('fɪnɪʃ) *v.* 完成；結束
  pad 是「平板電腦」的統稱，EPad 是一款平板電腦。
  swear (swɛr) *v.* 發誓　　leave (liv) *v.* 遺留
  maybe ('mebɪ) *adv.* 也許　　borrow ('baro) *v.* 借用
  at work 在工作中　　unless (ən'lɛs) *conj.* 除非

14. (**C**) Tipping started as a way of rewarding good service. Tips were viewed as gifts to servants. Today, tips are a part of

the way we pay for things. Different countries have different customs on tipping (in China, for example, it's an insult to tip). Here in Taiwan, tips are expected only in certain situations. It's helpful to know when it's appropriate to tip so that as you get older and go out in the world, you'll know what to do.

給小費一開始是種獎賞良好服務的方式。小費被認為是給服務員的禮物。現在，小費是我們付錢買東西的一部份。不同的國家有不同的給小費的習俗（以中國為例，給小費是一種侮辱）。在台灣這裡，只有在某些情況要給小費。知道何時給小費才適當是有幫助的，這樣當你長大以後出社會，就會知道該怎麼做。

Question：When is it appropriate to tip in China?

在中國，何時給小費最適當？

(A) Only in certain situations. 只有在某些情況。

(B) Only to servants. 只有給服務員。

(C) Never. 任何時候都不適當。

* tip〔tɪp〕v. 給小費　n. 小費　　reward〔rɪ'wɔrd〕v. 獎賞
　service〔'sɜvɪs〕n. 服務　　***be viewed as*** 被視為
　gift〔gɪft〕n. 禮物　　servant〔'sɜvənt〕n. 僕人；佣人
　today〔tə'de〕adv. 現在　　***pay for*** 支付⋯的錢
　different〔'dɪfrənt〕adj. 不同的　　country〔'kʌntrɪ〕n. 國家
　custom〔'kʌstəm〕n. 習俗　　on〔ɑn〕prep. 關於
　for example 例如　　insult〔'ɪnsʌlt〕n. 侮辱
　expect〔ɪk'spɛkt〕v. 期待　　certain〔'sɜtn̩〕adj. 某些
　situation〔ˌsɪtʃʊ'eʃən〕n. 情況
　helpful〔'hɛlpfəl〕adj. 有幫助的
　appropriate〔ə'proprɪɪt〕adj. 適當的　　***so that*** 以便於
　world〔wɜld〕n. 世界；社會

15. (**C**) W：Happy birthday, Robert! Do you have any special plans for today?

女：生日快樂，羅伯特！你今天有任何特別的計畫嗎？

M : Thanks, Elaine. No, I don't have anything special
planned. My brother's birthday is the day after
tomorrow, so my family will celebrate both birthdays
over the weekend.

男：謝謝，依蓮。沒有，我沒什麼特別的計畫。我弟弟的生日是
後天，所以我們全家人會在週末一起慶祝兩個人的生日。

W : Oh, I see. How old is your brother?

女：喔，我知道了。你弟弟幾歲？

M : He's two years younger than me, so 13.

男：他比我小兩歲，所以是十三歲。

Question : How old is Robert? 羅伯特幾歲？

(A) 13. 十三。

(B) 14. 十四。

(C) 15. 十五。

* special (ˈspɛʃəl) adj. 特別的   plan (plæn) n. v. 計劃
  the day after tomorrow 後天   celebrate (ˈsɛləˌbret) v. 慶祝
  weekend (ˈwikˈɛnd) n. 週末   see (si) v. 知道

16. (**B**) W : This garden is beautiful. I didn't know you had a
green thumb.

女：這個花園好美。我不知道你有園藝的才能。

M : I grew up on a farm, so I've always worked with the
land. This is just a hobby, though.

男：我在農場長大，所以我一直都在務農。不過這只是個嗜好。

W : Some of these flowers I've never seen in person
before. Is that a Comet Orchid?

女：有些花我以前從未親眼看過。那是彗星蘭嗎？

M : Yes, it is. It took me a long time to find the bulbs.
It's probably the rarest type of orchid for home
gardening.

男：是的，它是。我花了很長的時間才找到球莖。對家庭園藝來
　　說，它可能是最稀有的蘭花品種。

W : That's really cool!

女：眞是太酷了！

Question : What does the man like to do?

　　　　　這位男士喜歡做什麼？

(A) Work with children. 照顧小孩。

(B) Work with plants. 照顧植物。

(C) Work with animals. 照顧動物。

* garden〔'gardn〕*n.* 花園　　thumb〔θʌm〕*n.* 拇指
  a green thumb 園藝的才能　　***grow up*** 長大
  farm〔farm〕*n.* 農場
  work with 和…一起工作；（因工作關係）處理
  land〔lænd〕*n.* 土地；農業工作　　***work with the land*** 務農
  hobby〔'habɪ〕*n.* 嗜好　　though〔ðo〕*adv.*【置於句尾】不過
  comet〔'kamɪt〕*n.* 彗星　　orchid〔'ɔrkɪd〕*n.* 蘭花
  Comet Orchid 彗星蘭　　bulb〔bʌlb〕*n.* 球莖
  rare〔rɛr〕*adj.* 罕見的；稀有的　　type〔taɪp〕*n.* 類型
  gardening〔'gardnɪŋ〕*n.* 園藝　　cool〔kul〕*adj.* 酷的

17. (**C**) W : Would you like one more hamburger?

　　　　　女：你要再吃一個漢堡嗎？

　　　　　M : I would, but I'm full already.

　　　　　男：我想要，但是我已經飽了。

　　　　　Question : What does the man mean? 男士的意思是什麼？

(A) He wants to open a hamburger store.
　　他想開一間漢堡店。

(B) He'll ask for one more hamburger. 他會再要一個漢堡。

(C) He can't eat any more hamburgers.
　　他無法再吃更多的漢堡。

* ***would like*** 想要 　　hamburger〔'hæmbɝgɚ〕*n.* 漢堡
full〔fʊl〕*adj.* 飽的 　　mean〔min〕*v.* 意思是
open〔'opən〕*v.* 使開張 　　***ask for*** 要求

18. (**C**) M：Do you have any medicine for a headache?

　　　男：你有任何頭痛藥嗎？

　　　W：I do, but what's wrong? Are you sick?

　　　女：我有，但怎麼了？你生病了嗎？

　　　M：I don't think so. I've just had this headache for a
　　　　　couple of days.

　　　男：我想不是。我只是這樣頭痛好幾天了。

　　　W：Have you been to see the doctor?

　　　女：你去看過醫生了嗎？

　　　M：No, it's nothing serious.

　　　男：沒有，沒那麼嚴重。

　　Question：What is the man's problem? 男士的問題是什麼？

　　(A) He has a sore throat. 他喉嚨痛。

　　(B) He has a fever. 他發燒。

　　(C) He has a headache. 他頭痛。

* medicine〔'mɛdəsn̩〕*n.* 藥 　　headache〔'hɛd,ek〕*n.* 頭痛
What's wrong? 怎麼了？ 　　sick〔sɪk〕*adj.* 生病的
a couple of 兩三個；幾個 　　serious〔'sɪrɪəs〕*adj.* 嚴重的
sore〔sor〕*adj.* 疼痛的 　　throat〔θrot〕*n.* 喉嚨
have a sore throat 喉嚨痛 　　fever〔'fivɚ〕*n.* 發燒

19. (**C**) W：Hi, David. Why the glum look?

　　　女：嗨，大衛。爲什麼看起來悶悶不樂的？

　　　M：I just found out that my best friend, Al, is moving
　　　　　away at the end of the summer.

　　　男：我剛剛發現，我最好的朋友艾爾，夏天結束時要搬走了。

　　　W：He is? That's too bad. Why is he moving?

女：是嗎？眞是太糟了。爲什麼他要搬家？

M : I guess his mom got a better job in a different town.

男：我猜是因爲他媽媽在另一個城市找到更好的工作。

W : What about his dad?

女：那他的爸爸呢？

M : He lives with his mom.　His parents are divorced.

男：他和他的媽媽一起住。他的父母離婚。

Question : Why is David sad?　爲什麼大衛會難過？

(A) His parents are getting a divorce. 他的父母要離婚了。

(B) His parents are getting back together.

　　他的父母要復合了。

(C) His best friend is moving away. 他最好的朋友要搬走了。

* glum〔glʌm〕*adj.* 悶悶不樂的　　look〔lʊk〕*n.* 臉色；樣子
  find out 發現　***move away*** 搬走
  different〔'dɪfrənt〕*adj.* 不同的　　town〔taʊn〕*n.* 城鎮；城市
  What about…? …如何？　　divorced〔də'vɔrst〕*adj.* 離婚的
  sad〔sæd〕*adj.* 難過的　　***get back together*** 復合

20. (**B**) M : Are you going to the bank?

　　　男：妳要去銀行嗎？

　　　W : No, I'm going to the supermarket.

　　　女：不，我要去超市。

　　　M : Are you going to pass by the cleaners?

　　　男：妳會經過乾洗店嗎？

　　　W : I could.　Why?

　　　女：我可以。爲什麼這麼問？

　　　M : Would you pick up my suit?

　　　男：妳能幫我拿西裝嗎？

　　　W : OK.

　　　女：好。

Question： What does the man ask the woman to do?

這位男士要求女士做什麼？

(A) Give him a ride. 讓他搭便車。

(B) Pick up some clothing. 拿一些衣服。

(C) Buy some milk. 買一些牛奶。

* bank〔bæŋk〕*n.* 銀行　　supermarket〔'supɚˏmɑrkɪt〕*n.* 超市
pass by 經過　　*the cleaners* 乾洗店　　*pick up* 拿
suit〔sut〕*n.* 西裝　　*give sb. a ride* 讓某人搭便車
clothing〔'kloðɪŋ〕*n.* 衣服

21. (**A**)　W：May I see your boarding pass, sir?

女：我能看你的登機證嗎，先生？

M：Here it is. What's the problem, ma'am?

男：在這裡。有什麼問題嗎，女士？

W：You're sitting in 7B, sir. Your seat is 8B.

女：你坐在 7B，先生。你的座位是 8B。

M：Oh, I'm sorry. I must have misread the ticket.

男：喔，很抱歉。我一定是把票看錯了。

Question： What is the man's problem?

這位男士的問題是什麼？

(A) He's sitting in the wrong seat. 他坐錯位子。

(B) He's on the wrong flight. 他搭錯班機。

(C) He's headed in the wrong direction.

他朝錯誤的方向前進。

* board〔bord〕*v.* 上（車、船、飛機）
pass〔pæs〕*n.* 通行證　　*boarding pass* 登機證
Here it is. 你要的東西在這裡；拿去吧。
ma'am〔mæm〕*n.* 女士　　*must have + p.p.* 當時一定…
misread〔mɪs'rid〕*v.* 看錯　　flight〔flaɪt〕*n.* 班機
head〔hɛd〕*v.* 使前進　　direction〔də'rɛkʃən〕*n.* 方向
in ~ direction 朝～方向

🎧 TEST 5 ▶ 詳解

第一部分：辨識句意（第 1-3 題）

1. (**B**) (A)　　　　　(B)　　　　　(C)

Judy is at the farmer's market, where she wants to buy some fruit. 茱蒂在農夫市場，她想買些水果。

* farmer〔'fɑrmɚ〕*n.* 農夫　　　market〔'mɑrkɪt〕*n.* 市場
　fruit〔frut〕*n.* 水果

2. (**B**) (A)　　　　　(B)　　　　　(C)

The man wants to buy some flowers for his lovely wife's birthday. 男士因為可愛的老婆生日，所以想買一些花給她。

* lovely〔'lʌvlɪ〕*adj.* 可愛的　　　birthday〔'bɝθˌde〕*n.* 生日

3. (**B**) (A)　　　　　(B)　　　　　(C)

At dinner, they drank one bottle of soda, three cans of beer, and two glasses of wine.

晚餐時，他們喝了一瓶汽水、三罐啤酒，和兩杯葡萄酒。

* bottle〔'batḷ〕*n.* 瓶子　　soda〔'sodə〕*n.* 汽水
can〔kæn〕*n.* 罐子　　beer〔bɪr〕*n.* 啤酒
glass〔glæs〕*n.* 玻璃杯　　wine〔waɪn〕*n.* 葡萄酒

第二部分：基本問答（第 4-10 題）

4. (**C**) Were there many other kids at the park this afternoon?
今天下午公園有很多其他的小孩嗎？

(A) All of them.　他們全部。

(B) None of them.　他們一個都沒有。

(C) There were a few.　<u>有一些。</u>

* kid〔kɪd〕*n.* 小孩　　park〔pɑrk〕*n.* 公園

5. (**A**) Is that your jacket on the back of the chair?
在椅背上的那件是你的夾克嗎？

(A) No, it's not mine.　<u>不，不是我的。</u>

(B) Yes, they were here.　是的，它們在那裡。

(C) I didn't see him yesterday.　我昨天沒看到他。

* jacket〔'dʒækɪt〕*n.* 夾克　　back〔bæk〕*n.* 背部；背面

6. (**B**) How much time do you spend on the Internet every day?
你每天花多少時間上網？

(A) On Friday.　在星期五。

(B) Maybe an hour.　<u>也許一個小時。</u>

(C) Last week.　上星期。

* spend〔spɛnd〕*v.* 花費　　Internet〔'ɪntɚ.nɛt〕*n.* 網際網路
maybe〔'mebɪ〕*adv.* 也許

7. (**A**)　We are going to Hualien this weekend.
　　　　我們這個週末要去花蓮。

　　(A)　Enjoy your time there.　祝你們在那裡玩得愉快。

　　(B)　Can you join us?　你能加入我們嗎？

　　(C)　I'm sorry to hear that.　聽到這件事我很遺憾。

　　* weekend〔'wik'ɛnd〕*n.* 週末
　　　enjoy your time 祝你玩得愉快　　join〔dʒɔɪn〕*v.* 加入

8. (**A**)　Hi, Rex.　What seems to be the problem?
　　　　嗨，瑞克斯。有什麼問題嗎？

　　(A)　My computer froze and won't shut down.
　　　　我的電腦當機，而且無法關機。

　　(B)　I'm really enjoying myself here.
　　　　我在這裡真的玩得很愉快。

　　(C)　At least twice.　至少兩次。

　　* seem〔sim〕*v.* 似乎　　computer〔kəm'pjutɚ〕*n.* 電腦
　　　freeze〔friz〕*v.* 結冰；不動了【過去式是 froze】
　　　shut down 關機　　***enjoy*** *oneself* 玩得愉快
　　　at least 至少　　twice〔twaɪs〕*adv.* 兩次

9. (**B**)　Are you close with any of your siblings?
　　　　你跟任何一位兄弟姊妹關係親密嗎？

　　(A)　No, it shouldn't take that long.
　　　　不，這不應該花那麼久的時間。

　　(B)　Sure.　My family is very tight.
　　　　當然。我們全家人都非常親密。

　　(C)　Yes, it was pretty close.　是的，這相當接近。

　　* close〔klos〕*adj.* 親密的；接近的
　　　siblings〔'sɪblɪŋz〕*n. pl.* 兄弟姊妹　　take〔tek〕*v.* 花費
　　　long〔lɔŋ〕*n.* 長時間　　tight〔taɪt〕*adj.* 緊密的；關係親密的
　　　pretty〔'prɪtɪ〕*adv.* 相當

10. (**A**) Did you have a good time at the baseball game?
　　 你在棒球比賽玩得愉快嗎？

　　　 (A) Yes, it was a great game. 是的，那是很棒的比賽。

　　　 (B) Yes, I enjoyed my meal. 是的，我很喜歡我的餐點。

　　　 (C) Yes, they did a good job. 是的，他們做得很好。

　　　 * *have a good time* 玩得愉快　 game〔gem〕*n.* 比賽
　　　 great〔gret〕*adj.* 很棒的　 enjoy〔ɪn'dʒɔɪ〕*v.* 喜歡；享受
　　　 meal〔mil〕*n.* 一餐　 *do a good job* 做得好

第三部分：言談理解（第 11-21 題）

11. (**C**) W：Mr. Martin, I have a favor to ask.
　　　 女：馬丁先生，我要請你幫個忙。

　　　 M：Sure, Leslie. What can I do for you?
　　　 男：當然可以，萊斯莉。我能幫妳什麼忙？

　　　 W：My grandmother is visiting from Alabama next weekend, and I was wondering if I could have Saturday off.
　　　 女：我奶奶下週末要從阿拉巴馬州來，我想知道是否週六能休假。

　　　 M：That shouldn't be a problem, Leslie. Let me look at the schedule and see what I can do. I'll let you know later in the afternoon.
　　　 男：這應該不是問題，萊斯莉。讓我看一下時間表，然後看看能怎麼做。我下午晚一點再跟妳說。

　　　 Question：What is Leslie asking for? 萊斯莉要求什麼？

　　　 (A) A raise. 加薪。

　　　 (B) A different position. 一個不同的職位。

　　　 (C) Time off. 休假。

* favor〔'fevɚ〕n. 恩惠　　***ask a favor*** 請求幫忙
　sure〔ʃur〕adv. 當然；好
　grandmother〔'græn,mʌðɚ〕n. 祖母　　visit〔'vɪzɪt〕v. 作客
　Alabama〔,ælə'bæmə〕n. 阿拉巴馬州
　wonder〔'wʌndɚ〕v. 想知道　　off〔ɔf〕adv. 休息
　schedule〔'skɛdʒul〕n. 時間表　　later〔'letɚ〕adv. 稍後
　raise〔rez〕n. 加薪　　position〔pə'zɪʃən〕n. 職位

12. (**C**) W : Would you please stop making so much noise? I'm
　　　　　　 trying to study.
　　　　女：可以請你停止製造這麼多的噪音嗎？我想要唸書。
　　　　M : Sorry. I'm looking for my house keys.
　　　　男：抱歉。我正在找我家的鑰匙。
　　　　Question : Why is the woman angry?
　　　　　　　　　這位女士為什麼生氣？
　　　(A) She can't find her keys. 她找不到她的鑰匙。
　　　(B) She is locked out of the house. 她被鎖在房子外面。
　　　(C) The man is making noise. 這位男士正在製造噪音。

　　　* ***make noise*** 製造噪音　　***look for*** 尋找
　　　　lock〔lɑk〕v. 鎖　　***out of*** 在⋯外面

13. (**A**) W : I'm making a pot of tea. Would you like a cup?
　　　　女：我正在泡一壺茶。你要不要喝一杯？
　　　　M : No, thanks. I'm a coffee drinker.
　　　　男：不，謝謝。我喜歡喝咖啡。
　　　　W : Oh, I think I have some instant coffee in the freezer.
　　　　女：噢，我想我冰箱裡有些即溶咖啡。
　　　　M : Hmm. OK, I think I'll have a cup.
　　　　男：嗯。好，我想我要一杯。
　　　　W : Cream and sugar?
　　　　女：要加奶精和糖嗎？

M : No, black, please.

男：不，請給我黑咖啡。

W : Coming right up.　How about some biscuits?

女：馬上來。要一些餅乾嗎？

Question : How does the man prefer his coffee?

　　　　　這位男士喜歡什麼樣的咖啡？

(A) Black.　黑咖啡。

(B) With cream.　加奶精。

(C) With sugar.　加糖。

* pot〔pɑt〕*n.* 壺　　***make a pot of tea*** 泡一壺茶
　drinker〔ˈdrɪŋkɚ〕*n.* 愛喝（某種飲料）的人
　a coffee drinker 愛喝咖啡的人
　instant〔ˈɪnstənt〕*adj.* 速食的；即食的
　instant coffee 即溶咖啡　　freezer〔ˈfrizɚ〕*n.* 冰箱
　hmm〔m〕*interj.* 嗯　　cream〔krim〕*n.* 奶油；奶精
　sugar〔ˈʃugɚ〕*n.* 糖　　black〔blæk〕*adj.* 黑的；不加奶精的
　come up 出現　　right〔raɪt〕*adv.* 立即；馬上
　biscuit〔ˈbɪskɪt〕*n.* 餅乾　　prefer〔prɪˈfɝ〕*v.* 比較喜歡

14. (**B**) W : Uh-oh.　Here comes Coach Peterson.

　　　　　女：喔噢。彼得生教練來了。

M : What in the world?　Is he wearing one of our uniforms?

男：那究竟是什麼？他正穿著我們的制服嗎？

W : He looks like he's ready to join the team!

女：他看起來像是準備要加入隊伍！

M : Maybe we're short of a few players today.

男：也許我們今天少了幾個球員。

Question : What is the most probable reason Coach
　　　　　 Peterson is wearing a uniform?

　　　　　彼得生教練穿制服最有可能的原因是什麼？

(A) It's Halloween.　今天是萬聖節。

(B) He will play with the team today.

　　他今天會跟球隊一起打球。

(C) To end a losing streak.　爲了終止連輸。

* uh-oh (ˈʌˌo) *interj.* 喔噢　　coach (kotʃ) *n.* 教練
in the world 究竟　　uniform (ˈjunəˌfɔrm) *n.* 制服
team (tim) *n.* 隊伍　　short (ʃɔrt) *adj.* 短缺的；不足的
be short of 缺少　　player (ˈpleɚ) *n.* 球員
probable (ˈprɑbəbḷ) *adj.* 可能的　　reason (ˈrizṇ) *n.* 原因
Halloween (ˌhæloˈin) *n.* 萬聖節　　play (ple) *v.* 打球
end (ɛnd) *v.* 結束；終止　　losing (ˈluzɪŋ) *adj.* 輸的；失敗的
streak (strik) *n.* (輸、贏的) 連續
a losing streak 連輸（↔ *a winning streak* 連贏）

15. (**A**) Pop quiz: What is Voxer?　If you're scratching your head,
it's time to read up on the trendy new social media apps
kids are using.

隨堂測驗：Voxer 是什麼？如果你不知道的話，該是時候去研究
小孩在用的，最新流行的社交媒體應用程式了。

Question：What is Voxer?　Voxer 是什麼？

(A) A social media app.　一種社交媒體應用程式。

(B) A cordless telephone.　一種無線電話。

(C) A telecom company.　一間通訊公司。

* quiz (kwɪz) *n.* 小考　　***pop quiz*** 突擊測驗；突擊考試
scratch (skrætʃ) *v.* 抓；搔　　***scratch*** *one's* ***head*** 抓頭；傷腦筋
read up on 研究；用功研讀
trendy (ˈtrɛndɪ) *adj.* 非常流行的；時髦的
social (ˈsoʃəl) *adj.* 社交的　　media (ˈmidɪə) *n. pl.* 媒體
app (æp) *n.* 應用程式 (= *application*)
cordless (ˈkɔrdlɪs) *adj.* 無線的　　telecom (ˈtɛləˌkɑm) *n.* 通訊
company (ˈkʌmpənɪ) *n.* 公司

16. (**C**) M : How long have you lived in Jacksonville?

男：妳在傑克森村住多久了？

W : I moved here last year. How about you?

女：我去年搬來的。你呢？

M : Me? I was born here. I've never lived anywhere else.

男：我？我在這裡出生。我從來沒有住過別的地方。

Question : How long has the man lived in Jacksonville?

這位男士已經在傑克森村住了多久？

(A) One year. 一年。

(B) Since January. 從一月起。

(C) His whole life. <u>一輩子。</u>

* move〔muv〕*v.* 搬家　　born〔bɔrn〕*adj.* 出生的

else〔ɛls〕*adj.* 其他的；別的　　since〔sɪns〕*prep.* 自從

whole〔hol〕*adj.* 整個的　　***whole life*** 一輩子

17. (**A**) M : Hello!

男：哈囉！

W : Hello, David. Where are you guys? I've been
waiting for twenty minutes.

女：哈囉，大衛。你們在哪裡？我已經等二十分鐘了。

M : I'm on the bus. Are you already at the museum?

男：我在公車上。妳已經在博物館了嗎？

W : The museum? I'm at the school gate! I thought we
were meeting here at nine.

女：博物館？我在學校大門！我以為我們約九點在這裡見面。

M : No! We are meeting at the museum at ten.

男：不！我們約十點在博物館見面。

W : What?! Who decided that?

女：什麼?! 誰決定的？

M : Didn't Lucy call you last night?

男：露西昨晚沒打電話給妳嗎？

W : No, she did not.

女：不，她沒有。

Question : Why is the girl at the school gate?

這位女孩為什麼在學校大門？

(A) Lucy didn't call her. 露西沒打電話給她。

(B) David told her to be there. 大衛告訴她要去那裡。

(C) She's going to school. 她正要去學校。

* guy〔gaɪ〕*n.* 人；傢伙　*you guys* 你們
museum〔mju'ziəm〕*n.* 博物館　　gate〔get〕*n.* 大門
meet〔mit〕*v.* 會面　　decide〔dɪ'saɪd〕*v.* 決定
call〔kɔl〕*v.* 打電話給（某人）

18. (**B**) W : Welcome to The Matterhorn. My name is Debbie
and I'll be your server tonight.

女：歡迎來到馬特洪。我的名字是黛比，是你們今晚的服務員。

M : Hello there, Debbie. I think I'm ready to order.

男：嗨，黛比。我想我準備好要點餐了。

W : Would you like to hear about our specials, sir?

女：你想聽聽我們的特餐嗎，先生？

M : Thanks, but my mind is made up. I know what I
want.

男：謝謝，但我已經決定好了。我知道我要什麼。

Question : What do we know about the man?

我們知道這位男士的什麼事？

(A) He's been to this restaurant before.

他以前去過這間餐廳。

(B) He's ready to order his meal. 他準備好要點餐了。

(C) He wants to hear about the specials.

他想聽聽特餐是什麼。

* **server** (ˋsɝvɚ) *n.* 服務員　　***hello there*** 嗨；喂
  ready (ˋrɛdɪ) *adj.* 準備好的　　**order** (ˋɔrdɚ) *v.* 點（餐）
  hear about 聽到關於⋯的事　　**special** (ˋspɛʃəl) *n.* 特餐
  one's mind is made up 某人已經做好決定了
  【***make up one's mind*** 下定決心】
  have been to 去過　　**restaurant** (ˋrɛstərənt) *n.* 餐廳

19. (**A**) This form of transportation has two wheels but no engine.
    It is powered by the rider. You use your feet and legs to
    create motion. It is good exercise, and since it doesn't
    create any pollution, it's good for the environment, too.
    Most people learn to ride one of these when they are still
    young, but they are very popular with people of all ages.
    這種交通工具有兩個輪子，但沒有引擎。它是由騎的人供給動
    力。你用你的腳和腿使它移動。它是個好運動，而且因為它不
    會製造任何污染，所以也對環境有益。大部份的人都在小時候
    就學會騎它，但它們在所有年齡層都很受歡迎。

    Question：What is the speaker describing?
    　　　　　說話者在描述的是什麼？

    (A) A bicycle. 腳踏車。
    (B) A motorcycle. 摩托車。
    (C) An automobile. 汽車。

    * **form** (fɔrm) *n.* 形式
      transportation (͵trænspɚˋteʃən) *n.* 交通工具
      wheel (hwil) *n.* 輪子　　**engine** (ˋɛndʒən) *n.* 引擎
      power (ˋpauɚ) *v.* 提供動力　　**rider** (ˋraɪdɚ) *n.* 騎乘者
      create (krɪˋet) *v.* 創造　　**motion** (ˋmoʃən) *n.* 移動；運轉
      exercise (ˋɛksɚ͵saɪz) *n.* 運動
      pollution (pəˋluʃən) *n.* 污染
      environment (ɪnˋvaɪrənmənt) *n.* 環境
      still (stɪl) *adv.* 仍然　　**popular** (ˋpɑpjələ) *adj.* 受歡迎的

be popular with 受…歡迎   age〔edʒ〕*n.* 年齡
describe〔dɪ'skraɪb〕*v.* 描述;形容
motorcycle〔'motɚ,saɪkḷ〕*n.* 摩托車
automobile〔,ɔtəmə'bil〕*n.* 汽車

20. (**B**) M : Three of the messages on the answering machine are for Bill. Another four are for Kim.
　　　男:電話答錄機有三個留言是給比爾的。另外四個是給金的。
　　　W : What about the other two?
　　　女:那另外兩個呢?
　　　M : One was for me and the other was a wrong number.
　　　男:一個是給我的,而另一個是打錯電話。
　　　Question : How many messages were on the answering machine? 電話答錄機上共有幾個留言?
　　　(A) Eight. 八個。
　　　(B) Nine. 九個。
　　　(C) Ten. 十個。

　　　* message〔'mɛsɪdʒ〕*n.* 訊息;留言
　　　machine〔mə'ʃin〕*n.* 機器
　　　answering machine 電話答錄機   *What about~?* ~如何?
　　　one…the other~ (兩者)一個…,另一個~
　　　number〔'nʌmbɚ〕*n.* 號碼   *a wrong number* 打錯電話

21. (**A**) M : Hi, Jenny. Great to see you. It's been a while, huh?
　　　男:嗨,珍妮。很高興看到妳。好久不見了,對吧?
　　　W : What a pleasant surprise, Oscar!
　　　女:真是個愉快的驚喜,奧斯卡!
　　　M : So what have you been up to since graduation?
　　　男:畢業之後妳都在忙些什麼?
　　　W : Not much. Looking for a job.
　　　女:沒什麼。正在找工作。

M : I guess you haven't found one yet.

男：我猜妳還沒找到。

W : Nope. But I have been on a few interviews.

女：還沒。但我已經在進行一些面試。

M : I'm in the same boat.

男：我跟妳一樣。

Question : What does the man mean by "I'm in the same boat"?

這位男士說「我跟妳一樣」是什麼意思？

(A) He's having similar problems finding a job.

他同樣有找工作的問題。

(B) He's headed in the woman's direction.

他朝著那位女士的方向前進。

(C) He's on the same ferry boat as the woman.

他跟那位女士在同一艘渡船上。

* *a while* 一段時間　　*It's been a while.* 很久了；好久不見。
huh〔hʌ〕*interj.* 嗯；啊　　pleasant〔'plɛzn̩t〕*adj.* 令人愉快的
surprise〔sə'praɪz〕*n.* 驚奇；驚訝　　*be up to* 忙於
graduation〔,grædʒu'eʃən〕*n.* 畢業　　*not much* 沒什麼
look for 尋找　　guess〔gɛs〕*v.* 猜
not yet 尚未；還沒　　nope〔nop〕*adv.* 不（= *no*）
on〔ɑn〕*prep.* 處於…情況中　　*a few* 一些
interview〔'ɪntɚ,vju〕*n.* 面試　　boat〔bot〕*n.* 船
be in the same boat 處境相同　　mean〔min〕*v.* 意思是
have problems (*in*) + *V-ing* 做…有問題
similar〔'sɪmələ〕*adj.* 類似的　　head〔hɛd〕*v.* 使前進
direction〔də'rɛkʃən〕*n.* 方向
be headed in…direction 朝…方向前進
ferry〔'fɛrɪ〕*n.* 渡船（= *ferry boat*）

🎧 TEST 6 ▶ 詳解

第一部分：辨識句意（第 1-3 題）

1. (**C**) (A) 　(B) 　(C)

Bob is enjoying a big lunch of a cheeseburger, French fries, fried chicken, and a large soda.

鮑伯正在享用豐盛的午餐，有起士漢堡、薯條、炸雞，和大杯可樂。

* enjoy〔ɪnˈdʒɔɪ〕v. 享用　　big〔bɪɡ〕adj. 豐盛的
cheeseburger〔ˈtʃizˌbɝɡɚ〕n. 起士漢堡
French fries 薯條　　fried〔fraɪd〕adj. 炸的
soda〔ˈsodə〕n. 汽水

2. (**C**) (A) 　(B) 　(C)

Today is Children's Day in Taiwan, and many people celebrate by going to a festival.

今天是台灣的兒童節，許多人藉由參加慶典活動來慶祝。

* **Children's Day** 兒童節　　celebrate〔ˈsɛləˌbret〕v. 慶祝
festival〔ˈfɛstəvḷ〕n. 慶典

3. (**C**) (A)  (B)  (C)

Gloria went to the store, where she bought some sugar and 20 eggs. 葛洛麗亞去商店買了一些糖和二十顆蛋。

* sugar (ˈʃugɚ) *n.* 糖

第二部分：基本問答 (第 4-10 題)

4. (**B**) Have they finished repairing the Guandu Bridge?
他們修理好關渡大橋了嗎？

   (A) Sometimes. 有時候。

   (B) Not yet. 還沒。

   (C) Always. 總是這樣。

   * finish (ˈfɪnɪʃ) *v.* 完成   repair (rɪˈpɛr) *v.* 修理
   bridge (brɪdʒ) *n.* 橋   ***not yet*** 尚未；還沒

5. (**A**) I really like your jacket, Mary.
瑪莉，我真的很喜歡妳的夾克。

   (A) Thanks. 謝謝。

   (B) Sure. 當然。

   (C) You're welcome. 不客氣。

   * jacket (ˈdʒækɪt) *n.* 夾克

6. (**A**) Who is your favorite athlete? 你最喜愛的運動員是誰？

   (A) Kobe Bryant. 柯比・布萊恩。

   (B) TGI Fridays. 星期五餐廳。

   (C) Science. 科學。

* favorite〔'fevərɪt〕*adj.* 最喜愛的
athlete〔'æθlit〕*n.* 運動員　　science〔'saɪəns〕*n.* 科學

7. (**A**) That's a cool watch, Alan.　Where did you get it?
那支錶很酷，艾倫。你在哪裡買的？

(A) It was a gift from my brother.　這是我哥哥送我的禮物。

(B) It runs on a solar battery.　它是用太陽能電池運作。

(C) It cost one month's salary.　它花了我一個月的薪水。

* cool〔kul〕*adj.* 酷的　　get〔gɛt〕*v.* 買
gift〔gɪft〕*n.* 禮物　　run〔rʌn〕*v.* 運作
solar〔'solɚ〕*adj.* 太陽能的　　battery〔'bætərɪ〕*n.* 電池
cost〔kɔst〕*v.* 花費　　salary〔'sælərɪ〕*n.* 薪水

8. (**C**) Will there be enough food for everyone who attends the
party?　會有足夠的食物給參加派對的人嗎？

(A) The invitations have already been sent out.
邀請函已經寄出去了。

(B) Somewhere between 50 and 75 people.
大約有五十到七十五人。

(C) There should be more than enough.　應該綽綽有餘。

* attend〔ə'tɛnd〕*v.* 參加　　invitation〔ˌɪnvə'teʃən〕*n.* 邀請函
send out 寄出去　　somewhere〔'sʌmˌhwɛr〕*adv.* 大約
more than enough 夠多；綽綽有餘

9. (**A**) Why did Claire storm out like that?
為什麼克萊兒那樣氣沖沖地離開？

(A) I don't know.　Was it something I said?
我不知道。是我說了什麼嗎？

(B) That's right.　Could it be any louder?
沒錯。還能更大聲嗎？

(C) Of course.　Wait until the storm clears.
當然。你可以等到暴風雨過去。

* storm〔stɔrm〕*v.* 猛衝　*n.* 暴風雨
  storm out 氣沖沖地衝出　　loud〔laʊd〕*adj.* 大聲的
  clear〔klɪr〕*v.*（天氣）放晴；離開

10.（ **B** ） It looks like Stanley is running late. Should we start
without him?

看起來史丹利好像快要遲到了。沒有他我們還是照樣開始嗎？

(A) You never know. 這很難說。

(B) We might as well. 我們不妨這樣做。

(C) They didn't ask about it. 他們沒問那個。

* run〔rʌn〕*v.* 變得　　late〔let〕*adj.* 遲到的
  you never know 很難說；很難預料
  might as well 不妨；最好

第三部分：言談理解（第 11-21 題）

11.（ **A** ） Here's your local weather forecast. Today will continue
to be warm and sunny with highs in the upper 20s.
Tonight will be cooler as a cold front moves in from the
north. Expect rain showers tomorrow and highs in the
low to mid 20s. And now, here's John Edwards with your
noon drive-time traffic report.

以下是本地的天氣預報。今天將持續溫暖與晴朗，高溫二十八、
九度。由於今晚有冷鋒從北方移入，天氣將會比較涼。預計明天
會有陣雨，高溫會是二十一、二至二十四、五度左右。現在是由
約翰‧愛德華茲爲您播報中午開車時間的交通狀況。

Question：What will happen next? 接下來會出現什麼？

(A) A traffic report. 交通報導。

(B) A sports report. 運動報導。

(C) A special report. 特別報導。

* local〔'lokḷ〕*adj.* 本地的　　weather〔'wɛðɚ〕*n.* 天氣
  forecast〔'for͵kæst〕*n.* 預報　　continue〔kən'tɪnju〕*v.* 持續

warm〔wɔrm〕*adj.* 溫暖的　　sunny〔'sʌnɪ〕*adj.* 晴朗的
highs〔haɪz〕*n.pl.* 最高溫　　*in the upper 20s* 二十八、二十九
cool〔kul〕*adj.* 涼爽的　　*cold front* 冷鋒
move in 進來　　north〔nɔrθ〕*n.* 北方
expect〔ɪk'spɛkt〕*v.* 預期　　shower〔'ʃauɚ〕*n.* 陣雨
in the low to mid 20s 二十一、二至二十四、五
noon〔nun〕*n.* 中午　　drive-time *adj.* 開車時間的
traffic〔'træfɪk〕*n.* 交通　　report〔rɪ'port〕*n.* 報導
sports〔sports〕*adj.* 運動的　　special〔'spɛʃəl〕*adj.* 特別的

12. (**C**)　M：The Internet isn't working.
　　　　男：網路不能使用。
　　　　W：Did you check the router?
　　　　女：你有檢查線路嗎？
　　　　M：Yes. I even reset the whole network.
　　　　男：有。我甚至重設整個網路。
　　　　W：It must be a problem with the server.
　　　　女：這一定是伺服器有問題。
　　　　M：Do you have the phone number for tech support?
　　　　男：你有沒有技術支援的電話？
　　　　W：Here it is. 1-800-567-5566.
　　　　女：在這裡。1-800-567-5566。
　　　　M：Thanks. I'll call and find out what's going on.
　　　　男：謝謝。我會打去，並查明發生了什麼事。

　　　　Question：What will the man most likely do next?
　　　　　　　　　這位男士接下來最有可能做什麼？

　　　(A) Reset the Internet connection. 重設網路連線。
　　　(B) Install a new program. 安裝新的程式。
　　　(C) Call the helpline. 打服務熱線。

　　* Internet〔'ɪntɚ,nɛt〕*n.* 網際網路　　work〔wɝk〕*v.* 運作
　　　check〔tʃɛk〕*v.* 檢查
　　　router〔'rutɚ〕*n.* 路由器【連接數個區域網路的中繼裝置】

reset〔ri'sɛt〕 *v.* 重新設定　　whole〔hol〕 *adj.* 整個的
network〔'nɛt,wɝk〕 *n.* 網路　　server〔'sɝvɚ〕 *n.* 伺服器
tech〔tɛk〕 *adj.* 技術的（= *technical*）
support〔sə'port〕 *n.* 支持；援助　　***tech support*** 技術支援
find out 查明　　***go on*** 發生　　likely〔'laɪklɪ〕 *adv.* 可能
next〔nɛkst〕 *adv.* 接下來　　connection〔kə'nɛkʃən〕 *n.* 連結
install〔ɪn'stɔl〕 *v.* 安裝　　program〔'progræm〕 *n.* 程式
helpline〔'hɛlp,laɪn〕 *n.* 服務熱線

13. (**B**)　W：Shall we go and visit Mr. Miller in the hospital?
　　　　女：我們要去醫院探望米勒先生嗎？
　　　　M：What happened to him?
　　　　男：他發生了什麼事？
　　　　W：He got hurt in an accident near Coco Café.
　　　　女：他在可可咖啡廳附近出車禍受傷。
　　　　M：Sure. Let's go.
　　　　男：當然好。我們走吧。

　　　　Question：Where's Mr. Miller? 米勒先生在哪裡？

　　　　(A) In the office. 在辦公室。
　　　　(B) In the hospital. 在醫院。
　　　　(C) At Coco Café. 在可可咖啡廳。

　　　　* visit〔'vɪzɪt〕 *v.* 拜訪；探望　　happen〔'hæpən〕 *v.* 發生
　　　　hospital〔'hɑspɪtl〕 *n.* 醫院　　***get hurt*** 受傷
　　　　accident〔'æksədənt〕 *n.* 意外　　near〔nɪr〕 *prep.* 在…附近
　　　　café〔kə'fe〕 *n.* 咖啡廳　　office〔'ɔfɪs〕 *n.* 辦公室

14. (**C**)　M：What are you doing after this?
　　　　男：妳做完這個之後要做什麼？
　　　　W：No plans. I don't really feel like going home. It's
　　　　　　such a nice day.
　　　　女：沒有計畫。我不是很想回家。今天天氣真好。
　　　　M：Exactly. That's why I was thinking about going to
　　　　　　the outdoor shopping mall in Woodridge.

男：的確。這就是為什麼我正在考慮要去伍德里奇戶外購物中心的原因。

W : How are you planning to get there?

女：你打算要怎麼去那裡？

M : The number 12 bus goes there. I could also take the subway. Want to come?

男：十二號公車會到那裡。我也可以搭地鐵。要去嗎？

W : Sure, why not?

女：當然，為什麼不？

Question : Why does the man want to go to the shopping mall? 男士為什麼想要去購物中心？

(A) He has a part-time job in the food court.
他在美食廣場有個兼職工作。

(B) He can take the subway. 他可以搭地鐵。

(C) It's a nice day. 天氣很好。

* ***feel like*** 想要　　exactly〔ɪgˋzæktlɪ〕*adv.* 對的；沒錯
think about 考慮　　outdoor〔ˋaʊtˌdor〕*adj.* 戶外的
shopping mall 購物中心　　subway〔ˋsʌbˌwe〕*n.* 地鐵
part-time〔ˋpɑrtˌtaɪm〕*adj.* 兼差的　　***food court*** 美食廣場

15. (**C**) M : Where are you leaving for, Linda?

男：妳要去哪裡，琳達？

W : I'm leaving for Nantou to visit my grandsons. By the way, could you walk my dog while I'm out, Harry?

女：我要去南投看我的孫子。對了，哈利，我不在的時候你可以幫我遛狗嗎？

M : No problem.

男：沒問題。

Question : Who is in Nantou? 誰在南投？

(A) Linda. 琳達。

(B) Harry's grandsons. 哈利的孫子。

(C) Linda's grandsons. 琳達的孫子。

* ***leave for*** 動身前往　　grandson〔'grænd,sʌn〕*n.* 孫子
  by the way 順便一提　　***walk*** *one's* ***dog*** 幫某人遛狗
  out〔aut〕*adv.* 外出；不在

16. (**B**) W：That was a great movie! I loved it!
   女：那是一部很棒的電影！我非常喜愛！
   M：Seriously? It couldn't end soon enough for me.
   男：眞的嗎？我迫不及待要它趕快結束。
   W：Really? Why?
   女：眞的嗎？爲什麼？
   M：I knew who the killer was from the start. Why did we
   　　waste 90 minutes waiting for them to figure it out?
   男：我一開始就知道兇手是誰。爲什麼我們要浪費九十分鐘等他
   　　們弄清楚呢？
   Question：What does the woman think of the movie?
   　　　　　女士覺得電影怎麼樣？
   (A) She hated it. 她討厭這部電影。
   (B) She liked it. 她喜歡這部電影。
   (C) She thought it was too short. 她認爲這部電影太短了。

   * seriously〔'sɪrɪəslɪ〕*adv.* 認眞地　　***not ~ enough*** 不夠～
     soon〔sun〕*adv.* 快　　killer〔'kɪlɚ〕*n.* 殺人者；殺手
     from the start 從一開始　　***figure out*** 了解；弄清楚

17. (**A**) Lunch is at noon and lasts for one hour. You may choose
   to eat in our cafeteria or elsewhere. All employees are
   expected to be back at their desks at one o'clock. There
   are two 15-minute break periods at 10:30 and 3:30. You
   are free to leave the building; however, please stay on
   company property unless there's an emergency.
   午餐時間是中午一小時。你可以選擇在我們的自助餐廳，或去其
   他地方吃。所有的員工都要一點鐘回到自己的辦公桌前。有兩個

十五分鐘的休息時間，分別是在十點半和三點半。你可以自由離
開這棟大樓；然而，除非有緊急情況，否則請待在公司的範圍
內。

Question：What is happening? 現在正在發生什麼事？

(A) A manager is explaining company rules.
　　<u>經理正在說明公司的規定。</u>

(B) A teacher is explaining a test format.
　　老師正在說明考試的形式。

(C) A doctor is explaining an illness.
　　醫生正在解釋一種疾病。

* noon〔nun〕*n.* 中午　　last〔læst〕*v.* 持續
choose〔tʃuz〕*v.* 選擇　　cafeteria〔ˌkæfə'tɪrɪə〕*n.* 自助餐廳
elsewhere〔'ɛlsˌhwɛr〕*adv.* 在別處
employee〔ˌɛmplɔɪ'i〕*n.* 員工
expect〔ɪk'spɛkt〕*v.* 預期；要求　　desk〔dɛsk〕*n.* 辦公桌
break〔brek〕*n.* 休息　　period〔'pɪrɪəd〕*n.* 期間
free〔fri〕*adj.* 自由的　　building〔'bɪldɪŋ〕*n.* 大樓
company〔'kʌmpənɪ〕*n.* 公司
property〔'prɑpətɪ〕*n.* 財產；地產
unless〔ən'lɛs〕*conj.* 除非
emergency〔ɪ'mɝdʒənsɪ〕*n.* 緊急情況
manager〔'mænɪdʒɚ〕*n.* 經理
explain〔ɪk'splen〕*v.* 解釋；說明
rule〔rul〕*n.* 規定　　format〔'fɔrmæt〕*n.* 形式
illness〔'ɪlnɪs〕*n.* 疾病

18. (**C**) W：Have you tried the new YouBike system?
　　女：你試過新的微笑單車系統嗎？
　　M：Not yet.　I'm not sure how it works.
　　男：還沒。我還不確定它是怎麼運作的。
　　W：It's actually really simple.　All you need is an Easy
　　　　Card and a cellphone number.
　　女：它其實非常簡單。你只需要一張悠遊卡和一個手機號碼。

M : And is it true that you can return the bikes to any MRT station?

男：而且真的可以在任何捷運站歸還腳踏車嗎？

W : Yes. It's really quite convenient.

女：對。它真的很方便。

M : Maybe I will give it a try this weekend.

男：也許這個週末我會試一試。

Question : What do you need to use the YouBike system?

使用微笑單車系統會需要什麼？

(A) Two forms of photo ID and an ATM card.

兩張有照片的證件和一張提款卡。

(B) A copy of your passport and a home address.

一份護照影本和住家地址。

(C) An Easy Card and a cellphone number.

一張悠遊卡和一個手機號碼。

* ***not yet*** 尚未；還沒　　actually〔'æktʃʊəlɪ〕*adv.* 事實上
simple〔'sɪmpḷ〕*adj.* 簡單的　　***Easy Card*** 悠遊卡
cellphone〔'sɛl,fon〕*n.* 手機　　return〔rɪ'tɜn〕*v.* 歸還
MRT station 捷運站　　convenient〔kən'vinjənt〕*adj.* 方便的
give it a try 試試看　　weekend〔'wik'ɛnd〕*n.* 週末
system〔'sɪstəm〕*n.* 系統　　form〔fɔrm〕*n.* 形式；種類
photo〔'foto〕*n.* 照片　　***ID card*** 身分證（= *identity card*）
ATM　*n.* 提款機（= *automated-teller machine*）
ATM card 提款卡　　copy〔'kɑpɪ〕*n.* 影本
passport〔'pæs,port〕*n.* 護照　　address〔ə'drɛs〕*n.* 地址

19. (**C**) W : What's that smell?

女：那是什麼味道？

M : Umm…. Where is it coming from?

男：嗯…。是從哪裡傳來的？

W : Anything on your shoes?

女：會不會是你鞋子上的東西？

M : Nope. Maybe the trash can?

男：沒有。或許是垃圾桶？

W : Don't think so. I took out the garbage yesterday.

女：我覺得應該不是。我昨天才倒垃圾。

M : Ohh, it's Tom's noodles! I think that bowl has been there for days.

男：噢，是湯姆的麵！我覺得那碗已經在那裡好幾天了。

Question : Where is the smell coming from?

味道是從哪裡傳來的？

(A) The trash can. 垃圾桶。

(B) The man's shoes. 男士的鞋子。

(C) Tom's noodles. <u>湯姆的麵。</u>

* smell〔smɛl〕*n.* 味道　　nope〔nop〕*adv.* 不（= *no*）
trash〔træʃ〕*n.* 垃圾　　***trash can*** 垃圾桶
Don't think so. 我認為不是。（= *I don't think so*）
garbage〔'gɑrbɪdʒ〕*n.* 垃圾　　***take out the garbage*** 倒垃圾
noodle〔'nudl〕*n.* 麵　　bowl〔bol〕*n.* 碗

20. (**A**) M : Mom, I'm thinking about joining the school soccer team.

男：媽，我在考慮要加入學校的足球隊。

W : Didn't you say that you don't have enough time to do your homework yesterday?

女：你昨天不是說你沒有足夠的時間做功課？

M : I did, but I really like soccer.

男：我的確有說，但我真的很喜歡足球。

Question : What does the woman wish the boy to do?

女士希望男孩做什麼？

(A) Spend more time studying. <u>花更多的時間讀書。</u>

(B) Help her with the housework. 幫她做家事。

(C) Join the school soccer team. 加入學校的足球隊。

> * join〔dʒɔɪn〕 *v.* 加入   soccer〔'sɑkə〕 *n.* 足球
> team〔tim〕 *n.* 隊   homework〔'hom,wɜk〕 *n.* 功課
> spend〔spɛnd〕 *v.* 花（時間）
> housework〔'haʊs,wɜk〕 *n.* 家事

21. (**A**) M : Good evening, everyone. Welcome to Kitchen
      Corner with Rick Moss. Joining me today is Lena
      Stevens.

   男：大家晚安。歡迎來到瑞克摩斯的角落廚房。我今天的貴賓是
   　　麗娜史蒂芬斯。

   W : Hello, Rick. It's a pleasure to be here. What I'm
      going to show you today is Indian chicken.

   女：哈囉，瑞克。很榮幸來到這裡。我今天要示範給你看的是印
   　　度雞肉。

   M : Hmm, sounds good!

   男：嗯，聽起來很棒！

   W : And it tastes good, too. Now, you'll need four
      chicken legs. You'll also need two eggs, butter,
      cream, and….

   女：它嚐起來也很棒。現在，你會需要四隻雞腿。你也會需要兩
   　　顆蛋、奶油、鮮奶油，還有…。

   Question : What is the woman going to do?

   　　　　　　　這位女士將要做什麼？

   (A) Prepare some food. 準備一些食物。

   (B) Sing a song. 唱一首歌。

   (C) Give a speech. 發表演說。

   * corner〔'kɔrnə〕 *n.* 角落   pleasure〔'plɛʒə〕 *n.* 榮幸
   show〔ʃo〕 *v.* 給…看   Indian〔'ɪndɪən〕 *adj.* 印度的
   sound〔saʊnd〕 *v.* 聽起來   taste〔test〕 *v.* 嚐起來
   chicken leg 雞腿   butter〔'bʌtə〕 *n.* 奶油
   cream〔krim〕 *n.* 鮮奶油   prepare〔prɪ'pɛr〕 *v.* 準備
   speech〔spitʃ〕 *n.* 演說   ***give a speech*** 發表演說

TEST 7 ▶ 詳解

第一部分：辨識句意（第 1-3 題）

1. (**C**) (A)　　　　　(B)　　　　　(C)

Tracy and Wayne are on the bus going to school.
崔西和偉恩在去學校的公車上。

2. (**C**) (A)　　　　　(B)　　　　　(C)

Mrs. Wilson is putting a pumpkin pie into the oven.
威爾森太太正要把一個南瓜派放進烤箱裡。

* pumpkin〔'pʌmpkɪn〕n. 南瓜　　pie〔paɪ〕n. 派
  oven〔'ʌvən〕n. 烤箱

3. (**A**) (A)　　　　　(B)　　　　　(C)

Kevin and Roger are racing on bicycles while their
friends cheer them on.

凱文和羅傑正在比賽騎腳踏車，同時他們的朋友正在幫他們加油打氣。

* race〔res〕*v.* 比賽　　while〔hwaɪl〕*conj.* 同時
cheer〔tʃɪr〕*v.* 歡呼　　***cheer sb. on*** 為某人加油打氣

第二部分：基本問答（第 4-10 題）

4. (**B**) How does Fanny go to school? 芬妮怎麼去學校？

　　(A) She does well. 她考得很好。

　　(B) By train. <u>搭火車。</u>

　　(C) Twenty minutes. 二十分鐘。

　　* ***do well*** 考得好；表現好

5. (**B**) Where are the markers we use for the dry-erase board?
我們用來寫乾擦板的麥克筆在哪裡？

　　(A) Meet me at the bus stop. 在公車站跟我會面。

　　(B) In the top drawer of the desk.
<u>在書桌最上面的抽屜。</u>

　　(C) Nothing for me, thanks. 我不用，謝謝。

　　* marker〔'markɚ〕*n.* 麥克筆　　dry-erase〔'draɪ ɪ'res〕*n.* 乾擦
board〔bord〕*n.* 黑板　　meet〔mit〕*v.* 與…會面
stop〔stap〕*n.* 候車站　　top〔tap〕*adj.* 最上面的
drawer〔'drɔɚ〕*n.* 抽屜

6. (**C**) Who left the kitchen lights on? 誰沒關廚房的燈？

　　(A) I don't. 我不會。

　　(B) I will. 我將會。

　　(C) I did. <u>是我。</u>

　　* leave〔liv〕*v.* 使處於（某種狀態）　　light〔laɪt〕*n.* 燈
on〔an〕*adj.* 開著的

7. (**C**) What do you think about ordering a pizza tonight?

你覺得今晚訂披薩如何？

(A) Not quite. 還差一點。

(B) Very late. 很晚。

(C) Sounds good. 聽起來不錯。

* order (ˈɔrdɚ) v. 訂購　pizza (ˈpitsə) n. 披薩
  not quite 還差一點　late (let) adj. 晚的
  sound (saʊnd) v. 聽起來

8. (**A**) Was the train crowded this morning?

今天早上火車很擁擠嗎？

(A) It wasn't too bad. I was able to get a seat.

還不算太糟。我有位子坐。

(B) I went to school this morning. 我今天早上去上學。

(C) It had a few problems. I got home late.

它有一些問題。我很晚才到家。

* crowded (ˈkraʊdɪd) adj. 擁擠的　**be able to V.** 能夠…
  seat (sit) n. 座位　**a few** 一些

9. (**C**) Nobody replied to my party invitations.

沒人回覆我的派對邀請函。

(A) Come here. I'll fix it for you. 過來。我幫你修。

(B) Hold your horses. I'm not ready yet.

別著急。我還沒準備好。

(C) Give it some time. You just sent them out.

慢慢來。你才剛寄出去。

* reply (rɪˈplaɪ) v. 回覆
  invitation (ˌɪnvəˈteʃən) n. 請帖；邀請函
  fix (fɪks) v. 修理　**hold your horses** 別著急
  not yet 尚未；還沒　**get it time** 慢慢來　send (sɛnd) v. 寄

10. (**B**) The neighbor's dog has been digging up my garden.

鄰居的狗一直在挖我的花園。

(A) I grow flowers. 我種花。

(B) Is there anything we can do about it?

<u>我們能為此做點什麼嗎？</u>

(C) The cat is outside. 貓在外面。

* neighbor〔'nebɚ〕*n.* 鄰居　　dig〔dɪg〕*v.* 挖＜*up*＞
garden〔'gɑrdn̩〕*n.* 花園　　grow〔gro〕*v.* 種植
outside〔'aʊt,saɪd〕*adv.* 在外面

第三部分：言談理解（第 11-21 題）

11. (**C**) M：Susan, nice to meet you.

男：蘇珊，很高興認識妳。

W：Nice to meet you, too, Neil. My brother always talks about you. He says you are his best friend.

女：我也很高興認識你，尼爾。我哥哥經常提到你。他說你是他最好的朋友。

M：Yeah, Jeff and I are good friends.

男：是啊，傑夫和我是好朋友。

Question：Who's Susan? 蘇珊是誰？

(A) Neil's girlfriend. 尼爾的女朋友。

(B) Neil's sister. 尼爾的妹妹。

(C) Jeff's sister. <u>傑夫的妹妹。</u>

* meet〔mit〕*v.* 認識　　yeah〔jɛ〕*adv.* 是（＝*yes*）
girlfriend〔'gɝl,frɛnd〕*n.* 女朋友

12. (**A**) M：Glenda, is everything going well at school? It's been two weeks, right?

男：格蘭達，在學校一切順利嗎？已經兩週了，對嗎？

W : Yeah. I've met three classmates who love playing volleyball, just like me!

女：是啊。我已經認識三個和我一樣愛打排球的同學！

M : How about your classes?

男：妳的課程如何？

W : Well, most of them are interesting, but I have much more homework here than at my last school.

女：嗯，大部份都很有趣，但我在這裡的功課比上一個學校還要多很多。

Question : What do we know about Glenda?

關於格蘭達我們知道什麼？

(A) She enjoys volleyball. <u>她喜歡排球。</u>

(B) She doesn't like school. 她不喜歡學校。

(C) She never has homework. 她從未有過功課。

* **go well** 進展順利　　volleyball (ˈvɑlɪ,bɔl) *n.* 排球
  just (dʒʌst) *adv.* 正好　　***How about~?***　~如何？
  interesting (ˈɪntrɪstɪŋ) *adj.* 有趣的
  enjoy (ɪnˈdʒɔɪ) *v.* 喜歡　　never (ˈnɛvɚ) *adv.* 從未

13. (**A**) W : Hi, I'm Wendy, the head of Sportex. You must be Reggie. Tell me something about your work experience.

女：嗨，我是溫蒂，史波特斯的總經理。你一定是瑞吉。跟我說說你的工作經驗。

M : Sure, I worked as a waiter for five years.

男：好，我當服務生當了五年。

W : Don't you think it's tiring to be a waiter?

女：你不覺得當服務生很累嗎？

M : Not at all. I love food and I like to see people enjoying their meals.

男：一點也不。我熱愛食物，而且我喜歡看人們享受他們的餐點。

W : Good. Can you tell me more about…

女：很好。你能跟我講更多關於…

Question：What does the man want to do?

　　　　男士想要做什麼？

(A) Get a job. 得到一份工作。

(B) Find an apartment. 找一間公寓。

(C) Order a meal. 點餐。

* head〔hɛd〕*n.* 主管；總經理
experience〔ɪk'spɪrɪəns〕*n.* 經驗
sure〔ʃʊr〕*adv.* 當然；好　***work as*** 擔任
waiter〔'wetɚ〕*n.* 服務生　tiring〔'taɪrɪŋ〕*adj.* 令人疲倦的
not at all 一點也不　meal〔mil〕*n.* 一餐
apartment〔ə'pɑrtmənt〕*n.* 公寓　order〔'ɔrdɚ〕*v.* 點（餐）

14.(**C**) M : Are you ready to order?

男：你準備好要點餐了嗎？

W : Yes. I'll have the fried chicken.

女：是的。我要炸雞。

M : Anything to drink?

男：需要任何飲料嗎？

W : Do you have lemonade?

女：你們有檸檬汁嗎？

Question：Where are the speakers? 說話者在哪裡？

(A) In a bank. 在銀行。

(B) In a library. 在圖書館。

(C) In a restaurant. <u>在餐廳。</u>

* fried〔fraɪd〕*adj.* 油炸的　　***fried chicken*** 炸雞
lemonade〔͵lemən'ed〕*n.* 檸檬汁　　bank〔bæŋk〕*n.* 銀行
library〔'laɪ͵brɛrɪ〕*n.* 圖書館　　restaurant〔'rɛstərənt〕*n.* 餐廳

15. (**B**)　W：This is a picture of my daughter.

女：這是我女兒的照片。

M：My goodness, she's a beautiful girl!

男：我的天啊，她真是個美麗的女孩！

W：Thank you.　She's very charming and a great student, too.

女：謝謝你。她非常迷人，而且也是個好學生。

M：Wow, you really hit the jackpot!

男：哇，妳真的是中頭獎了！

Question：What does the man mean when he says, "You really hit the jackpot!"? 當這位男士說「妳真的是中頭獎了！」，是什麼意思？

(A) The woman is rich. 女士很有錢。

(B) The woman is lucky. <u>女士很幸運。</u>

(C) The woman is smart. 女士很聰明。

* picture〔'pɪktʃɚ〕*n.* 照片　　daughter〔'dɔtɚ〕*n.* 女兒
My goodness! 我的天啊！　　beautiful〔'bjutəfəl〕*adj.* 美麗的
charming〔'tʃɑrmɪŋ〕*adj.* 迷人的　　great〔gret〕*adj.* 很棒的
hit〔hɪt〕*v.* 中　　jackpot〔'dʒæk͵pɑt〕*n.* 累積賭注獎金
hit the jackpot 中頭獎　　rich〔rɪtʃ〕*adj.* 有錢的
lucky〔'lʌkɪ〕*adj.* 幸運的　　smart〔smɑrt〕*adj.* 聰明的

16. (**A**)　W：How much did you spend at the shopping mall?

女：你在購物中心花了多少錢？

M：Nothing.　I was only browsing.

男：沒花錢。我只是去看看。

W：Then what do you have in the bag?

女：那你袋子裡的是什麼？

M：These are some old clothes I'm going to donate to charity.

男：這些是我要捐給慈善機構的一些舊衣服。

W：Oh, where can you do that?

女：喔，你要在哪裡捐？

M：There's a collection box in my neighborhood.

男：我家附近有一個舊衣回收箱。

Question：What is the man going to do? 男士將要做什麼？

(A) Give some clothing to needy people.

<u>把一些衣服給貧窮的人。</u>

(B) Return some items he bought at the mall.

退還一些他在購物中心買的東西。

(C) Visit a friend in the hospital. 去醫院探望朋友。

* spend〔spɛnd〕v. 花　　mall〔mɔl〕n. 購物中心
shopping mall 購物中心　　browse〔braʊz〕v. 瀏覽
donate〔'donet〕v. 捐贈　　charity〔'tʃærətɪ〕n. 慈善機構
collection〔kə'lɛkʃən〕n. 收集
neighborhood〔'nebɚ͵hʊd〕n. 鄰近地區
needy〔'nidɪ〕adj. 貧窮的　　return〔rɪ'tɝn〕v. 退還
item〔'aɪtəm〕n. 物品　　visit〔'vɪzɪt〕v. 探望
hospital〔'hɑspɪtḷ〕n. 醫院

17. (**B**) W：Mr. Evans, I don't feel well. My throat is sore and I feel dizzy.

女：伊凡斯先生，我覺得不太舒服。我喉嚨痛，而且覺得頭暈。

M：OK, maybe you should go see the school nurse. Hold on a minute and I'll write you a permission slip.

男：好，也許你應該去看一下學校護士。妳等一下，我寫張批准
　　單給妳。

W : Thank you, Mr. Evans.

女：謝謝你，伊凡斯先生。

Question : What does Mr. Evans think should happen?

　　　　伊凡斯先生認為應該怎麼做？

(A) The girl should go home. 女孩應該要回家。

(B) The girl should see a nurse. 女孩應該要去找護士。

(C) The girl should study harder. 女孩應該更用功讀書。

* throat〔θrot〕*n.* 喉嚨　　sore〔sor〕*adj.* 疼痛的
  dizzy〔'dɪzɪ〕*adj.* 頭暈的　　*go see* 去看（= *go and see*）
  nurse〔nɝs〕*n.* 護士　　*hold on a minute* 等一下
  permission〔pɚ'mɪʃən〕*n.* 允許　　slip〔slɪp〕*n.* 便條紙
  hard〔hard〕*adv.* 努力地

18. (**B**) Father's Day is fast approaching—do you know what
you're getting the dad in your life? At Mick's
Electronics, we make it easy to find the perfect present.
It doesn't matter whether the dad in your life is totally
tech-savvy or not. With a range of great gifts to choose
from, you're sure to discover a fabulous deal that will
match Dad's interests and your budget.
父親節很快就到了—你知道要買什麼給你的爸爸嗎？在米克電器
行，我們讓你輕鬆找到完美的禮物。你的父親是否非常了解科技
產品都沒關係。這裡有一系列很棒的禮物可以選，你一定能找到
讓你父親有興趣，而且又符合你預算，很棒的產品。

Question : What is coming soon? 什麼節日即將來臨？

(A) Mother's Day. 母親節。

(B) Father's Day. 父親節。

(C) Christmas. 聖誕節。

* approach〔ə'protʃ〕v. 接近　　get〔gɛt〕v. 買

get sb. sth. 買某物給某人

the dad in your life 你的爸爸 (= *your father*)

electronics〔ɪ,lɛk'trɑnɪks〕*n. pl.* 電子設備

perfect〔'pɝfɪkt〕*adj.* 完美的　　present〔'prɛzn̩t〕*n.* 禮物

matter〔'mætɚ〕*v.* 有關係；重要　　totally〔'totl̩ɪ〕*adv.* 完全地

tech〔tɛk〕*n.* 科技　　savvy〔'sævɪ〕*adj.* 精通的

range〔rendʒ〕*n.* (同種類的)一套物品

a range of 一系列的　　***choose from*** 從中挑選

be sure to V. 一定會…　　discover〔dɪ'skʌvɚ〕*v.* 發現

fabulous〔'fæbjələs〕*adj.* 很棒的　　deal〔dil〕*n.* 交易

match〔mætʃ〕*v.* 符合　　interest〔'ɪntrɪst〕*n.* 興趣

budget〔'bʌdʒɪt〕*n.* 預算

19. (**A**) M : Excuse me, ma'am. I'm looking for the Crown Plaza Hotel.

男：不好意思，小姐。我正在找皇冠廣場飯店。

W : Hmm. It doesn't ring a bell. There are dozens of hotels in the downtown area.

女：嗯。聽起來沒什麼印象。市中心有太多家飯店了。

M : It's supposed to be across from Burns Park.

男：它應該在伯恩斯公園的對面。

W : Oh, right. I know the place you're talking about. It's over on South Third Street.

女：噢，對。我知道你說的那個地方。它在南三街上。

M : Is that within walking distance?

男：走路能到嗎？

W : It's about a 10-minute walk from here.

女：從這裡走大約十分鐘。

Question : What does the man want to do?

男士想要做什麼？

(A) Walk to the hotel. 走路到飯店。

(B) Take a taxi to the airport. 搭計程車去機場。

(C) Buy a city map. 買一張市區地圖。

* *ring a bell* 聽起來耳熟　　dozen〔'dʌzn̩〕*n.* 一打；十二個
dozens of 幾十個；很多個
downtown〔'daʊn͵taʊn〕*adj.* 市中心的　　area〔'ɛrɪə〕*n.* 地區
be supposed to 應該　　*across from* 在…對面
over〔'ovɚ〕*prep.* 在（街道）的那一邊
south〔saʊθ〕*n.* 南；南方　　within〔wɪð'ɪn〕*prep.* 在～之內
walk〔wɔk〕*v. n.* 走路　　distance〔'dɪstəns〕*n.* 距離；路程
airport〔'ɛr͵port〕*n.* 機場　　city〔'sɪtɪ〕*n.* 城市
map〔mæp〕*n.* 地圖

20. (**C**) M : Hi, Lucy. What are you doing?

男：嗨，露西。妳在做什麼？

W : Just studying for the exam tomorrow. By the way, do you know our book reports are due tomorrow instead of Monday?

女：只是在讀明天要考的試。對了，你知道我們的讀書報告是明天到期而不是星期一嗎？

M : Yes, I know. I finished mine last night.

男：是的，我知道。我昨晚就把我的寫完了。

Question : What will NOT happen tomorrow?

明天不會發生什麼事？

(A) Lucy will take an exam. 露西將會參加考試。

(B) Lucy will turn in her book report.

露西將會交她的讀書報告。

(C) Lucy will go on a field trip. 露西將去戶外教學。

* exam〔ɪgˈzæm〕*n.* 考試　　*by the way* 順便一提；對了
report〔rɪˈport〕*n.* 報告　　due〔du〕*adj.* 到期的
instead of 而不是　　finish〔ˈfɪnɪʃ〕*v.* 做完
happen〔ˈhæpən〕*v.* 發生　　*take an exam* 參加考試
turn in 繳交　　field〔fild〕*n.* 田野
field trip 戶外教學　　*go on a field trip* 去戶外教學

21. (**A**) Scientists have often linked a healthy body with a healthy
mind. Getting enough exercise is often a problem for
today's students. Some parents don't see the value in
physical education, so they don't encourage their kids to
be active.

科學家常把健康的身體與健康的心理連結在一起。對現在的學生
而言，要有足夠的運動常常是個問題。有些家長不知道體育課的
重要，所以他們不會鼓勵他們的孩子要運動。

Question： What does the speaker say about today's
students? 關於現在的學生，說話者說了什麼？

(A) They don't get enough exercise.

他們沒有足夠的運動。

(B) They don't eat right. 他們吃得不健康。

(C) They don't study hard enough. 他們讀書不夠用功。

* scientist〔ˈsaɪəntɪst〕*n.* 科學家　　link〔lɪŋk〕*v.* 連結
healthy〔ˈhɛlθɪ〕*adj.* 健康的　　mind〔maɪnd〕*n.* 心；精神
enough〔əˈnʌf〕*adj.* 足夠的　　exercise〔ˈɛksə͵saɪz〕*n.* 運動
see〔si〕*v.* 看到；知道　　value〔ˈvælju〕*n.* 價值；重要性
physical〔ˈfɪzɪkḷ〕*adj.* 身體的
education〔͵ɛdʒəˈkeʃən〕*n.* 教育
physical education 體育　　encourage〔ɪnˈkɝɪdʒ〕*v.* 鼓勵
active〔ˈæktɪv〕*adj.* 活動的　　*eat right* 吃得對；吃得健康

TEST 8 ▶ 詳解

第一部分：辨識句意（第 1-3 題）

1. (**B**) (A)　　　　　(B)　　　　　(C)

A whole chicken costs seven hundred dollars, while a whole fish only costs two hundred dollars.

一整隻雞要七百元，然而一整條魚只要兩百元。

* whole〔hol〕*adj.* 整個的　　cost〔kɔst〕*v.* 值～（錢）
　while〔hwaɪl〕*conj.* 然而

2. (**A**) (A)　　　　　(B)　　　　　(C)

The family is seated at a large round table where they are enjoying a meal together.　一家人坐在大圓桌前一起享用餐點。

* seat〔sit〕*v.* 使就座　　enjoy〔ɪn'dʒɔɪ〕*v.* 享受
　meal〔mil〕*n.* 一餐　　together〔tə'gɛðɚ〕*adv.* 一起

3. (**C**) (A)　　　　　(B)　　　　　(C)

Mr. Miller has a seven-year-old son named Billy.
米勒先生有個七歲大的兒子叫比利。
* son〔sʌn〕*n.* 兒子 　　***named~*** 名叫~

第二部分：基本問答（第 4-10 題）

4. (**A**) I wonder if school will be cancelled tomorrow because of
the typhoon. 我想知道明天學校是否會因颱風而放假。

   (A) Probably. It's supposed to be a big one.
　　　有可能。它應該會是個很大的颱風。

   (B) Sometimes. If it's really dangerous.
　　　有時候。如果真的很危險的話。

   (C) Usually. If it's close enough. 通常。如果它夠靠近的話。

* wonder〔'wʌndɚ〕*v.* 想知道 　　cancel〔'kænsḷ〕*v.* 取消；放假
typhoon〔taɪ'fun〕*n.* 颱風 　　probably〔'prɑbəblɪ〕*adv.* 可能
be supposed to 應該 　　dangerous〔'dendʒərəs〕*adj.* 危險的
close〔klos〕*adj.* 靠近的 　　enough〔ə'nʌf〕*adv.* 足夠地

5. (**A**) How long is the bus ride from Taipei to Keelong?
搭巴士從台北到基隆要多久？

   (A) About 45 minutes. 大約四十五分鐘。

   (B) On Saturday. 在星期六。

   (C) We sometimes take the bus. 我們有時候會搭公車。

* ride〔raɪd〕*n.* 搭乘

6. (**C**) Did you enjoy the concert last night?
你喜歡昨晚的演唱會嗎？

   (A) I'm the pitcher. 我是投手。

   (B) You've been a great teammate. 你一直是很棒的隊友。

   (C) It was better than I thought it would be.
　　　它比我想像的還要好。

* concert〔'kɑnsɜt〕*n.* 演唱會　　pitcher〔'pɪtʃə〕*n.* 投手
　great〔gret〕*adj.* 很棒的　　teammate〔'tim,met〕*n.* 隊友

7. (**B**) Would it be possible for you to give me a ride home from
　 school? 你能從學校載我回家嗎？

　 (A) See you. 再見。

　 (B) Sure. 當然。

　 (C) No, thanks. 不，謝謝。

　 * possible〔'pɑsəbḷ〕*adj.* 可能的　　***give*** *sb.* ***a ride*** 載某人一程

8. (**B**) What's your uncle doing? 你的叔叔正在做什麼？

　 (A) Yes, he's standing over there. 是的，他正站在那裡。

　 (B) He's playing with the hula hoop. 他正在玩呼拉圈。

　 (C) He's in the dining room. 他在飯廳。

　 * ***over there*** 在那裡　　hula hoop〔'hulə,hʊp〕*n.* 呼拉圈
　 dining room 飯廳

9. (**A**) Do you like funny or scary movies?
　 你喜歡喜劇還是恐怖電影？

　 (A) I like funny movies. 我喜歡喜劇電影。

　 (B) Chocolate. 巧克力。

　 (C) All the time. 一直都是。

　 * funny〔'fʌnɪ〕*adj.* 好笑的　　scary〔'skɛrɪ〕*adj.* 可怕的；恐怖的
　 chocolate〔'tʃɔkəlɪt〕*adj.* 巧克力的
　 all the time 一直；總是

10. (**C**) I like to practice boxing on the weekend.
　 我週末喜歡打拳擊。

　 (A) I do. 我喜歡。

　 (B) Me neither. 我也不。

　 (C) Me too. 我也是。

* practice〔'præktɪs〕*v.* 練習；實行　boxing〔'bɑksɪŋ〕*n.* 拳擊
practice boxing 打拳擊　weekend〔'wik'ɛnd〕*n.* 週末
neither〔'niðɚ〕*adv.* 也不

第三部分：言談理解（第 11-21 題）

11. (**A**)　M：My goodness! Look at the line.

　　男：天啊！你看這個隊伍。

　　W：I told you it was going to be crowded.

　　女：我告訴過你會擠滿人。

　　M：But we're an hour early! The movie starts at nine o'clock.

　　男：但我們已經提早一小時了！電影九點才開始。

　　W：Is there an eleven o'clock showing?

　　女：十一點還會有一場嗎？

　　Question：What time is it now? 現在幾點？

　　(A) Eight o'clock. <u>八點。</u>

　　(B) Nine o'clock. 九點。

　　(C) Eleven o'clock. 十一點。

　　* ***My goodness!*** 天啊！　***look at*** 看
　　line〔laɪn〕*n.* 排隊的隊伍　　crowded〔'kraʊdɪd〕*adj.* 擁擠的
　　showing〔'ʃoɪŋ〕*n.* (電影) 放映；播出

12. (**B**)　M：What seems to be the problem?

　　男：有什麼問題嗎？

　　W：I have a bad cough and chest pains.

　　女：我咳得很嚴重，而且胸痛。

　　M：Is that all?

　　男：就這樣嗎？

　　W：A headache, fever, and dizziness.

　　女：頭痛、發燒，和暈眩。

M : Sounds like the flu. Take this medication for seven
　　days and get plenty of rest.

男：聽起來像流感。這個藥吃七天，並且要多休息。

Question : Who are the speakers? 說話者是誰？

(A) Brother and sister. 兄妹。

(B) Doctor and patient. 醫生和病人。

(C) Teacher and student. 老師和學生。

* seem〔sim〕*v.* 似乎　　bad〔bæd〕*adj.* 嚴重的
  cough〔kɔf〕*n.* 咳嗽　　chest〔tʃɛst〕*n.* 胸腔
  pain〔pen〕*n.* 疼痛　　headache〔'hɛd,ek〕*n.* 頭痛
  fever〔'fivɚ〕*n.* 發燒　　dizziness〔'dɪzɪnɪs〕*n.* 暈眩
  sound〔saʊnd〕*v.* 聽起來　　flu〔flu〕*n.* 流行性感冒
  take〔tek〕*v.* 服用　　medication〔,mɛdɪ'keʃən〕*n.* 藥物
  plenty of 許多的　　rest〔rɛst〕*n.* 休息
  patient〔'peʃənt〕*n.* 病人

13. (**B**) Welcome to Columbia House. The program will begin in
fifteen minutes. If you want to use the restroom, turn left
when you walk out of the room. Please don't drink or eat
inside. Be sure to turn off your cell phone, and don't take
photos during the show. We hope you have a wonderful
time tonight.

歡迎來到哥倫比亞之家。節目將於十五分鐘後開始。如果你想使
用洗手間，走出房間後左轉。在裡面請勿飲食。務必將手機關
機，節目進行中請勿拍照。我們希望你今晚有個美好的時光。

Question : What are listeners getting ready to do?
　　　　　聽眾準備要做什麼？

(A) Board a plane. 登機。

(B) Watch a show. 看一場表演。

(C) Leave a building. 離開一棟建築物。

* program〔'progræm〕*n.* 節目
restroom〔'rɛst,rum〕*n.* 洗手間
turn left 左轉　　inside〔'ɪn'saɪd〕*adv.* 在裡面
turn off 關掉（電源）　　***take photos*** 拍照
show〔ʃo〕*n.* 表演　　hope〔hop〕*v.* 希望
wonderful〔'wʌndəfəl〕*adj.* 極好的；很棒的
board〔bord〕*v.* 上（飛機）　　plane〔plen〕*n.* 飛機
building〔'bɪldɪŋ〕*n.* 建築物

14. (**A**) W：How long have you been waiting?

女：你等多久了？

M：About 25 minutes.

男：大約二十五分鐘。

W：Oh, my goodness! I thought the Broadway Express was supposed to run every five to seven minutes.

女：噢，我的天啊！我以為百老匯快車應該要每五至七分鐘一班。

M：It is, but apparently not today. There's some kind of rally in Times Square this afternoon, so that's causing traffic problems all over the city. If you're going uptown, you might want to take the subway.

男：是啊，但今天似乎不是這樣。今天下午在時代廣場有某種示威，所以造成整個城市都有交通問題。如果你要到住宅區，你可能會想要搭地鐵。

Question：Where are the speakers? 說話者在哪裡？

(A) At a bus stop. 在公車站。

(B) At a train station. 在火車站。

(C) At a bank. 在銀行。

* Broadway〔'brɔd,we〕*n.* 百老匯　　express〔ɪk'sprɛs〕*n.* 快車
be supposed to V. 應該…　　run〔rʌn〕*v.* 行駛
apparently〔ə'pærəntlɪ〕*adv.* 似乎　　***some kind of*** 某種的
rally〔'rælɪ〕*n.* 示威　　***Times Square*** 時代廣場
cause〔kɔz〕*v.* 造成　　traffic〔'træfɪk〕*adj.* 交通的

uptown〔ˋʌpˋtaʊn〕*adv.* 在住宅區　subway〔ˋsʌb͵we〕*n.* 地鐵
stop〔stɑp〕*n.* 候車站　station〔ˋsteʃən〕*n.* 車站

15. (**B**)　W : How old are you, Nick?

女：你今年幾歲，尼克？

M : That's kind of a rude question, Liz.

男：那個問題有一點失禮，麗茲。

W : No, it's only rude for you to ask a woman.　Men are fair game.

女：不，這問題你問女士才失禮。男士是適合問的對象。

M : Oh, really?　I didn't know that.　How about my weight?　Is it OK to ask me that?

男：喔，眞的嗎？我不知道。那我的體重呢？問我這個問題是可以的嗎？

W : Umm… that… wasn't my question.

女：嗯…那…不是我問的問題。

M : Anyway, I'm 38, Liz.

男：隨便啦，我三十八歲，麗茲。

W : Uh-huh.　I thought so.　Did you know that Mr. Foster is 60 years old?

女：嗯。我想也是。你知道福斯特先生今年六十歲嗎？

M : You're kidding!　He doesn't look a day over 40.

男：妳在開玩笑吧！他看起來不超過四十歲。

Question : What does the man mean?　男士是什麼意思？

(A) Mr. Foster has poor eyesight. 福斯特先生的視力很差。

(B) Mr. Foster looks young for his age.

　　福斯特先生看起來比實際年齡年輕。

(C) Mr. Foster is getting old. 福斯特先生越來越老了。

* ***kind of*** 有點　　rude〔rud〕*adj.* 粗魯的；無禮的
fair game （有正當理由可嘲笑、攻擊的）對象；目標

How about~? ～如何？　weight〔wet〕*n.* 體重
kid〔kɪd〕*v.* 開玩笑
doesn't look a day over 看起來不超過（某個年齡）
poor〔pʊr〕*adj.* 差勁的　　eyesight〔'aɪ͵saɪt〕*n.* 視力

16. (**C**) W : Is Jason out of bed yet?

女：傑森起床了沒？

M : I think I heard him in the shower.

男：我好像聽到他在淋浴。

W : It's already seven-thirty.　He's going to be late for
　　school again.

女：已經七點半了。他上學又要遲到了。

M : Don't worry.　I'll drive him.

男：別擔心。我會開車載他。

Question : Why is the woman worried?

　　　　　女士為什麼會擔心？

(A) Jason might be ill.　傑森可能生病了。

(B) Jason might be hungry.　傑森可能肚子餓了。

(C) Jason might be late for school.　<u>傑森可能上學會遲到。</u>

* *be out of bed* 起床　　yet〔jɛt〕*adv.* 已經
　shower〔'ʃaʊɚ〕*n.* 淋浴　　late〔let〕*adj.* 遲到的
　worried〔'wɜɪd〕*adj.* 擔心的　　drive〔draɪv〕*v.* 開車載
　ill〔ɪl〕*adj.* 生病的　　hungry〔'hʌŋgrɪ〕*adj.* 飢餓的

17. (**C**) M : Can I help you?

男：我可以幫妳嗎？

W : Yes.　I'd like to buy a birthday cake.

女：是的。我想要買一個生日蛋糕。

M : We have many to choose from.　How about this one?
　　It's strawberry cheesecake.

男：我們有很多可以選。這個如何呢？這是草莓起司蛋糕。

W : Can you make it say, "Happy Birthday, Brian"?

女：你能在上面寫：「生日快樂，布萊恩」嗎？

M : Sure. No problem.

男：當然。沒問題。

Question : What does the woman want to buy?

　　　　　女士想買什麼？

(A) A wedding present. 一個結婚禮物。

(B) A Christmas gift. 一個聖誕禮物。

(C) A birthday cake. <u>一個生日蛋糕。</u>

* *choose from* 從…中選擇　　strawberry〔'strɔ,bɛrɪ〕*n.* 草莓
cheesecake〔'tʃiz,kek〕*n.* 起司蛋糕　　say〔se〕*v.* 寫著
wedding〔'wɛdɪŋ〕*n.* 婚禮　　present〔'prɛznt〕*n.* 禮物
gift〔gɪft〕*n.* 禮物

18. (**B**) M : I have an extra ticket for the movies tonight.
　　　　　Interested?

男：今晚的電影我有多一張票。有興趣嗎？

W : Thanks for the offer, but I'm really tired. Why don't
you ask Jill? She loves movies.

女：謝謝你的邀約，但我眞的好累。你何不問問吉兒？她熱愛電
影。

M : I know, that's why I asked her first. She's studying
for a test, so I thought you might like to come instead.

男：我知道，這就是爲什麼我會先問過她。她正在爲考試唸書，
所以我才覺得妳可能會想來。

Question : Why did the woman turn the man down?

　　　　　爲什麼女士拒絕了男士？

(A) She has already seen the movie. 她已經看過那部電影。

(B) She is tired. <u>她很累。</u>

(C) She needs to work. 她必須工作。

* extra〔ˋɛkstrə〕 *adj.* 額外的　　ticket〔ˋtɪkɪt〕 *n.* 票
interested〔ˋɪntrɪstɪd〕 *adj.* 有興趣的　　offer〔ˋɔfə〕 *n.* 提議
tired〔taɪrd〕 *adj.* 疲倦的；累的
instead〔ɪnˋstɛd〕 *adv.* 代替；取而代之　　***turn down*** 拒絕

19. (**C**)　How much water should you drink each day? It's a
simple question with no easy answers. Studies have
produced varying results over the years, but in truth, your
water needs depend on many factors, including your
health, how active you are and where you live. Although
no single formula fits everyone, knowing more about
your body's need for fluids will help you estimate how
much water to drink each day.

你每天應該喝多少水？這是個簡單的問題，卻沒有容易的答案。
多年來，研究產生了不同的結果，但事實上，你的水量需求取決
於很多因素，包括你的健康、你有多活躍，和你住在哪裡。雖然
沒有一個公式適用每個人，但多了解你身體對水份的需求，將會
幫助你估計每天該喝多少水。

Question：Which of the following is NOT a factor that
determines how much water you need to
drink？ 下列何者不是決定你需要喝多少水的因素？

(A) How much exercise you get. 你做多少運動。

(B) Where you live. 你住在哪裡。

(C) Using the correct formula. <u>使用正確的公式。</u>

* simple〔ˋsɪmpḷ〕 *adj.* 簡單的　　study〔ˋstʌdɪ〕 *n.* 研究
produce〔prəˋdjus〕 *v.* 生產
varying〔ˋvɛrɪɪŋ〕 *adj.* 不同的；變化的
result〔rɪˋzʌlt〕 *n.* 結果　　***over the years*** 多年來
in truth 事實上 (= *in fact*)　　need〔nid〕 *n.* 需求
depend on 取決於；視…而定　　factor〔ˋfæktə〕 *n.* 因素
including〔ɪnˋkludɪŋ〕 *prep.* 包括　　health〔hɛlθ〕 *n.* 健康

active〔'æktɪv〕*adj.* 活躍的；活動的
single〔'sɪŋɡḷ〕*adj.* 單一的　　formula〔'fɔrmjələ〕*n.* 公式
fit〔fɪt〕*v.* 適合　　fluid〔'fluɪd〕*n.* 液體；水份
estimate〔'ɛstə,met〕*v.* 估計　　determine〔dɪ'tɜmɪn〕*v.* 決定
exercise〔'ɛksɚ,saɪz〕*n.* 運動　　correct〔kə'rɛkt〕*adj.* 正確的

20. (**B**)　M：Why is the back door open?

　　　　　男：為什麼後門是開著的？

　　　　　W：I was taking out the trash when the phone rang.

　　　　　女：我正要去倒垃圾時電話就響了。

　　　　　M：Can I close it?　I don't want the dog to get out.

　　　　　男：我能關上嗎？我不想讓狗跑出去。

　　　　　W：Suit yourself.

　　　　　女：隨你的便。

　　　　　Question：What does the woman mean by "Suit
　　　　　　　　　　yourself"?　女士說「隨你的便」是什麼意思？

　　(A)　She doesn't want the dog to get out.

　　　　她不想讓狗跑出去。

　　(B)　She doesn't care if the door is open or closed.

　　　　<u>她不在乎門是開著或關著。</u>

　　(C)　She doesn't like having to take out the trash.

　　　　她不喜歡必須要倒垃圾。

　*　***back door*** 後門　　trash〔træʃ〕*n.* 垃圾
　　take out the trash 倒垃圾　　ring〔rɪŋ〕*v.* (鈴)響
　　suit〔sut〕*v.* 適合　　***suit yourself*** 隨你的便
　　mean〔min〕*v.* 意思是　　care〔kɛr〕*v.* 在乎
　　if〔ɪf〕*conj.* 是否

21. (**B**)　W：Are Mom and Dad going to pick up Grandpa from
　　　　　　　the airport?

　　　　　女：爸媽會去機場接爺爺嗎？

M : Dad will pick him up. Mom has to work.

男： 爸爸會去接他。媽媽要上班。

W : What time does the flight arrive?

女： 班機幾點抵達？

M : Sometime around six. Six-thirty? I don't know.

男： 大概六點左右。六點半？我不知道。

W : So I guess we're on our own for dinner.

女： 那我猜我們要自己解決晚餐了。

M : Oh, I almost forgot. Dad left some money and a note for us on the kitchen counter. The note says no fast food.

男： 喔，我差點忘了。爸在廚房的餐台上留了一些錢和一張紙條給我們。紙條上寫著不准吃速食。

W : Darn it! I really wanted Burger Champion!

女： 該死！我真的很想吃冠軍漢堡！

Question： Why is the woman upset? 為什麼女士不高興？

(A) She can't meet Grandpa at the airport.

她不能去機場接爺爺。

(B) She can't eat fast food for dinner. 她晚餐不能吃速食。

(C) She can't get a ride home from the park.

沒人從公園載她回家。

* **pick up** 接   airport〔'ɛr͵port〕*n.* 機場
  flight〔flaɪt〕*n.* 班機   arrive〔ə'raɪv〕*v.* 抵達
  sometime〔'sʌm͵taɪm〕*adv.* 某時
  around〔ə'raʊnd〕*adv.* 大約   guess〔gɛs〕*v.* 猜
  on one's **own** 獨自；靠自己   almost〔'ɔl͵most〕*adv.* 幾乎
  leave〔liv〕*v.* 留下   note〔not〕*n.* 紙條
  counter〔'kaʊntɚ〕*n.*（餐廳等的）細長櫃台
  fast food 速食   **Darn it!** 該死！（= *Damn it!*）
  burger〔'bɝgɚ〕*n.* 漢堡   champion〔'tʃæmpɪən〕*n.* 冠軍
  upset〔ʌp'sɛt〕*adj.* 不高興的   ride〔raɪd〕*n.* 搭乘；搭便車

 TEST 9 ▶ 詳解

第一部分：辨識句意（第 1-3 題）

1. (**C**) (A)　　　　　(B)　　　　　(C)

Joan will go roller-skating at four o'clock, but she will be home for dinner at seven o'clock.

瓊安四點會去溜冰，但她七點會回家吃晚餐。

* roller-skate〔'rolɚˌsket〕v. 穿輪式溜冰鞋溜冰

2. (**A**) (A)　　　　　(B)　　　　　(C)

Today is October 10th in both Taiwan and Japan.

台灣和日本今天都是十月十日。

3. (**B**) (A)　　　　　(B)　　　　　(C)

Ms. Franklin made a cake from eggs, sugar, flour, and bananas.

富蘭克林女士用雞蛋、糖、麵粉，和香蕉做了一個蛋糕。

* sugar〔ˈʃʊgɚ〕*n.* 糖　　flour〔flaʊr〕*n.* 麵粉

第二部分：基本問答（第 4-10 題）

4. (**A**) That was a great film, wasn't it? 那部電影很棒，不是嗎？

(A) I was really impressed by the special effects.
<u>我真的對那個特效印象很深刻。</u>

(B) I wouldn't be surprised if it costs more.
如果它更貴我也不會感到驚訝。

(C) Shh, it's about to start. 噓，快要開始了。

* great〔gret〕*adj.* 很棒的　　film〔fɪlm〕*n.* 電影
impress〔ɪmˈprɛs〕*v.* 使印象深刻
special〔ˈspɛʃəl〕*adj.* 特別的　　effect〔ɪˈfɛkt〕*n.* 效果
surprised〔səˈpraɪzd〕*adj.* 驚訝的　　cost〔kɔst〕*v.* 值（…錢）
shh〔ʃ〕*interj.* 噓　　***be about to V.*** 即將…

5. (**A**) I did great on the entrance exam. Now I can go to the top
high school. 我入學考試考得很好。現在我可以上最好的高中。

(A) Good for you. You earned it. <u>你真棒。這是你應得的。</u>

(B) I will go tomorrow. Wish me luck.
我明天會去。祝我好運。

(C) Take a break. You need to rest.
休息一下。你需要休息。

* do〔du〕*v.* 表現　　***do great***（考試）考得好
entrance〔ˈɛntrəns〕*n.* 進入；入學　　top〔tɑp〕*adj.* 最頂級的
good for you 你真棒　　earn〔ɝn〕*v.* 贏得；獲得；應得
wish〔wɪʃ〕*v.* 祝　　luck〔lʌk〕*n.* 運氣
take a break 休息一下　　rest〔rɛst〕*v.* 休息

6. (**C**) Do you know the head cook at the cafeteria?
你認識自助餐廳的主廚嗎？

(A) I did. She said no. 我以前認識。她否認。

(B) I am. Maybe she will call later.

我是。也許她晚一點會打來。

(C) I do. Her name is Ms. Wilson.

我認識。她的名字是威爾森女士。

* ***head cook*** 主廚 ***say no*** 說「不」；否認
cafeteria (ˌkæfə'tırıə) *n.* 自助餐廳

7. (**A**) Would you like a slice of pizza? 你要一片披薩嗎？

(A) No, thanks. 不，謝謝。

(B) What kind of tea? 哪一種茶？

(C) You're welcome. 不客氣。

* slice (slaıs) *n.* 片 pizza ('pitsə) *n.* 披薩
kind (kaınd) *n.* 種類

8. (**B**) How are you going to spend the summer vacation?

你要如何度過暑假？

(A) I'll probably take the day off. 我那天可能會休假。

(B) I'll most likely visit my family in the South.

我很可能會回南部看我的家人。

(C) I'll never forget that summer. 我絕不會忘記那個夏天。

* spend (spɛnd) *v.* 度過 probably ('prɑbəblı) *adv.* 可能
take a day off 休一天假 likely ('laıklı) *adv.* 可能
visit ('vızıt) *v.* 探望 south (sauθ) *n.* 南方
never ('nɛvɚ) *adv.* 絕不 forget (fɚ'gɛt) *v.* 忘記

9. (**C**) Sorry. I'm late. 抱歉。我遲到了。

(A) All right. 好吧。

(B) That's right. 沒錯。

(C) That's all right. 沒關係。

10. (**B**) Shall we go to the museum on Sunday?

我們星期天去博物館好嗎？

(A) I have to work on Saturday. 我星期六必須工作。

(B) That's a good idea. 那是個好主意。

(C) No, let's go. 不，我們走吧。

* museum〔mju'ziəm〕*n.* 博物館

第三部分：言談理解（第 11-21 題）

11. (**A**) Jimbo's is having a special sale. When you buy three muffins, we will give you a fourth one free. Choose from a wide range of flavors including chocolate, blueberry, and our specialty, peanut butter. Also, we are offering 10 percent off on all cakes, pies, and cookies.

金寶正在特賣。當你買三個馬芬，我們會免費送你一個。有許多口味可挑選，包括巧克力、藍莓，和我們特製的花生醬。另外，我們所有的蛋糕、派，和餅乾，都有九折優惠。

Question：What type of business is Jimbo's?

金寶是什麼類型的行業？

(A) A bakery. 麵包店。

(B) A print shop. 印刷店。

(C) A shoemaker. 裝鞋業者。

* ***special sale*** 特賣　　muffin〔'mʌfɪn〕*n.* 馬芬；鬆餅
fourth〔forθ〕*adj.* 第四的　　free〔fri〕*adv.* 免費地
choose〔tʃuz〕*v.* 選擇　　wide〔waɪd〕*adj.* 廣泛的
range〔rendʒ〕*n.* 範圍　　flavor〔'flevə〕*n.* 口味
including〔ɪn'kludɪŋ〕*prep.* 包括
blueberry〔'blu,bɛrɪ〕*n.* 藍莓
specialty〔'spɛʃəltɪ〕*n.* 特製品
peanut butter〔'pi,nʌt'bʌtə〕*n.* 花生醬
also〔'ɔlso〕*adv.* 並且；另外　　offer〔'ɔfə〕*v.* 提供
percent〔pə'sɛnt〕*n.* 百分之…　　off〔ɔf〕*adv.* 打折
pie〔paɪ〕*n.* 派　　cookie〔'kukɪ〕*n.* 餅乾
type〔taɪp〕*n.* 類型　　business〔'bɪznɪs〕*n.* 行業
bakery〔'bekərɪ〕*n.* 麵包店　　print〔prɪnt〕*n.* 印刷
shoemaker〔'ʃu,mekə〕*n.* 鞋匠；裝鞋業者

12. (**B**)　M：Have you spoken with Victor Tsai's parents about his behavior?

男：妳有跟蔡維克的父母談論過他的行為嗎？

W：Not yet.　How has he been in your class?

女：還沒。他在你的課堂上表現得如何？

M：He never stops talking.

男：他從未停止說話。

W：I guess somebody will have to call his parents.

女：我想必須要有人打電話給他的父母了。

M：If it were up to me, I would have called them weeks ago.

男：如果我能決定，我早在前幾週就打了。

W：Well, I really hoped we could solve the problem through other means.

女：嗯，我原本希望我們能用其他的方式來解決這個問題。

Question：Who are the speakers?　說話者是誰？

(A) Students.　學生。

(B) Teachers.　老師。

(C) Parents.　父母。

* behavior〔bɪ'hevjɚ〕*n.* 行為　　***not yet***　尚未；還沒
  guess〔gɛs〕*v.* 猜；想；認為　　***be up to sb.***　由某人決定
  solve〔sɑlv〕*v.* 解決　　through〔θru〕*prep.* 透過
  means〔minz〕*n. pl.* 方法；手段

13. (**C**)　M：Mary, there are cookies in the kitchen if you're interested.　Mom just made them so they're still warm and fresh.

男：瑪麗，廚房有餅乾，如果妳有興趣的話。媽媽剛做好，所以還熱的，而且很新鮮。

W：No, thanks, Dad.　I'm on a diet.

女：不了，謝謝，爸。我在節食。

M：What on earth for?　You're not fat.

男：到底為什麼要節食？妳又不胖。

W : Dad… there's a lot of pressure on girls to stay thin. Don't you know that? I'm not trying to lose weight. I'm just trying not to gain any.

女：爸…女生有很大的壓力，要保持苗條。你不知道嗎？我不是要減重。我只是試著不要增重。

M : Oh, I see. Well, your loss. That means more cookies for me.

男：喔，我知道了。好吧，這是妳的損失。這代表我有更多的餅乾可以吃。

Question：What is true about Mary? 關於瑪麗，何者正確？

(A) She is getting bullied at school. 她在學校被霸凌。

(B) She has been gaining a lot of weight.
她的體重增加了很多。

(C) She is not fat. 她不胖。

* interested (ˈɪntrɪstɪd) *adj.* 有興趣的
warm (wɔrm) *adj.* 溫暖的；暖熱的　　fresh (frɛʃ) *adj.* 新鮮的
on a diet 節食　　***What…for***? 為什麼…? (= *Why*… ?)
on earth 究竟　　fat (fæt) *adj.* 胖的
pressure (ˈprɛʃɚ) *n.* 壓力　　thin (θɪn) *adj.* 瘦的
lose (luz) *v.* 減少　　weight (wet) *n.* 體重
gain (gen) *v.* 增加　　see (si) *v.* 知道
loss (lɔs) *n.* 損失　　bully (ˈbʊlɪ) *v.* 霸凌

14. (**A**) W : Hello, Jimmy. What seems to be bothering you today?

女：哈囉，吉米。今天有什麼事讓你這麼困擾？

M : It's my foot, Dr. Norton. It aches even when I'm not walking.

男：是我的腳，諾頓醫生。即使我不走路也會痛。

W : Let me see your foot.

女：讓我看看你的腳。

M : Do you think it might be something serious?
男：妳覺得會很嚴重嗎？
W : It's hard to say, Jimmy, but I don't think it's broken.
女：這很難說，吉米，但我不認爲它斷了。
Question : What's bothering Jimmy? 什麼困擾著吉米？
(A) His foot. 他的腳。
(B) His ankle. 他的腳踝。
(C) His hips. 他的屁股。

* seem〔sim〕v. 似乎　　bother〔'baðɚ〕v. 困擾
ache〔ek〕v. 疼痛　　serious〔'sɪrɪəs〕adj. 嚴重的
It's hard to say. 很難說。　　broken〔'brokən〕adj. 折斷的
ankle〔'æŋkļ〕n. 腳踝　　hips〔hɪps〕n. pl. 屁股

15. (**B**) Hi, Stephanie, it's Todd. I'm so excited that you're going to Danny's party tomorrow! I'm bringing chips and salad. Could you please bring something for everyone to drink? Enough for 20 people. Any kind of soda will do. Iced tea is good. It's up to you. Mix it up if you like. Thanks a bunch. See you tomorrow!
嗨，史蒂芬妮，我是陶德。妳明天要去丹尼的派對讓我感到非常興奮！我會帶洋芋片跟沙拉。妳能帶些喝的給大家嗎？足夠給二十人的。任何汽水都行。冰紅茶也不錯。由妳決定。如果妳想要，混著帶也行。非常感謝。明天見！
Question : What will Stephanie probably bring to the party tomorrow?
史蒂芬妮最有可能會帶什麼去明天的派對？
(A) Food. 食物。
(B) Drinks. 飲料。
(C) Entertainment. 娛樂。

* excited〔ɪk'saɪtɪd〕adj. 興奮的
chips〔tʃɪps〕n. pl. 洋芋片（= *potato chips*）

salad〔'sæləd〕*n.* 沙拉　　kind〔kaɪnd〕*n.* 種類
soda〔'sodə〕*n.* 汽水　　iced〔aɪsd〕*adj.* 冰的
mix〔mɪks〕*v.* 混合　　***mix up*** 使…混雜在一起
bunch〔bʌntʃ〕*n.* 一群；許多；大量
thanks a bunch 非常感謝
entertainment〔ˌɛntə'tenmənt〕*n.* 娛樂

16. (**A**) M：How much is a ticket to London?

男：去倫敦的票要多少錢？

W：That depends.　When are you planning to go?

女：那要看情況。你打算什麼時候去？

M：I don't have a specific plan.　I was just curious.

男：我沒有明確的計畫。我只是好奇。

W：Well, if you book online during the slow season, you can probably get a round-trip fare for less than a thousand bucks.

女：嗯，如果你在淡季線上訂票，你可能可以買到一張票價不到一千美元的來回票。

M：What about during the busy season?

男：那旺季呢？

W：Double that.

女：那個的兩倍。

Question：What does the woman mean by "double that"?

這位女士說「那個的兩倍」是什麼意思？

(A) The price is twice as high. 價格是兩倍高。

(B) The flights are twice as full. 班機是兩倍的滿。

(C) The seasons are twice as long. 季節是兩倍的長。

* ticket〔'tɪkɪt〕*n.* 票　　depend〔dɪ'pɛnd〕*v.* 取決於；視…而定
That depends. 那要看情況。　　plan〔plæn〕*v. n.* 計畫；打算
specific〔spɪ'sɪfɪk〕*adj.* 特定的；明確的
curious〔'kjʊrɪəs〕*adj.* 好奇的　　book〔bʊk〕*v.* 預訂
online〔ɑn'laɪn〕*adv.* 在線上　　season〔'sizn̩〕*n.* 季節；時期
slow season 淡季　　round-trip *adj.* 來回的

fare〔fɛr〕*n.* 車資；(交通工具的)票價
buck〔bʌk〕*n.* 一美元　　***busy season*** 旺季
double〔'dʌbḷ〕*adj.* 兩倍的　　twice〔twaɪs〕*adv.* 兩倍地
high〔haɪ〕*adj.* 高的　　flight〔flaɪt〕*n.* 班機
full〔fʊl〕*adj.* 客滿的

17.(**A**)　W：Hello, Mr. Logan?
　　　　女：哈囉，是羅根先生嗎？
　　　　M：Yes?
　　　　男：妳是？
　　　　W：This is Tammy with Franklin Auto Shop.
　　　　女：我是法蘭克林汽車修理廠的泰咪。
　　　　M：Oh, hi, Tammy.　How are you doing?
　　　　男：噢，嗨，泰咪。妳好嗎？
　　　　W：I'm great, thanks.　I'm calling because we've made
　　　　　　the repairs and your car is ready to be picked up.
　　　　女：我很好，謝謝。我打來是因為我們已經把車修理好了，你的
　　　　　　車子已經可以開走了。
　　　　M：It is?!　I didn't bring my car to the shop.
　　　　男：修好了？！我沒有把我的車送去修理廠。
　　　　W：Oh, um…　Ms. Logan brought it in this morning.
　　　　　　There was some minor damage to the front bumper.
　　　　女：喔，嗯…是羅根太太今天早上開來的。車子的前保險桿有些
　　　　　　微損傷。
　　　　M：That's news to me!
　　　　男：我不知道這件事！
　　　　Question：Why is the man surprised?
　　　　　　　　　為什麼男士會感到驚訝？
　　　(A)　His wife didn't tell him the car needed repairs.
　　　　　　他的太太沒有告訴他車子需要修理。
　　　(B)　His car is usually very reliable.
　　　　　　他的車通常是非常可靠的。

(C) His friend was supposed to give him a ride.

他的朋友應該要載他一程。

* auto (ˈɔto) *n.* 汽車　***auto shop*** 汽車修理廠
great (gret) *adj.* 極好的　　repair (rɪˈpɛr) *n.* 修理
ready (ˈrɛdɪ) *adj.* 準備好的　***pick up*** 領取
minor (ˈmaɪnə) *adj.* 較小的　　damage (ˈdæmɪdʒ) *n.* 損傷
front (frʌnt) *adj.* 前面的　　bumper (ˈbʌmpə) *n.* 保險桿
*sth. **is news to** sb.* 某人原本不知道某件事
wife (waɪf) *n.* 妻子　　reliable (rɪˈlaɪəbḷ) *adj.* 可靠的
be supposed to V. 應該⋯　***give sb. a ride*** 載某人一程

18. (**C**) M : Next week our class will take a trip to the beach.

男：下週我們班要去海邊旅行。

W : Really? Wow, what day is the trip?

女：眞的嗎？哇，哪一天要旅行？

M : Next Thursday.

男：下週四。

W : Be careful not to stay in the sun too long.

女：小心別在陽光下待太久。

Question : What will the boy do next Thursday?

男孩下週四要做什麼？

(A) Visit a museum. 參觀博物館。

(B) Take an exam. 參加考試。

(C) Go to the beach. 去海邊。

* trip (trɪp) *n.* 旅行　***take a trip*** 去旅行
beach (bitʃ) *n.* 海邊　　careful (ˈkɛrfəl) *adj.* 小心的
stay (ste) *v.* 停留　　sun (sʌn) *n.* 太陽；陽光
in the sun 在陽光下　　visit (ˈvɪzɪt) *v.* 參觀
museum (mjuˈziəm) *n.* 博物館　　exam (ɪgˈzæm) *n.* 考試
take an exam 參加考試

19. (**B**) W : The door is unlocked. That's strange.

女：門沒鎖。眞奇怪。

M：I bet Grandpa's home.　Bingo ended at 8:30.

男：我肯定阿公一定在家。賓果遊戲八點半就結束了。

W：He never locks the door.　It's very dangerous.

女：他從不鎖門。這樣很危險。

M：His memory isn't what it used to be.

男：他的記性已經跟以往不同了。

Question：What do we know about the speakers?

　　　　　關於說話者我們知道什麼？

(A) They are not at home. 他們不在家。

(B) They live with their grandfather. <u>他們和祖父一起住。</u>

(C) They enjoy bingo. 他們喜歡賓果遊戲。

* unlocked〔ʌn'lɑkt〕*adj.* 沒有鎖的
  strange〔strendʒ〕*adj.* 奇怪的　　bet〔bɛt〕*v.* 打賭；斷定
  grandpa〔'grændpɑ〕*n.* 祖父（= *grandfather*）
  bingo〔'bɪŋgo〕*n.* 賓果遊戲　　lock〔lɑk〕*v.* 鎖
  dangerous〔'dendʒərəs〕*adj.* 危險的
  memory〔'mɛmərɪ〕*n.* 記憶力　　***used to*** 以前
  sth. ***isn't what it used to be*** 某事物已經跟以前不同
  enjoy〔ɪn'dʒɔɪ〕*v.* 喜歡

20. (**C**)　M：Where did you get these delicious oranges?

　　　　　男：妳在哪裡買到這些美味的柳橙？

　　　　　W：At the produce market on Fulton Street.

　　　　　女：在富頓街的農產品市場。

　　　　　M：There's a produce market on Fulton?　I didn't know that.

　　　　　男：富頓街有個農產品市場？我並不知道。

　　　　　W：It's new.　They took over the spot that used to be Danny's Café.

　　　　　女：是新開的。他們接管了以前丹尼咖啡廳的地點。

　　　　　M：Good to know.　I'll do my shopping there from now on.

男： 很高興知道這個消息。我從現在起都要去那裡購物。

Question： What do we know about the produce market?

關於農產品市場我們知道什麼？

(A) It employs many people. 它雇用了很多人。

(B) It sells more than produce. 它賣的不只是農產品。

(C) It is located on Fulton Street. 它位於富頓街。

* get〔gɛt〕v. 買　　delicious〔dɪ'lɪʃəs〕adj. 美味的
orange〔'ɔrɪndʒ〕n. 柳橙　　produce〔'prɑdjus〕n. 農產品
market〔'mɑrkɪt〕n. 市場　　**take over** 接管；接收
spot〔spɑt〕n. 地點　　**used to V.** 以前…
café〔kə'fe〕n. 咖啡廳　　**do** one's **shopping** 去購物
from now on 從現在起　　employ〔ɪm'plɔɪ〕v. 雇用
sell〔sɛl〕v. 賣　　**more than** 不只是
locate〔'loket〕v. 使位於　　**be located on** 位於

21. (**C**) W： Who made the mess in the kitchen and didn't clean it up?

女： 是誰把廚房弄得一團亂，而且沒打掃乾淨？

M： Not me.

男： 不是我。

W： Where's Jim?

女： 吉姆在哪裡？

M： In his bedroom.

男： 在他的房間裡。

Question： What do we know about Jim?

關於吉姆我們知道什麼？

(A) He made the mess. 是他弄亂的。

(B) He will clean the kitchen. 他會把廚房清理乾淨。

(C) He is not in the kitchen. 他不在廚房。

* mess〔mɛs〕n. 混亂；亂七八糟　　**clean up** 打掃乾淨；整理
bedroom〔'bɛd,rum〕n. 臥室

🎧 TEST 10 ▶ 詳解

第一部分：辨識句意（第 1-3 題）

1. (**B**) (A)　　　　　(B)　　　　　(C)

Irene jumps rope for 30 minutes every day from 5:30 to 6:00. 艾琳每天從五點半到六點都會跳繩三十分鐘。

* jump〔dʒʌmp〕v. 跳　　rope〔rop〕n. 繩子
jump rope 跳繩

2. (**B**) (A)　　　　　(B)　　　　　(C)

Nancy loves fast food but Howard won't eat it.
南西熱愛速食，但霍華德不願意吃。

* ***fast food*** 速食

3. (**A**) (A)　　　　　(B)　　　　　(C)

Olivia ordered a forty-five dollar cup of tea, and gave the clerk sixty dollars.

奧莉薇亞點了一杯四十五元的茶，然後給了店員六十元。

* order〔ˈɔrdɚ〕*v.* 點（餐）　　clerk〔klɜk〕*n.* 店員

第二部分：基本問答（第 4-10 題）

4. (**A**) Shall we go shopping at First Mall tonight?

我們今晚要不要去第一購物中心購物？

(A) Good idea. I need a new dress.
<u>好主意。我需要一件新洋裝。</u>

(B) It's my pleasure. 這是我的榮幸。

(C) Have a good time. 玩得愉快。

* mall〔mɔl〕*n.* 購物中心；商場　　dress〔drɛs〕*n.* 洋裝
pleasure〔ˈplɛʒɚ〕*n.* 榮幸　　***have a good time*** 玩得愉快

5. (**A**) What does your father do for a living? 你父親以什麼謀生？

(A) He's a pilot. <u>他是飛行員。</u>

(B) He's German and English. 他是德國和英國混血。

(C) He's about six-two. 他大約六呎二吋。

* living〔ˈlɪvɪŋ〕*n.* 生活；生計　　pilot〔ˈpaɪlət〕*n.* 飛行員
German〔ˈdʒɜmən〕*adj.* 德國人的
English〔ˈɪŋglɪʃ〕*adj.* 英國人的
six-two *adj.* 六呎二吋的（= *six feet and two inches*）

6. (**A**) What was the date yesterday? 昨天是幾月幾日？

(A) It was November sixteenth. <u>昨天是十一月十六日。</u>

(B) It was summer. 昨天是夏天。

(C) It was a sunny day. 昨天天氣晴朗。

* date〔det〕*n.* 日期　　sunny〔ˈsʌnɪ〕*adj.* 晴朗的

7. (**B**) What's your phone number? 你的電話號碼幾號？

(A) 220 Oak Street. 橡樹街 220 號。

(B) 2555-2345. 2555-2345。

(C) Ben Smith. B-E-N, S-M-I-T-H.
班‧史密斯。班，史—密—斯。

* oak〔ok〕*n.* 橡樹

8. (**B**) Excuse me. Which bus goes to Main Station?
不好意思。哪一班公車會到車站？

(A) Yes, you can go there by bus.
是的，你能搭公車去那裡。

(B) The number 74 bus. 74 號公車。

(C) That's all the same. 都一樣。

* main〔men〕*adj.* 主要的   station〔'steʃən〕*n.* 車站

9. (**A**) Do you know how to swim? 你會游泳嗎？

(A) No. But I really want to learn. 不會。但我真的很想學。

(B) OK. But don't get me wet. 好。但不要把我弄濕。

(C) Yes. But he's not sure. 會。但他不確定。

* wet〔wɛt〕*adj.* 濕的   sure〔ʃur〕*adj.* 確定的

10. (**A**) Excuse me. Am I headed in the right direction for the MRT station?
不好意思。我要前往捷運站，這個方向是對的嗎？

(A) Yes, keep walking straight. You can't miss it.
是的，繼續直走。你不會錯過的。

(B) Yes, you're doing it right. Keep your hand steady.
是的，你做得對。手要保持穩定。

(C) Yes, the MRT stops here. Don't be late.
是的，捷運會停在這裡。不要遲到。

* ***be headed for*** 前往　　direction〔dəˈrɛkʃən〕 *n.* 方向
MRT *n.* 捷運（ = *Mass Rapid Transit*）
keep〔kip〕*v.* 持續　　straight〔stret〕 *adv.* 直直地
miss〔mɪs〕*v.* 錯過　　right〔raɪt〕 *adv.* 正確地
steady〔ˈstɛdɪ〕*adj.* 穩定的　　late〔let〕 *adj.* 遲到的

第三部分：言談理解（第 11-21 題）

11.(**B**)　M：Brandon just told us a very funny story.

男：布蘭登剛剛告訴我們一個非常有趣的故事。

W：Oh, yeah?

女：喔，是嗎？

M：Yeah.　Yesterday, Brandon and his brother Luke went fishing and Luke fell out of the boat.

男：是的。昨天布蘭登和他的弟弟路克去釣魚，然後路克掉出船外。

W：That's funny, I guess.

女：我猜，那應該很有趣。

M：What's funny is that Luke doesn't know how to swim

男：有趣的是路克不會游泳。

Question：What were Brandon and Luke doing yesterday? 布蘭登和路克昨天在做什麼？

(A) Swimming. 游泳。

(B) Fishing. 釣魚。

(C) Hunting. 打獵。

funny〔ˈfʌnɪ〕 *adj.* 有趣的　　yeah〔jæ〕 *adv.* 是的（ = *yes*）
fish〔fɪʃ〕*v.* 釣魚　　fall〔fɔl〕 *v.* 掉落
guess〔gɛs〕*v.* 猜　　hunt〔hʌnt〕 *v.* 打獵

12. (**B**)　Milk is important for healthy bones because it contains a
lot of vitamins that help your body grow strong. Some
milk comes from cows and can be made into cheese.
Other types of milk include goat and soybean milk.
Cow's milk is the most popular and my favorite way to
enjoy milk is with a plate of freshly-baked cookies.
Mm, delicious!

牛奶對於健康的骨頭來說很重要，因為它含有許多維生素，能幫
助你的身體變得很強壯。有些牛奶來自乳牛，能被製成起司。其
他種類的牛奶包括山羊奶和豆漿。乳牛的牛奶是最受歡迎的，而
且我最喜歡用牛奶搭配一盤剛烤好的餅乾。嗯，眞美味！

Question：What does the speaker enjoy with milk?
　　　　　說話者喜歡用牛奶搭配什麼？

(A) Soybeans. 大豆。

(B) Cookies. 餅乾。

(C) Cheese. 起司。

* important〔ɪm'pɔrtn̩t〕*adj.* 重要的
　healthy〔'hɛlθɪ〕*adj.* 健康的　　bone〔bon〕*n.* 骨頭
　contain〔kən'ten〕*v.* 包含　　***a lot of*** 很多的
　vitamin〔'vaɪtəmɪn〕*n.* 維生素　　grow〔gro〕*v.* 變得
　strong〔strɔŋ〕*adj.* 強壯的　　cow〔kaʊ〕*n.* 母牛；乳牛
　cheese〔tʃiz〕*n.* 起司　　type〔taɪp〕*n.* 種類
　include〔ɪn'klud〕*v.* 包括　　goat〔got〕*n.* 山羊
　soybean〔'sɔɪ,bin〕*n.* 黃豆；大豆　　***soybean milk*** 豆漿
　popular〔'pɑpjələ〕*adj.* 受歡迎的
　favorite〔'fevərɪt〕*adj.* 最喜愛的　　way〔we〕*n.* 方式
　enjoy〔ɪn'dʒɔɪ〕*v.* 享受　　plate〔plet〕*n.* 盤子；一盤的份量
　freshly〔'frɛʃlɪ〕*adv.* 新近；新鮮地
　bake〔bek〕*v.* 烘烤　　freshly-baked *adj.* 剛出爐的
　mm〔m〕*interj.* 嗯　　delicious〔dɪ'lɪʃəs〕*adj.* 美味的

13. (**B**) W : My sister is moving back in with my parents next week.

女：我姊姊下週要搬回來跟我的爸媽住。

M : What happened? Did she break up with her boyfriend or something?

男：發生了什麼事？她和她的男朋友分手了，還是怎麼了嗎？

W : No, their apartment was damaged in the typhoon. So they're both moving home until it gets fixed.

女：不是，他們的公寓在颱風期間損壞了。所以他們兩人都要搬回家，直到房子修好。

M : So, you sister's boyfriend is moving in with your parents, too?

男：所以，你姊姊的男朋友也要搬來跟你的爸媽住嗎？

W : No, he's going to his parents' house.

女：不，他會去他的父母家。

Question : What are the speakers mainly discussing?

說話者主要在討論什麼？

(A) Their parents. 他們的父母。

(B) The woman's sister. <u>這位女士的姊姊。</u>

(C) The recent typhoon. 最近的颱風。

* move〔muv〕*v.* 搬家　　***move in*** 搬進新居
move back in 搬回來　　happen〔'hæpən〕*v.* 發生
break up 分手　　boyfriend〔'bɔɪˌfrɛnd〕*n.* 男朋友
or something 或什麼的　　apartment〔ə'pɑrtmənt〕*n.* 公寓
damage〔'dæmɪdʒ〕*v.* 損壞　　typhoon〔taɪ'fun〕*n.* 颱風
fix〔fɪks〕*v.* 修理　　mainly〔'menlɪ〕*adv.* 主要地
discuss〔dɪ'skʌs〕*v.* 討論　　recent〔'risn̩t〕*adj.* 最近的

14. (**A**) M : Do you ride your bike to school every day?

男：你每天都騎腳踏車去上學嗎？

W : Unless it's raining. Then I take the bus.

女：除非下雨。那時我就會搭公車。

Question : How does the woman get to school if it's not
raining? 如果沒下雨，這位女士如何去學校？

(A) She rides her bike. 她騎她的腳踏車。

(B) She walks. 她走路。

(C) She takes the bus. 她搭公車。

* ride〔raɪd〕v. 騎   bike〔baɪk〕n. 腳踏車
 unless〔ən'lɛs〕conj. 除非   ***get to*** 抵達

15. (**C**) W : What are you looking for?

女：你在找什麼？

M : My cell phone. Have you seen it?

男：我的手機。你有看到嗎？

W : No. Have you tried calling the phone so it will ring?

女：沒有。你有試過打電話讓它響嗎？

M : That won't help. It's on vibrate.

男：那沒用的。它現在是震動模式。

W : Give it a shot. Sometimes the vibration is just loud
enough to hear it.

女：試試看。有時候震動的聲音大到能聽得見。

M : Let me see your phone.

男：讓我看一下妳的手機。

Question : What will the man most likely do next?
接下來男士很有可能要做什麼？

(A) Put his phone on vibrate. 把他的手機調成震動模式。

(B) Call the woman. 打給女士。

(C) Use the woman's cell phone. <u>用女士的手機。</u>

* *look for* 尋找　*cell phone* 手機　ring〔rɪŋ〕*v.* （鈴）響
vibrate〔'vaɪbret〕*v.* 震動
be on vibrate （手機）是震動模式
give it a shot 試試看　vibration〔vaɪ'breʃən〕*n.* 震動
loud〔laʊd〕*adj.* 大聲的　likely〔'laɪklɪ〕*adv.* 可能
put〔pʊt〕*v.* 使處於（某種狀態）

16. (**B**) W : There's something wrong with my computer. Could
you take a look at it?

女：我的電腦出了點問題。你能看一下嗎？

M : Sure. But I don't know much about computers.

男：當然。但我對電腦懂得不多。

W : You probably know more than me. I just learned
how to use e-mail.

女：你也許懂得比我多。我才剛學會怎麼使用電子郵件。

Question : What do we know about the woman?

關於女士我們知道什麼？

(A) She is a computer expert. 她是電腦專家。

(B) She knows how to send an e-mail.
<u>她知道如何寄電子郵件。</u>

(C) She owns several computers. 她擁有好幾台電腦。

* wrong〔rɔŋ〕*adj.* 故障的　computer〔kəm'pjutɚ〕*n.* 電腦
take a look at 看一眼
probably〔'prɑbəblɪ〕*adv.* 可能；也許
e-mail〔'i,mel〕*n.* 電子郵件　expert〔'ɛkspɝt〕*n.* 專家
send〔sɛnd〕*v.* 寄　own〔on〕*v.* 擁有
several〔'sɛvərəl〕*adj.* 幾個的

17. (**C**) M : Where should we hold the meeting?

男： 我們應該在哪裡舉行會議？

W : How about right here in my office?

女： 在我的辦公室這裡如何？

M : No, that's not going to work. There isn't room for ten people.

男： 不行，妳的辦公室不行。空間容納不下十個人。

W : The conference room is already occupied.

女： 會議室已經被佔用了。

M : Then let's do it in the employee break room.

男： 那我們就去員工休息室開吧。

W : Good idea. I'll let the receptionist know we'll be using it.

女： 好主意。我會讓接待員知道我們要用那裡。

Question : Where will they hold the meeting?

他們將在哪裡舉行會議？

(A) In the woman's office. 在女士的辦公室。

(B) In the reception area. 在接待區。

(C) In the break room. <u>在休息室。</u>

* hold〔hold〕v. 舉行　　meeting〔ˈmitɪŋ〕n. 會議
  office〔ˈɔfɪs〕n. 辦公室　　work〔wɜk〕v. 行得通
  room〔rum〕n. 空間　　conference〔ˈkɑnfərəns〕n. 會議
  occupy〔ˈɑkjəˌpaɪ〕v. 占據　　employee〔ˌɛmplɔɪˈi〕n. 員工
  break〔brek〕n. 休息　　***employee break room*** 員工休息室
  receptionist〔rɪˈsɛpʃənɪst〕n. 接待員
  reception〔rɪˈsɛpʃən〕n. 接待　　area〔ˈɛrɪə〕n. 區域

18. (**C**) W : Can you have my car ready by tomorrow morning?

女： 你能在明天早上準備好我的車嗎？

M : I don't know about that, ma'am. The parts won't be here until this evening. I can have my guy stay late, but there's no guarantee he'll finish.

男：我不知道，女士。零件要今天傍晚才會到。我可以要我的員工加班，但不保證他能夠完成。

W : I really need the car tomorrow.

女：我明天真的需要用這部車。

M : We'll do our best.

男：我們會盡力。

Question : What does the man say? 男士說了什麼？

(A) He has the parts to fix the car. 他有修車要用的零件。

(B) The woman will have to pay extra.

　　女士必須要付額外的錢。

(C) They will try to have the car ready on time.

　　他們會試著準時把車子準備好。

* ready〔'rɛdɪ〕*adj.* 準備好的　　ma'am〔mæm〕*n.* 女士
part〔part〕*n.* 零件　　***not…until***~ 直到~才…
guy〔gaɪ〕*n.* 人　　***stay late*** 加班（= *work overtime*）
guarantee〔,gærən'ti〕*n.* 保證　　finish〔'fɪnɪʃ〕*v.* 完成
do one's ***best*** 盡力　　pay〔pe〕*v.* 支付
extra〔'ɛkstrə〕*adv.* 額外地　　***on time*** 準時

19. (**A**) M : How many exams do you have left to take this semester?

男：這個學期妳還剩下幾個考試要考？

W : I took the final in English yesterday. I'm finished.

女：我昨天考了英文期末考。我現在都考完了。

M : Really? I thought you had at least one more to go.

男：真的嗎？我以為妳至少剩一科。

W：Nope.

女：沒有。

Question：What is true about the woman?

　　　　關於女士何者正確？

(A) She is finished with exams for the semester.

　　她這學期的考試都考完了。

(B) She hasn't taken her English exam yet.

　　她還沒參加英文考試。

(C) She has two exams left to take.

　　她還剩下兩場考試要考。

* leave〔liv〕*v.* 剩下　　take〔tek〕*v.* 參加（考試）
  semester〔sə'mɛstɚ〕*n.* 學期　　final〔'faɪn̩〕*n.* 期末考
  finished〔'fɪnɪʃt〕*adj.* 完成的　　***at least*** 至少
  to go 剩下；還有　　nope〔nop〕*adv.* 不（= *no*）
  not…yet 尚未；還沒　　left〔lɛft〕*adj.* 剩下的

20. (**C**) M：So? I'm dying to know. Who won the basketball
　　　　　　　game?

男：所以呢？我超想知道。是誰贏了籃球比賽？

W：We lost.

女：我們輸了。

M：Aw, that's too bad. Well, there's always next year.

男：噢，真糟糕。嗯，反正還有明年。

Question：What does the man imply about the basketball
　　　　　team? 關於籃球隊男士暗示了什麼？

(A) They can still make the play-offs.

　　他們還有機會打延長賽。

(B) They could use a few new players.

　　他們想要一些新球員。

(C) They are done playing for the season.

他們這一季打完了。

* ***be dying*** 很想要；渴望　　win〔wɪn〕*v.* 贏
lose〔luz〕*v.* 輸　　aw〔ɔ〕*interj.* 噢
imply〔ɪm'plaɪ〕*v.* 暗示　　make〔mek〕*v.* 獲得；贏得
play-off〔'ple͵ɔf〕*n.* 延長賽；季後賽　　***could use*** 想要
player〔'pleɚ〕*n.* 球員　　done〔dʌn〕*adj.* 結束的
season〔'sizn̩〕*n.* 季；(運動等的) 活動時期

21. (**B**) It lives in a pond. When it was young, it had a tail but no legs. Now its tail is gone and it has four legs. Its hind legs help it jump far, and its webbed feet help it swim well. After supper it likes to sing, but some people do not like its voice.

它住在池塘裡。當牠年幼時，有尾巴但沒有腿。現在牠的尾巴不見了，卻有四條腿。牠的後腿能幫助牠跳得很遠，而牠有蹼的腳能幫助牠游泳游得很好。晚餐後，牠喜歡唱歌，但有些人不喜歡牠的聲音。

Question：What is it? 牠是什麼？

(A) It is a turtle. 牠是一隻烏龜。

(B) It is a frog. 牠是一隻青蛙。

(C) It is a goldfish. 牠是一條金魚。

* pond〔pɑnd〕*n.* 池塘　　young〔jʌŋ〕*adj.* 年幼的
tail〔tel〕*n.* 尾巴　　gone〔gɔn〕*adj.* 消失的
hind〔haɪnd〕*adj.* 後面的　　webbed〔wɛbd〕*adj.* 有蹼的
supper〔'sʌpɚ〕*n.* 晚餐　　voice〔vɔɪs〕*n.* 聲音
turtle〔'tɝtl̩〕*n.* 烏龜　　frog〔frɑg〕*n.* 青蛙
goldfish〔gold'fɪʃ〕*n.* 金魚

 TEST 11 ▶ 詳解

第一部分：辨識句意（第 1-3 題）

1. (**A**) (A)   (B)   (C)

Mr. and Mrs. Chen are having lunch with their grandson, Kyle. 陳先生和陳太太正在和他們的孫子凱爾吃午餐。

　* have〔hæv〕v. 吃　　grandson〔ˈgrænd͵sʌn〕n. 孫子

2. (**A**) (A)   (B)   (C)

 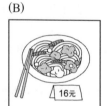 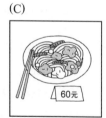

An order of pasta at this restaurant costs one hundred and sixty dollars. 這家餐廳一份義大利麵要 160 元。

　* order〔ˈɔrdɚ〕n. 一份　　pasta〔ˈpɑstə〕n. 義大利麵
　　cost〔kɔst〕v. 需要⋯金額；值⋯價錢

3. (**B**) (A)   (B)   (C)

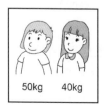 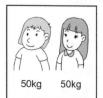 

Betty and Charlotte both weigh fifty kilograms.

貝蒂和夏綠蒂兩人的體重都是 50 公斤。

* weigh〔we〕*v.* 重~　　kilogram〔ˈkɪləˌgræm〕*n.* 公斤

第二部分：基本問答（第 4-10 題）

4. (**B**) Why aren't you getting ready for the basketball game?

你爲何還沒準備好去看籃球比賽？

　　(A) I don't know. Usually basketball.

　　　　我不知道。通常是籃球。

　　(B) I'm not going. I have too much homework to do.

　　　　我沒有要去。我有太多功課要做。

　　(C) I think so. But I will ask my mom.

　　　　我想是的。但是我要問我媽。

　　* *get ready for* 爲…做好準備　　game〔gem〕*n.* 比賽

5. (**C**) Dad, I did all the dishes in the kitchen sink and took out the trash.

爸爸，我洗了廚房水槽裡所有的碗盤，也倒了垃圾。

　　(A) You got one already. 你已經有一個了。

　　(B) I'm sorry about that. 我對那件事感到抱歉。

　　(C) Good job. 做得好。

　　* *do the dishes* 洗碗　　sink〔sɪŋk〕*n.* 水槽

　　take out the trash 倒垃圾　　*good job* 做得好

6. (**B**) Where is your office? 你的辦公室在哪裡？

　　(A) I'm in my office. 我在我的辦公室裡。

　　(B) It's on the fourth floor. 在四樓。

　　(C) This is her office. 這是她的辦公室。

　　* floor〔flor〕*n.* 樓；層

7. (**A**) Did you finish writing your essay, or do you need some more time? 你短文寫完了嗎，還是你還需要一些時間？

(A) I need more time. 我需要更多時間。

(B) I want more sleep. 我想要更多的睡眠。

(C) I have more money. 我有更多的錢。

* finish〔'fɪnɪʃ〕 *v.* 做完；完成
  essay〔'ɛse〕 *n.* 短文；論說文

8. (**C**) I'm brewing a pot of coffee, so you're welcome to have a cup when it's ready.

我正在泡一壺咖啡，所以泡好後歡迎你來喝一杯。

(A) Me neither. 我也不。

(B) He said with a bit of sugar. 他說加一點糖。

(C) Thanks, but don't make it too strong.

謝謝，但是別泡得太濃。

* brew〔bru〕 *v.* 泡；沏　　pot〔pat〕 *n.* 一壺
  neither〔'niðɚ〕 *adv.* 也不　　***a bit of*** 一點
  sugar〔'ʃʊgɚ〕 *n.* 糖　　strong〔strɔŋ〕 *adj.* 濃的

9. (**A**) Have you met the new kid, John, yet?

你見到新來的小孩約翰了嗎？

(A) No, not yet. What's he like?

不，還沒。他人怎麼樣？

(B) Yes, I'm John. What do you want?

是的，我是約翰。你想要什麼？

(C) Sure, I'll do it. Where do you want me?

當然，我會做。你需要我去哪裡？

* kid〔kɪd〕 *n.* 小孩　　yet〔jɛt〕 *adv.* 已經
  not yet 還沒；尚未　　sure〔ʃʊr〕 *adv.* 當然

10. (**A**) Do we need anything for the party?

　　　我們派對需要什麼東西嗎？

　　(A) We will probably need more chairs.

　　　　我們可能會需要更多的椅子。

　　(B) We will probably need to see it. 我們可能會需要看它。

　　(C) It's a birthday party. 這是個生日派對。

　　* probably〔'prɑbəblɪ〕*adv.* 可能　　chair〔tʃɛr〕*n.* 椅子

第三部分：言談理解（第 11-21 題）

11. (**C**) M : License and registration, please.

　　　男：請出示駕照和車輛登記證。

　　　W : Here you go.

　　　女：拿去吧。

　　　M : Do you know why I pulled you over, ma'am?

　　　男：妳知道我為什麼要妳靠路邊停車嗎，女士？

　　　W : No, I don't, officer.

　　　女：不，我不知道，警官。

　　　M : You ran the red light back there.

　　　男：妳剛在後面那裡闖了紅燈。

　　　W : Oh, no, sir, it was yellow when I entered the intersection.

　　　女：喔，不，先生，我到十字路口時還是黃燈。

　　　M : Actually, ma'am, it had been red for a couple of seconds.

　　　男：事實上，女士，那時候已經紅燈好幾秒了。

　　　W : I'm sorry, officer. Could you give me a warning this time?

　　　女：我很抱歉，警官。你這次可以給我個警告嗎？

M : Seeing as how there wasn't a lot of traffic at this hour, I'll cut you a break.

男：看在這個時間沒有什麼車，我就饒過妳。

Question : What did the woman do?

女士做了什麼？

(A) She made an illegal turn. 她違規轉彎。

(B) She gave the officer a warning. 她給警官一個警告。

(C) She ran a red light. 她闖了紅燈。

* license (ˈlaɪsṇs) *n.* 執照

registration (ˌrɛdʒɪˈstreʃən) *n.* 登記；車輛登記證

Here you go. 你要的東西在這裡；拿去吧。(= *Here you are.*)

pull over 令 (某人) 停靠路邊　　ma'am (mæm) *n.* 女士

officer (ˈɔfəsə) *n.* 警官　　*run a red light* 闖紅燈

back (bæk) *adv.* 在後面　　sir (sə) *n.* 先生

intersection (ˌɪntəˈsɛkʃən) *n.* 十字路口

actually (ˈæktʃuəlɪ) *adv.* 事實上　　*a couple of* 幾個

second (ˈsɛkənd) *n.* 秒　　warning (ˈwɔrnɪŋ) *n.* 警告

time (taɪm) *n.* 次

seeing as how 看在；既然 (= *seeing that*)

traffic (ˈtræfɪk) *n.* 交通；往來的車輛

hour (aʊr) *n.* 時刻　　*at this hour* 在這個時候

cut sb. a break 饒過某人 (= *give sb. a break*)

make a turn 轉彎　　illegal (ɪˈligl) *adj.* 違法的；非法的

12. (**A**) W : Ow! Watch where you're going. Can't you see I'm using a knife?

女：啊！要注意你往哪裡走。你沒看到我在用刀子嗎？

M : Oh, I'm sorry. I didn't realize you were cutting fruit. Are you OK?

男：喔，我很抱歉。我不知道妳剛剛在切水果。妳還好嗎？

W：No, I've sliced my finger. See, it's bleeding now.

女：不好，我已經切到手指了。你看，現在在流血了。

M：Quick! Run it under cold water. I'll go get you a band-aid.

男：快點！用冷水沖洗手指。我去幫妳拿 OK 繃。

Question：What happened first?

一開始發生了什麼事？

(A) The man bumped into the woman. <u>男士撞到了女士。</u>

(B) The woman cut herself. 女士割傷了自己。

(C) The woman ran her finger under cold water.

女士用冷水沖洗手指。

* ow〔aʊ〕*interj.*（表示疼痛、驚訝）唉呀；啊
  watch〔wɑtʃ〕*v.* 注意　　knife〔naɪf〕*n.* 刀子
  realize〔ˈriəˌlaɪz〕*v.* 了解；知道　　slice〔slaɪs〕*v.* 切到
  bleed〔blid〕*v.* 流血　　quick〔kwɪk〕*adv.* 快地
  run *sth.* **under water** 用水沖洗某物
  go + *V.* 去～（= *go to V.*）　　**get** *sb. sth.* 拿某物給某人
  band-aid〔ˈbændˌed〕*n.* OK 繃　　happen〔ˈhæpən〕*v.* 發生
  first〔fɜst〕*adv.* 最先地　　**bump into** 撞上
  cut〔kʌt〕*v.* 切；割

13. (**A**) W：OK, I'll meet you in the lobby at six.

女：好的，我六點會在大廳跟你見面。

M：Don't be late.

男：不要遲到了。

W：Gee, that was one time. You don't have to always remind me.

女：哎呀，那只發生過一次。你不需要每次都提醒我。

Question：What does the woman imply? 女士暗示什麼？

(A) She has been late before. <u>她以前曾經遲到過。</u>

(B) She will probably be late again. 她可能會再遲到。

(C) She is never late. 她從未遲到過。

* lobby〔'lɑbɪ〕*n.* 大廳　　gee〔dʒi〕*interj.* 哎呀
remind〔rɪ'maɪnd〕*v.* 提醒　　imply〔ɪm'plaɪ〕*v.* 暗示

14. (**B**)　M : What would you like to eat?

男：妳想要吃什麼？

W : French fries and corn soup.

女：薯條和玉米湯。

M : Anything to drink?

男：想要喝什麼嗎？

W : Coke, please.

女：可口可樂，謝謝。

M : OK. I will order them for you.

男：好的。我會幫妳點。

Question : What didn't the woman order?

女士沒有點什麼？

(A) French fries. 薯條。

(B) Rice. <u>飯。</u>

(C) Coke. 可口可樂。

* ***would like to V.*** 想要~　　***French fries*** 薯條
corn soup 玉米湯　　Coke〔kok〕*n.* 可口可樂
order〔'ɔrdɚ〕*v.* 點（餐）　　rice〔raɪs〕*n.* 米飯

15. (**A**)　M : Can I borrow your car tonight, Mom?

男：媽，我今晚可以跟妳借車嗎？

W : Why?

女：為什麼？

M : Why? I have a date with Kimberly, that super hot
cheerleader I was telling you about. She's incredible.
Wait until you see her. She looks like a supermodel!

男： 爲什麼？我和金柏莉有約會，就是我跟你說過的那位超級辣
的啦啦隊隊長。她很棒。等等妳就會見到她。她看起來像個
超級名模！

W : Where are you taking her?

女： 你要帶她去哪裡？

M : To a movie and then maybe grab a bite afterwards.

男： 去看電影，然後，或許會吃點東西。

W : Hmm. I don't know. This Kimberly sounds…

女： 嗯。我不知道。這個金柏莉聽起來…。

M : Don't worry, Mom. She's a good girl.

男： 別擔心，媽。她是個好女孩。

Question : Why does the man want to borrow the car?

男士爲何要借車？

(A) He has a date. 他有約會。

(B) He has to work. 他必須工作。

(C) He wants to go shopping. 他想去購物。

* borrow〔'baro〕*v.* 借　date〔det〕*n.* 約會
Kimberly〔'kımbəlı〕*n.* 金柏莉
super〔'supɚ〕*adj.* 非常的；超級的
hot〔hat〕*adj.* 辣的；很正的；受人喜愛的
cheerleader〔'tʃɪr,lidɚ〕*n.* 啦啦隊隊長
incredible〔ın'krɛdəbl̩〕*adj.* 令人難以置信的；很棒的
supermodel〔'supɚ,madl̩〕*n.* 超級名模
maybe〔'mebɪ〕*adv.* 可能　grab〔græb〕*v.* 急抓
bite〔baɪt〕*n.* 食物；小吃；點心
grab a bite 隨便吃點東西

afterwards〔'æftəwədz〕*adv.* 之後

hmm〔hm〕*interj.* 嗯　　sound〔saʊnd〕*v.* 聽起來

16. (**B**) W：Are you busy this weekend?

女：你這個週末忙嗎？

M：No plans. Why?

男：沒有計畫。爲什麼問？

W：I was wondering if I might ask a favor.

女：我在想我是否能請你幫個忙。

M：No harm in asking.

男：問問無妨。

W：I have to work on Sunday and I need someone to walk my dog in the afternoon.

女：我週日得上班，而我需要有人在下午幫我遛狗。

M：No problem. I'll do it.

男：沒問題。我來做。

Question：What will the man do on Sunday?

　　　　　男士週日會做什麼？

(A) Attend a meeting. 參加一場會議。

(B) Walk the woman's dog. 幫女士遛狗。

(C) Ask a favor. 請求幫忙。

* busy〔'bɪzɪ〕*adj.* 忙碌的　　weekend〔'wik'ɛnd〕*n.* 週末
plan〔plæn〕*n.* 計畫　　wonder〔'wʌndə〕*v.* 想知道
favor〔'fevə〕*n.* 幫忙；請求　　***ask a favor*** 請求幫忙
harm〔hɑrm〕*n.* 傷害；妨礙；不妥 < *in* >
walk a dog 遛狗　　attend〔ə'tɛnd〕*v.* 參加
meeting〔'mitɪŋ〕*n.* 會議

17. (**B**) While many kids are lucky enough to become the best of friends with their siblings, it's very common for brothers and sisters to fight. It's also common for them to swing back and forth between adoring and detesting one another. Often, sibling rivalry starts even before the second child is born, and continues as the kids grow and compete for everything from toys to attention. As kids reach different stages of development, their evolving needs can significantly affect how they relate to one another.

雖然很多小孩很幸運，可以和他們的兄弟姊妹成爲最好的朋友，但是兄弟姊妹吵架是非常普遍的。也很常見的是，他們時而喜愛和時而討厭彼此。兄弟姊妹的對立，甚至常常在第二個小孩出生前就開始了，而且這會隨著孩子成長而持續，會爲了從玩具到關注的任何事物競爭。隨著小孩達到不同的發展階段，他們不斷改變的需求，會大大地影響他們彼此之間的關係。

Question：What is more common among siblings?

兄弟姊妹之間什麼是更常見的？

(A) Honesty. 誠實。

(B) Arguing. 爭論。

(C) Luck. 運氣。

* while〔hwaɪl〕*conj.* 雖然（= *though*）
  enough to V. 足以～
  the best of friends 最好的朋友；摯友
  sibling〔'sɪblɪŋ〕*n.* 兄弟姊妹
  common〔'kɑmən〕*adj.* 常見的；普遍的
  fight〔faɪt〕*v.* 打架；吵架　　swing〔swɪŋ〕*v.* 搖擺；來回
  back and forth 來回地；反覆地　　adore〔ə'dor〕*v.* 喜愛
  detest〔dɪ'tɛst〕*v.* 討厭；憎惡　　***one another*** 彼此
  rivalry〔'raɪvḷrɪ〕*n.* 競爭；對立

continue〔kən'tɪnju〕v. 繼續　　grow〔gro〕v. 成長

compete〔kəm'pit〕v. 競爭　　toy〔tɔɪ〕n. 玩具

attention〔ə'tɛnʃən〕n. 關注

reach〔ritʃ〕v. 達到　　stage〔stedʒ〕n. 階段

development〔dɪ'vɛləpmənt〕n. 發展；發育

evolving〔ɪ'vɑlvɪŋ〕adj. 逐漸發展的；不斷變化的

significantly〔sɪg'nɪfɪkəntlɪ〕adv. 顯著地；大大地

affect〔ə'fɛkt〕v. 影響　　relate〔rɪ'let〕v. 有關連 < to >

honesty〔'ɑnɪstɪ〕n. 誠實　　argue〔'ɑrgju〕v. 爭論

luck〔lʌk〕n. 運氣

18.（**A**）M：I'd like to mail this package.

男：我想要寄這個包裹。

W：How would you like to send it?

女：你要怎麼寄？

M：I'm afraid I don't understand what you mean. I want to mail this package to the person it's addressed to, Bill Ross, in Houston, Texas.

男：恐怕我不了解妳的意思。我想要把這包裹寄給在德州休士頓的比爾·羅斯。

W：We have many options, sir. There's overnight, second-day air, and regular ground service.

女：我們有很多選擇，先生。有夜間郵寄、隔日空運，和平郵。

M：What are the rates? I want the cheapest method.

男：費用是多少？我要最便宜的寄法。

W：Regular ground service is the most affordable service, but it also takes the longest. A package to Houston would take up to a week.

女：平郵是最便宜的服務，但也是最久的。寄一個包裹到休士頓需要長達一個星期的時間。

M：Well, I thought the mail was delivered every day. A week is far too long!

男：嗯，我還以爲每天都有遞送郵件。一個星期也太久了！

Question：What is most likely true about the man?
關於這位男士何者最可能是正確的？

(A) He is not familiar with the mail system.
他對郵寄系統不熟悉。

(B) He has never been to Houston. 他從沒去過休士頓。

(C) He frequently visits the post office. 他經常去郵局。

* ***would like to V***. 想要～　　mail〔mel〕v. 郵寄　n. 郵件；郵寄
package〔'pækɪdʒ〕n. 包裹　　send〔sɛnd〕v. 寄
I'm afraid 恐怕　　mean〔min〕v. 意思是
address〔ə'drɛs〕v. 寄（信、包裹等）
Houston〔'hjustən〕n. 休士頓　　Texas〔'tæksəs〕n. 德州
option〔'ɑpʃən〕n. 選擇　　sir〔sɝ〕n. 先生
overnight〔'ovɚ'naɪt〕adj. 夜間的；晚上的
air〔ɛr〕n. 空運　　regular〔'rɛgjəlɚ〕adj. 一般的
ground〔graʊnd〕adj. 地面的；基本的　***gound service*** 平郵
rate〔ret〕n. 費用；價格　　method〔'mɛθəd〕n. 方法
affordable〔ə'fɔrdəbḷ〕adj. 負擔得起的；平價的
take〔tek〕v. 花（時間）　***up to*** 高達
well〔wɛl〕interj. 嗯　　deliver〔dɪ'lɪvɚ〕v. 遞送
far〔fɑr〕adv. 大大地　　likely〔'laɪklɪ〕adv. 可能
familiar〔fə'mɪljɚ〕adj. 熟悉的 < *with* >
system〔'sɪstəm〕n. 系統　***have been to*** 去過
frequently〔'frikwəntlɪ〕adv. 經常
visit〔'vɪzɪt〕v. 拜訪；去　***post office*** 郵局

19. (**A**) M：One fried chicken leg is forty dollars. I want two pieces, so that comes to eighty dollars, right?

男：一支炸雞腿是 40 元。我要兩支，所以總共是 80 元，對嗎？

W : Correct. I've received one hundred. Your change is twenty dollars. Enjoy your chicken.

女：對。我收到 100 元。找您 20 元。請享用您的炸雞。

Question : Who is the woman? 女士是誰？

(A) A cashier. 收銀員。

(B) A teacher. 老師。

(C) A chef. 主廚。

* fried〔fraɪd〕*adj.* 油炸的　　***chicken leg*** 雞腿
piece〔pis〕*n.* 片；塊；支　　***come to*** 總計為；加起來是
correct〔kə'rɛkt〕*adj.* 正確的
change〔tʃendʒ〕*n.* 零錢；找零
cashier〔kæ'ʃɪr〕*n.* 收銀員　　chef〔ʃɛf〕*n.* 主廚

20. (**A**) YouBike is a bicycle service in which you can rent a bike by using your Easy Card. The first 30 minutes are free; then it's 10NT$ for every 30 minutes. There is a station located next to Taipei 101, and it's convenient for transportation around the area.

微笑單車是種腳踏車服務，你可以用悠遊卡來租用腳踏車。前 30 分鐘免費；然後每 30 分鐘新台幣 10 元。在台北 101 旁邊有站，是附近地區很方便的交通工具。

Question : How much would it cost to rent a YouBike for one hour? 租用微笑單車一小時要多少錢？

(A) 10NT$. 新台幣 10 元。

(B) 30NT$. 新台幣 30 元。

(C) 60NT$. 新台幣 60 元。

* bicycle〔'baɪ,sɪkl̩〕*n.* 腳踏車　　service〔'sɝvɪs〕*n.* 服務
rent〔rɛnt〕*v.* 租　　***Easy Card*** 悠遊卡
free〔fri〕*adj.* 免費的　　***NT$*** 新台幣（= *New Taiwan Dollar*）

station〔'steʃən〕 *n.* 車站；站
located〔lo'ketɪd〕 *adj.* 位於…的　　***next to*** 在…旁邊
convenient〔kən'vinjənt〕 *adj.* 方便的
transportation〔ˌtrænspə'teʃən〕 *n.* 交通；運輸
around〔ə'raʊnd〕 *prep.* 在…附近　　area〔'ɛrɪə〕 *n.* 地區

21. (**A**) W：Should we leave now?

女：我們應該現在離開嗎？

M：It's rush hour now. Let's wait an hour or so.

男：現在是尖峰時間。我們等個一小時左右吧。

W：Alright, but don't blame me if we're late.

女：好吧，但是如果我們遲到不要怪我。

M：If we leave now, we'll just end up sitting in traffic.
I'd rather be late than waste gas and time.

男：如果我們現在離開，我們最後只會困在車陣中動彈不得。
我寧可遲到，也不要浪費汽油和時間。

Question：Why does the man not want to leave now?

男士為什麼不想要現在離開？

(A) Traffic is bad. 交通狀況不好。

(B) He's low on gas. 他快沒油了。

(C) He needs to stop at an ATM. 他需要在提款機停留一下。

* leave〔liv〕 *v.* 離開　　***rush hour*** 尖峰時間
or so 大約　　alright〔ɔl'raɪt〕 *adv.* 好的
blame〔blem〕 *v.* 責怪　　***end up*** + ***V-ing*** 最後…；結果…
sit〔sɪt〕 *v.* 坐；留在原地不動
traffic〔'træfɪk〕 *n.* 交通；往來的車輛
would rather…***than***~ 寧願…也不願~
waste〔west〕 *v.* 浪費　　gas〔gæs〕 *n.* 汽油
be low on …短缺的；…快耗盡的
ATM 自動提款機 (= *automated-teller machine*)

🎧 TEST 12 ▶ 詳解

第一部分：辨識句意（第 1-3 題）

1. (**A**) (A)　　　　(B)　　　　(C)

Amy is a thirty-year-old woman who doesn't wear fancy clothes or have any special talents.

艾咪是一位不穿華麗衣服，也沒有任何特殊才能的三十歲女士。

* wear〔wɛr〕*v.* 穿著　　fancy〔ˈfænsɪ〕*adj.* 華麗的
clothes〔kloz〕*n. pl.* 衣服　　special〔ˈspɛʃəl〕*adj.* 特別的
talent〔ˈtælənt〕*n.* 才能

2. (**B**) (A)　　　　(B)　　　　(C)

Emily has just hit the ball toward Ben, who is waiting to return her shot.

艾蜜莉剛剛才把球打向等待回擊的班。

* toward〔tord〕*prep.* 朝向　　wait〔wet〕*v.* 等待
return〔rɪˈtɜn〕*v.* 回擊；擊回　　shot〔ʃɑt〕*n.* 擊球
return a shot 擊回抽球

3. (**C**) (A) (B)  (C)

A large T-shirt will cost you three hundred dollars if you buy it at this store.

如果你在這間店買一件大 T 恤，要花三百元。

* T-shirt〔'ti.ʃɜt〕*n.* T 恤
　cost〔kɔst〕*v.* 使（人）花費

第二部分：基本問答（第 4-10 題）

4. (**B**) Oh, no! Tomorrow is Vanessa's birthday.
　　　喔，不！明天是凡妮莎的生日。

(A) Again? She just started that job.
　　又一次？她才剛開始那份工作。

(B) Uh-oh. You didn't get her a present?
　　哦。你沒買禮物給她？

(C) I see. Will Vanessa be there?
　　我知道了。凡妮莎會在那裡嗎？

* birthday〔'bɝθ,de〕*n.* 生日　　again〔ə'gɛn〕*adv.* 又；再
　just〔dʒʌst〕*adv.* 剛剛　　start〔stɑrt〕*v.* 開始
　job〔dʒɑb〕*n.* 工作　　uh-oh〔'ʌ,o〕*interj.* 喔
　get〔gɛt〕*v.* 買　　present〔'prɛzn̩t〕*n.* 禮物
　see〔si〕*v.* 明白；知道

5. (**A**) Excuse me, is this seat taken?
　　　不好意思，這個位子有人坐嗎？

(A) I'm afraid so. I'm saving it for my girlfriend.
　　恐怕有喔。我要把它留給我的女朋友。

(B) I wouldn't know. I'm not from here.
　　我不知道。我不是這裡的人。

(C) Go ahead. Nobody will notice.
　　做吧。沒有人會注意到。

　* seat〔sit〕*n.* 座位　　take〔tek〕*v.* 佔（位子）；就（座）
　　I'm afraid 恐怕　　save〔se〕*v.* 留…給
　　girlfriend〔'gɜl,frɛnd〕*n.* 女朋友　　*I wouldn't know* 我不清楚
　　sb. not from here 某人不是這裡的人；某人對這裡不熟
　　go ahead 做吧　　nobody〔'no,badɪ〕*pron.* 沒（有）人
　　notice〔'notɪs〕*v.* 注意到

6. (**A**) Look! There's Ronnie Bogan. 你看！那是隆尼・博根。

　　(A) Let's go say hello to him. <u>我們去跟他打個招呼吧。</u>

　　(B) My name is Thomas. 我的名字是湯瑪斯。

　　(C) Once in a while. 偶爾。

　* *say hello to sb.* 跟某人打招呼　　*once in a while* 偶爾；有時候

7. (**C**) How long will you be in Singapore? 你會在新加坡待多久？

　　(A) Wednesday. 星期三。

　　(B) As many as possible. 越多越好。

　　(C) I'm going home tomorrow. <u>我明天就要回家了。</u>

　* Singapore〔'sɪŋgə,por〕*n.* 新加坡
　　as…as possible 儘可能；儘量

8. (**A**) Could you make me a cup of tea? 你可以幫我泡一杯茶嗎？

　　(A) No problem. <u>沒問題。</u>

　　(B) Never mind. 沒關係。

　　(C) No, thanks. 不了，謝謝。

　* make〔mek〕*v.* 為（人）準備　　mind〔maɪnd〕*v.* 介意
　　Never mind. 沒關係。

9. (**B**) Why are you still in bed? You're going to be late for
　　school. 你為什麼還沒起床？你上學要遲到了。

(A) Set the alarm for seven. 把鬧鐘設七點。

(B) I don't feel well. <u>我覺得不太舒服。</u>

(C) Open the window. 把窗戶打開。

* late〔let〕*adj.* 遲到的　set〔sɛt〕*v.* 設定
alarm〔ə'lɑrm〕*n.* 鬧鐘（= *alarm clock*）
well〔wɛl〕*adj.* 健康的；安好的

10. (**A**) Mom, I'm supposed to go swimming tomorrow. Is it going to rain again? 媽，我明天應該要去游泳。會再下雨嗎？

(A) No, tomorrow is supposed to be nice.
<u>不會，明天應該是好天氣。</u>

(B) Good luck. I hope you are successful.
祝你好運。我希望你能成功。

(C) Whatever happens, just be cool.
無論發生什麼事，都要保持冷靜。

* ***be supposed to*** 應該　　***good luck*** 祝你好運
hope〔hop〕*v.* 希望　successful〔sək'sɛsfəl〕*adj.* 成功的
whatever〔hwɑt'ɛvɚ〕*pron.* 不論什麼事
happen〔'hæpən〕*v.* 發生　cool〔kul〕*adj.* 冷靜的

第三部分：言談理解（第 11-21 題）

11. (**C**) W : How long does it take to get to Wulai from here? I need to be there by one-thirty.

女：從這裡到烏來要多久？我一點半之前需要到那裡。

M : If you take the number 41 bus that departs from Taipei City Hall station, the trip usually takes 40 minutes, but sometimes there is heavy traffic. Give yourself about an hour to get there.

男：如果你搭從台北市政府站出發的 41 號公車，通常會需要四十分鐘，但有時候會塞車。給自己一個小時左右的時間去那裡。

Question：When does the woman need to be in Wulai?

這位女士需要何時抵達烏來？

(A) On Wednesday. 星期三。

(B) In 40 minutes. 再過在四十分鐘。

(C) At one-thirty. 一點半。

* take〔tek〕*v.* 花費；搭乘　　by〔baɪ〕*prep.* 在…之前
　number〔'nʌmbɚ〕*n.* …號　　depart〔dɪ'pɑrt〕*v.* 出發
　city hall 市政廳；市政府　　trip〔trɪp〕*n.* 行程
　station〔'steʃən〕*n.* 車站　　heavy〔'hɛvɪ〕*adj.* 大量的
　traffic〔'træfɪk〕*n.* 交通；往來的車輛　　***heavy traffic*** 塞車

12. (**C**)　M：Don't you just love ice cream?　What's your favorite
　　　　　　　flavor?

男：妳不是很愛吃冰淇淋？妳最喜愛什麼口味？

W：Chocolate, I guess.　That's the only flavor I know.
　My mom never lets me eat ice cream.　She says it's
　not healthy.

女：巧克力吧，我猜。那是我唯一知道的口味。我媽媽從不讓我
　　吃冰淇淋。她說那不健康。

M：But it's so delicious!

男：但是很好吃！

Question：Why is chocolate the woman's favorite flavor
　　　　　　of ice cream?

為什麼那女士最喜愛的冰淇淋口味是巧克力？

(A) Her mother says it's healthier than other flavors.
　她媽媽說它比其他的口味健康。

(B) She doesn't like fruit flavors. 她不喜歡水果口味。

(C) It's the only flavor she's ever tried.
　那是她唯一試過的口味。

* favorite〔'fevərɪt〕*adj.* 最喜愛的　　flavor〔'flevɚ〕*n.* 口味
　just〔dʒʌst〕*adv.* (用於否定句、疑問句) 很

chocolate (ˈtʃɔkəlɪt) *n.* 巧克力　　guess (gɛs) *v.* 猜
healthy (ˈhɛlθɪ) *adj.* 健康的　　delicious (dɪˈlɪʃəs) *adj.* 美味的
ever (ˈɛvɚ) *adv.* 曾經　　try (traɪ) *v.* 試嘗；試吃

13. (**A**) Students, we're almost there. Once the bus arrives at the
museum, you will have two hours to explore on your own,
or you can join me for a guided tour. Please remember,
no photographs; and keep your cell phone switched to
silent or vibrate. Those who wish to join me on a tour,
please line up on the sidewalk after we arrive.

同學們，我們快到了。一旦公車抵達博物館，你們就有兩小時自
由探索的時間，或是你們可以跟我一起加入導覽。請記住，不許
拍照並；並把手機轉成靜音或震動模式。凡是要跟我一起參加導
覽的，請在我們抵達後，在人行道上排成一列。

Question：Where is the speaker right now?
說話者現在在哪裡？

(A) On a bus. 在巴士上。

(B) In a museum. 在博物館。

(C) At school. 在學校。

* once (wʌns) *conj.* 一旦　　arrive (əˈraɪv) *v.* 到達
museum (mjuˈzɪəm) *n.* 博物館　　explore (ɪkˈsplor) *v.* 探險
on *one's* **own** 獨自　　join (dʒɔɪn) *v.* 參加；加入
guide (gaɪd) *v.* 引導　　***guided tour*** 有人引導的遊覽；導覽
photograph (ˈfotə،græf) *n.* 照片　　***cell phone*** 手機
switch (swɪtʃ) *v.* 使轉變
silent (ˈsaɪlənt) *adj.* 無聲的；安靜的
vibrate (ˈvaɪbret) *v.* 震動　　wish (wɪʃ) *v.* 希望；想要
line up 排隊　　sidewalk (ˈsaɪd،wɔk) *n.* 人行道
speaker (ˈspikɚ) *n.* 說話者　　***right now*** 現在

14. (**C**) M：Gloria, this casserole is delicious!
男：葛洛麗亞，這焗烤也太美味了吧！

W：Thanks, Ted.

女：謝謝你，泰德。

M : Where did you learn to cook like this?

男：妳在哪裡學會這樣做菜的？

W : Actually, I didn't.

女：事實上，我沒學。

M : What? You must be joking. Someone who doesn't know how to cook couldn't possibly have made this dish.

男：什麼？妳一定是在開玩笑吧。一個不知道如何做菜的人，不可能做得出這道菜。

W : I'll tell you how I did it. I went to the store, bought it, took it home, removed it from the packaging, put it in the microwave, and pressed a few buttons. Ten minutes later—it was done.

女：我來告訴你我怎麼做的。我去了商店，買了它，帶回家，拆掉包裝，放進微波爐，然後按了幾個按鈕。十分鐘之後──就完成了。

Question : What is true about the woman?

關於女士，何者正確？

(A) She is a good cook. 她很會做菜。

(B) She wants to learn how to cook. 她想學習如何做菜。

(C) She knows how to use a microwave.

她知道如何使用微波爐。

* casserole〔'kæsə‚rol〕*n.* 焗烤；砂鍋菜
  cook〔kʊk〕*v.* 煮；烹調　*n.* 廚師
  actually〔'æktʃʊəlɪ〕*adv.* 事實上　　joke〔dʒok〕*v.* 開玩笑
  possibly〔'pɑsəblɪ〕*adv.* 可能　　dish〔dɪʃ〕*n.* 菜餚
  remove〔rɪ'muv〕*v.* 移開
  packaging〔'pækɪdʒɪŋ〕*n.* 包裝；容器
  microwave〔'maɪkrə‚wev〕*n.* 微波爐　　press〔prɛs〕*v.* 壓；按
  a few 一些；幾個　　button〔'bʌtn̩〕*n.* 按鈕
  later〔'letə〕*adv.* …之後　　done〔dʌn〕*adj.* 完成的

15. (**C**) W : It was so nice of you to give me the gift, Oscar, but I can't accept it.

女：你真好，還送我禮物，奧斯卡，但我不能收下它。

M : Why not? It's your birthday!

男：為什麼不？今天是妳的生日！

W : My boyfriend is very jealous. He'll think there's something going on between us.

女：我男朋友會吃醋。他會覺得我們之間有曖昧。

Question : Why did the woman reject the man's gift?

　　　為何女士拒絕了男士的禮物？

(A) She already has a boyfriend. 她已經有男朋友了。

(B) She's not interested in him. 她對他沒興趣。

(C) Her boyfriend would not approve.

　　她的男朋友不會同意。

* nice〔naɪs〕*adj.* 好的　　accept〔əkˈsɛpt〕*v.* 接受
boyfriend〔ˈbɔɪˌfrɛnd〕*n.* 男朋友　　***go on*** 發生
jealous〔ˈdʒɛləs〕*adj.* 嫉妒的；吃醋的
something ***going on between*** 男女之間有曖昧
reject〔rɪˈdʒɛkt〕*v.* 拒絕
interested〔ˈɪntrɪstɪd〕*adj.* 感興趣的
approve〔əˈpruv〕*v.* 同意；贊成

16. (**C**) That's a very common question, and the answer is— writing well takes practice. Reading is very important to good writing, but the only way to get better as a writer is to write. You have to write every day, no matter what. As long as you are determined to improve, your writing will get better. A lot of young writers are afraid to take risks, but failure is nothing to fear. Making mistakes is how we learn. Most of my readers don't realize that before one of my books is published, it contains many mistakes which my editor helps me fix.

那是一個很常見的問題，而答案是——要寫得好就要練習。閱讀對於良好的寫作很重要，但要成爲一位更好的作家，唯一的方法就是寫作。無論如何，你每天都要寫。只要你有心想進步，你的文筆就會變好。很多年輕的作家都害怕冒險，但失敗沒什麼好怕的。要犯了錯我們才學得會。我的很多讀者都不知道，我的書在出版前，是有很多錯誤的，我的編輯會幫我修改。

Question : Who is the speaker?　說話者是誰？

(A) An architect.　一位建築師。

(B) An athlete.　一位運動員。

(C) An author.　<u>一位作家。</u>

* common〔'kɑmən〕*adj.* 常見的　　take〔tek〕*v.* 需要
practice〔'præktɪs〕*n.* 練習　　***no matter what*** 無論如何
as long as 只要　　determined〔dɪ'tɜmɪnd〕*adj.* 堅決的
improve〔ɪm'pruv〕*v.* 進步　　young〔jʌŋ〕*adj.* 年輕的
afraid〔ə'fred〕*adj.* 害怕的　　risk〔rɪsk〕*n.* 危險；風險
take a risk 冒險　　failure〔'feljə〕*n.* 失敗
fear〔fɪr〕*v.* 害怕　　mistake〔mə'stek〕*n.* 錯誤
make a mistake 犯錯　　how〔haʊ〕*adv.* (做…的) 方法
reader〔'ridə〕*n.* 讀者　　realize〔'riə,laɪz〕*v.* 了解
publish〔'pʌblɪʃ〕*v.* 出版　　contain〔kən'ten〕*v.* 包含
editor〔'ɛdɪtə〕*n.* 編輯　　fix〔fɪks〕*v.* 修改
architect〔'ɑrkə,tɛkt〕*n.* 建築師　　athlete〔'æθlit〕*n.* 運動員
author〔'ɔθə〕*n.* 作家 (= *writer*)

17. (**A**) M : Did you see Gary's report card?

男：你有看到蓋瑞的成績單嗎？

W : How did he do?

女：他考得如何？

M : I didn't think he could do any worse than last semester, but he did.

男：我以爲他不會考得比上學期差，但這次更差。

W : Oh, no.　Maybe we need to get him a tutor.

女：哦，不。也許我們必須給他找個家教。

Question：What is probably true about Gary's grades?
關於蓋瑞的成績，何者可能是正確的？

(A) They got worse. 變得更糟了。

(B) They improved. 進步了。

(C) They remained unchanged. 保持不變。

* *report card* 成績單（= *transcript*）　　***do worse*** 考得更差
　last〔 læst 〕*adj.* 上一個的　　semester〔 sə'mɛstə 〕*n.* 學期
　tutor〔'tutə 〕*n.* 家教　　grade〔 gred 〕*n.* 成績
　improve〔 ɪm'pruv 〕*v.* 改善；進步
　remain〔 rɪ'men 〕*v.* 依然；依舊；繼續
　unchanged〔 ʌn'tʃendʒd 〕*adj.* 不變的

18. (**B**) M：I'm going to have the Denver omelet, how about you?

男：我要吃丹佛煎蛋捲，你呢？

W：The pancakes look good. But I'm also looking at the waffles.

女：煎餅看起來不錯。但我也在考慮鬆餅。

M：Where's the server? We should probably order soon.

男：服務生在哪裡？我們可能要趕快點餐。

W：Relax. We have plenty of time.

女：放輕鬆。我們時間很多。

Question：What are the speakers most likely going to do next? 這兩位說話者接下來最可能會做什麼？

(A) Pay the bill. 結帳。

(B) Order breakfast. 點早餐。

(C) Have dessert. 吃甜點。

* have〔 hæv 〕*v.* 吃　　omelet〔'ɑmlɪt 〕*n.* 煎蛋捲
　pancake〔'pæn,kek 〕*n.* 鬆餅；薄煎餅　　look〔 lʊk 〕*v.* 看起來
　look at 看著；考慮　　waffle〔'wɑfḷ 〕*n.* 鬆餅
　server〔'sɝvə 〕*n.* 服務生　　order〔'ɔrdə 〕*v.* 點餐
　relax〔 rɪ'læks 〕*v.* 放鬆　　***plenty of*** 很多的

likely〔'laɪklɪ〕*adv.* 可能　　next〔nɛkst〕*adv.* 接下來

bill〔bɪl〕*n.* 帳單　***pay the bill*** 付錢；結帳

dessert〔dɪ'zɝt〕*n.* 甜點

19. (**B**) M：Can we meet sometime this afternoon?

　　　男：今天下午我們可以找個時間見面嗎？

　　　W：Sorry, I'm busy all day.　How about tomorrow?

　　　女：抱歉，我整天都很忙。明天如何？

　　　M：OK.　When is a good time?

　　　男：好。幾點比較好呢？

　　　W：Anytime before noon.

　　　女：中午之前都可以。

　　　Question：When will the man and woman most likely

　　　　　　　　meet?　男士和女士最有可能何時見面？

　　　(A) Tomorrow at 12:30.　明天十二點半。

　　　(B) Tomorrow at 9:30.　<u>明天九點半。</u>

　　　(C) Today at 5:00.　今天五點。

　　　* meet〔mit〕*v.* 見面　　sometime〔'sʌm,taɪm〕*adv.* 在某個時候

　　　　busy〔'bɪzɪ〕*adj.* 忙碌的　　***How about***~?　~如何？

　　　　anytime〔'ɛnɪ,taɪm〕*adv.* 隨時；任何時候

　　　　noon〔nun〕*n.* 中午

20. (**B**) M：There's nothing on television.　It's all reality shows

　　　　　　and religious programming.

　　　男：電視上沒什麼好看的。全都是實境秀和宗教節目。

　　　W：This is news to you?　There's never been anything

　　　　　good on TV.　Why don't you try reading a book?

　　　女：這你應該早就知道了吧？電視上從來沒有什麼好節目。爲什

　　　　　麼你不試著看點書？

　　　Question：What is the man complaining about?

　　　　　　　　男士在抱怨什麼？

　　　(A) A story on the news.　一則新聞報導。

(B) A lack of something he's interested in seeing.
缺乏他有興趣看的節目。

(C) An argument he had with another guy about religion.
他和另一個人關於宗教的爭論。

* ***reality show*** 眞人秀；實境秀
 religious〔rɪ'lɪdʒəs〕*adj.* 宗教的
 programming〔pro'græmɪŋ〕*n.* 節目的上演；節目的播送
 religious programming 宗教節目
 be news to *sb.* 對某人來說是新聞；某人不知道
 complain〔kəm'plen〕*v.* 抱怨　　story〔'storɪ〕*n.* 報導
 lack〔læk〕*n.* 缺乏　　argument〔'ɑrgjəmənt〕*n.* 爭論
 guy〔gaɪ〕*n.* 人；傢伙　　religion〔rɪ'lɪdʒən〕*n.* 宗教

21. (**C**) W : Oh, no! Becky left for school and forgot her lunch.
　　　　女：喔，不！貝姬上學去了，但忘了帶她的午餐。

　　　　M : That's OK. I'll drop it off on my way to work.
　　　　　　When is her lunch break?

　　　　男：沒關係。我上班途中順便拿給她。她午餐的時間是幾點？

　　　　W : After fourth period, so I guess that's about noon.
　　　　女：第四節課後，所以我猜大概是中午。

　　　　M : No problem.
　　　　男：沒問題。

　　　　Question : What did Becky forget this morning?
　　　　　　　　　　貝姬今天早上忘了什麼？

(A) Her backpack. 她的背包。

(B) Her wallet. 她的皮夾。

(C) Her lunch. 她的午餐。

* ***leave for*** 動身前往　　***drop off*** 把…放下
 on *one's* ***way to*** 在某人去…的途中　　***lunch break*** 午餐時間
 period〔'pɪrɪəd〕*n.* (上課的) 節；堂
 forget〔fə'gɛt〕*v.* 忘記　　backpack〔'bæk,pæk〕*n.* 背包
 wallet〔'wɑlɪt〕*n.* 皮夾

TEST 13 ▶ 詳解

第一部分：辨識句意（第 1-3 題）

1. (**B**) (A)　　　　　　(B)　　　　　　(C)

Debbie used to be skinny like a model but now she's super fat. 黛比以前像模特兒一樣非常瘦，但是她現在很胖。

> * **used to** 以前　　skinny〔ˋskɪnɪ〕adj. 皮包骨的；很瘦的
> model〔ˋmɑdḷ〕n. 模特兒　　super〔ˋsupɚ〕adj. 超級的
> fat〔fæt〕adj. 胖的

2. (**A**) (A)　　　　　　(B)　　　　　　(C)

The family of three is making an offering at the temple. 一家三口正在廟裡獻祭。

> * offering〔ˋɔfərɪŋ〕n. 供奉；奉獻；祭品
> **make an offering** （對神的）奉獻；獻祭
> temple〔ˋtɛmpḷ〕n. 廟

3. (**C**) (A)　　　　　　(B)　　　　　　(C)

Ann has just brought a gift to her neighbors.

安剛剛帶了禮物給她的鄰居。

* bring〔brɪŋ〕*v.* 帶　　gift〔gɪft〕*n.* 禮物
　neighbor〔'nebɚ〕*n.* 鄰居

第二部分：基本問答（第 4-10 題）

4.(**C**) Here's the money I borrowed last week.

這是我上禮拜借的錢。

(A) That's OK. Just take what you need.

沒關係。需要什麼就拿去吧。

(B) You're welcome. 不客氣。

(C) Thanks for paying me back. I appreciate it.

謝謝你還給我。我非常感激。

* borrow〔'baro〕*v.* 借（出）　　***That's OK***. 沒關係。
　pay back 償還　　appreciate〔ə'priʃɪ,et〕*v.* 感激

5.(**A**) Maybe you should bring a sweater. It's pretty chilly out there. 也許你應該帶一件毛衣。外面很冷。

(A) OK. I'll put one in my backpack.

好的。我會放一件在我的背包裡。

(B) Of course. They are my friends.

當然。他們是我的朋友。

(C) Sure. You can use it any time you like.

當然。你隨時都可以用它。

* maybe〔'mebɪ〕*adv.* 或許　　sweater〔'swɛtɚ〕*n.* 毛衣
　pretty〔'prɪtɪ〕*adv.* 相當　　chilly〔'tʃɪlɪ〕*adj.* 寒冷的
　out there 外面　　***of course*** 當然　　sure〔ʃʊr〕*adv.* 當然

6.(**C**) Wow, that girl is beautiful! Do you know who she is?

哇，那個女孩好漂亮！你知道她是誰嗎？

(A) I've never been here before. 我以前從沒來過這裡。

(B) I've never tried that before. 我以前從沒試過那個。

(C) I've never seen her before. <u>我以前從沒見過她。</u>

   * wow〔waʊ〕*interj.* 哇！   try〔traɪ〕*v.* 嘗試

7. (**A**) Would you like to stay for lunch? I made your favorite
pasta salad.
你要留下來吃午餐嗎？我做了你最愛的義大利冷麵。

   (A) Sure, I'd love to. <u>當然，我非常樂意。</u>

   (B) The weather is bad. 天氣不好。

   (C) We had chicken. 我們吃了雞肉。

   * stay〔ste〕*v.* 停留   favorite〔'fevərɪt〕*adj.* 最喜愛的
    pasta〔'pɑstə〕*n.* 義大利麵   salad〔'sæləd〕*n.* 沙拉
    pasta salad 義大利冷麵   ***I'd love to*** 我非常樂意
    weather〔'wɛðə˞〕*n.* 天氣   have〔hæv〕*v.* 吃
    chicken〔'tʃɪkɪn〕*n.* 雞肉

8. (**C**) Are you feeling better today than you did yesterday?
你今天有覺得比昨天好嗎？

   (A) Yes, I'm glad you did. 是的，我很高興你那麼做。

   (B) Didn't you see me? 你沒看到我嗎？

   (C) Much better. <u>好多了。</u>

   * glad〔glæd〕*adj.* 高興的

9. (**B**) Where are you? We've been waiting for almost 20
minutes. 你在哪裡？我們等了快二十分鐘了。

   (A) Why not? He didn't ask for it.
      為什麼不？他沒有要求那個東西。

   (B) I'm so sorry. I'm still stuck in traffic.
      <u>我很抱歉。我還塞在車陣中。</u>

(C) Good enough. Close the door on your way out.

已經夠好了。你出去時要把門關上。

* wait〔wet〕*v.* 等　　almost〔'ɔl,most〕*adv.* 幾乎
stuck〔stʌk〕*adj.* 卡住不能動彈的
traffic〔'træfɪk〕*n.* 交通；往來的車輛
be stuck in traffic 塞車　　***on one's way out*** 出去時

10. (**C**) If you're going to the comic book store, tell Kevin I said hello. 如果你要去漫畫書店，幫我跟凱文問好。

(A) I've read that book already. 我已經看過那本書了。

(B) I'm ready for another. 我準備好開始下一個了。

(C) I'll do that. 我會的。

* ***comic book*** 漫畫書　　store〔stor〕*n.* 商店
say hello to *sb.* 跟某人問好　　already〔ɔl'rɛdɪ〕*adv.* 已經
ready〔'rɛdɪ〕*adj.* 準備好的

第三部分：言談理解（第 11-21 題）

11. (**B**) M : Hey, Chloe. Here's your mail and the keys.

男：嘿，克蘿伊。這裡有妳的信件和鑰匙。

W : Thanks for watching my house while I was away, Trevor. I really appreciate it.

女：謝謝你當我不在的時候幫我看家，特雷弗。我真的很感激。

M : Anytime. It was no trouble at all. How was your vacation?

男：不客氣。根本沒什麼。妳假期過得如何？

Question : Where was the woman? 女士原本在哪裡？

(A) At work. 在工作。

(B) Out of town. 在城外。

(C) In the hospital 在醫院。

* hey〔he〕*interj.* 嘿　　mail〔mel〕*n.* 信件
key〔ki〕*n.* 鑰匙　　***while sb. is away*** 當某人不在的時候
no trouble at all 一點都不麻煩；沒問題的
vacation〔ve'keʃən〕*n.* 假期　　work〔wɜk〕*n.* 工作場所
town〔taʊn〕*n.* 城鎮；城市　　hospital〔'hɑspɪtl〕*n.* 醫院

12. (**C**) W：Skippy. Do you need a ride to school?

女：史奇比。你需要我載你去學校嗎？

M：If it's OK with you, Mom, Frank and I will ride our bikes together.

男：媽，如果妳覺得可以的話，法蘭克和我要騎我們的腳踏車一起去。

W：That's fine. Be careful.

女：可以。路上小心。

Question：How will Skippy get to school?

史奇比會怎麼去學校？

(A) He will get a ride from Frank. 他會被法蘭克載。

(B) He will take the bus. 他會搭公車。

(C) He will ride his bike. 他會騎他的腳踏車。

* ride〔raɪd〕*v. n.* 搭乘；騎乘
OK〔'o'ke〕*adj.* 可以的；沒問題的
together〔tə'gɛðɚ〕*adv.* 一起　　fine〔faɪn〕*adj.* 好的
get a ride from sb. 被某人載
bike〔baɪk〕*n.* 腳踏車（= *bicycle*）
careful〔'kɛrfəl〕*adj.* 小心的　　take〔tek〕*v.* 搭乘

13. (**B**) It's kind of tricky to find, but go straight to the next intersection and turn right. Be sure to cross over the intersection and then turn right. There's a bank about

halfway up the block and you'll come up on a narrow alley on the west side of the street. That's Grover Lane. OK, now, turn into the alley and you'll see a bunch of neon signs. The Hideaway is almost at the very end of the lane.

這有點難找，但你就直走到下一個十字路口，然後右轉。要確定你有過那個十字路口，然後右轉。大概走半條街後，有一家銀行，然後在街道的西邊，你會看到一條狹窄的巷子。那就是格羅弗里巷。好，現在在轉進巷子，你會看到一堆霓虹燈招牌。The Hideaway 幾乎就在巷子的盡頭。

Question：What is the woman doing? 女士正在做什麼？

(A) Asking for help. 尋求幫助。

(B) Giving directions. 指引方向。

(C) Playing the piano. 彈鋼琴。

---

* ***kind of*** 有點　　tricky〔'trɪkɪ〕*adj.* 棘手的；難以處理的
straight〔stret〕*adv.* 直直地
intersection〔ˌɪntɚ'sɛkʃən〕*n.* 十字路口
turn〔tɜn〕*v.* 轉　　***turn right*** 右轉
cross over 經過；越過
halfway〔'hæf'we〕*adv.* 在中途；到中途
up〔ʌp〕*adv.* 往；上…的途中；向…接近
block〔blɑk〕*n.* 街區　　***come up on*** 看見
narrow〔'næro〕*adj.* 狹窄的　　alley〔'ælɪ〕*n.* 小巷
west〔wɛst〕*adj.* 西方的　　lane〔len〕*n.* 巷子
bunch〔bʌntʃ〕*n.* 一堆　　neon〔'niɑn〕*n.* 霓虹燈
sign〔saɪn〕*n.* 招牌　　almost〔ɔl'most〕*adv.* 幾乎
very〔'vɛrɪ〕*adj.* 正是；就是　　end〔ɛnd〕*n.* 末端；盡頭
directions〔də'rɛkʃənz〕*n. pl.* 方向；指引
piano〔pɪ'æno〕*n.* 鋼琴

14. (**C**) M : I see you brought your own folding chair.

男：我看到妳帶了自己的摺疊椅。

W : Yes, I knew there would be a long line.

女：是的，我知道這裡會大排長龍。

M : Is this something you do often? I mean, the thing with the chair.

男：妳常這麼做嗎？我是說，妳帶椅子這件事。

W : I'm from the Philippines. We're used to waiting in long lines. But I don't think it's that unusual. You see people setting up tents outside of Wal-Mart the night before a big sale.

女：我來自菲律賓。我們習慣要排很長的隊。但我不覺得這有什麼不尋常的。你可以在沃爾瑪有大拍賣時的前一天晚上，看到大家在外面搭帳篷。

Question : What are the speakers doing?

說話者在做什麼？

(A) Camping. 露營。

(B) Buying furniture. 買家具。

(C) Waiting in line. 排隊。

* own〔on〕*adj.* 自己的　　fold〔fold〕*v.* 摺疊
  folding chair 摺疊椅　　line〔laɪn〕*n.* 行列
  mean〔min〕*v.* 意思是　　***the thing with*** 關於…的事
  the Philippines〔'fɪləˌpinz〕菲律賓
  be used to + ***V-ing*** … 習慣於…
  unusual〔ʌn'juʒʊəl〕*adj.* 不尋常的　　***set up*** 設立
  tent〔tɛnt〕*n.* 帳棚　　Wal-Mart〔'wɔlˌmɑrt〕*n.* 沃爾瑪
  the night before …的前一天晚上　　***big sale*** 大拍賣
  camp〔kæmp〕*v.* 露營　　furniture〔'fɝnɪtʃɚ〕*n.* 家具
  wait in line 排隊

15. (**A**) W：Did you get a new iPad?

女：你買了新的 iPad 嗎？

M：Kind of…

男：嗯，之類的…

W：Can I see it?

女：我可以看嗎？

M：Sure. Check it out.

男：當然。拿去看吧。

W：Oh, this isn't an Apple iPad.

女：喔，這不是蘋果的 iPad。

M：Nope. I bought it at the night market. Looks just like the real thing, doesn't it?

男：不是。我是在夜市買的。看起來就像真的一樣，不是嗎？

W：Maybe, but I noticed a couple of differences right away. It feels lighter than a normal tablet.

女：也許吧，但是我馬上就注意到有幾個不同點。它比一般的平板電腦還要輕。

Question：What does the woman notice about the tablet?

關於平板電腦女士發現了什麼？

(A) It's lighter than an iPad. 它比 iPad 輕。

(B) It's heavier than an iPad. 它比 iPad 重。

(C) It's cheaper than an iPad. 它比 iPad 便宜。

* get〔gɛt〕*v.* 買　　***kind of*** 之類的　　***check it out*** 看看
nope〔nop〕*adv.* 不；不是（= *no*）　　***night market*** 夜市
the real thing 原版的；真正的　　***a couple of*** 兩三個；幾個
difference〔'dɪfrəns〕*n.* 不同；差異
right away 立刻；馬上　　feel〔fil〕*v.* 使人感覺
light〔laɪt〕*adj.* 輕的
normal〔'nɔrml̩〕*adj.* 正常的；普通的

tablet〔ˈtæblɪt〕*n.* 平板電腦　　notice〔ˈnotɪs〕*v.* 注意到
heavy〔ˈhɛvɪ〕*adj.* 重的　　cheap〔tʃip〕*adj.* 便宜的

16. (**C**)　W : What kind of music do you listen to?
　　　女：你都聽什麼類型的音樂？
　　　M : I don't listen to a lot of music.
　　　男：我聽的音樂不多。
　　　W : Why not?
　　　女：為什麼不？
　　　M : I like reading. I'm a bookworm, so I prefer silence to
　　　　　noise.
　　　男：我喜歡閱讀。我很愛看書，所以比起吵鬧，我更喜歡安靜。
　　　W : What kind of books do you like to read?
　　　女：你喜歡讀什麼種類的書？
　　　M : Mostly science fiction.
　　　男：大多是科幻小說。

　　　Question：What is true about the man?
　　　　　　　　關於男士，何者正確？

　　　(A) He loves music.　他喜愛音樂。
　　　(B) He majored in science.　他主修自然科學。
　　　(C) He reads a lot.　<u>他讀很多書。</u>

　　*　kind〔kaɪnd〕*n.* 種類
　　　bookworm〔ˈbʊk͵wɝm〕*n.* 極愛讀書者；書呆子
　　　prefer〔prɪˈfɝ〕*v.* 比較喜歡　　***prefer A to B*** 喜歡 A 甚於 B
　　　silence〔ˈsaɪləns〕*n.* 安靜　　noise〔nɔɪz〕*n.* 噪音；吵鬧
　　　mostly〔ˈmostlɪ〕*adv.* 大多　　***science fiction*** 科幻小說
　　　major in 主修　　***a lot*** 許多

17. (**A**) Hi, Derek. I hope you had a good day at school. I went to pick up your father from the airport. Your dinner is in the microwave, so all you need to do is heat it up. Make sure you eat before doing your homework. Listening to music is fine, but remember—no computer games until your homework is finished. Call me on my cell phone if you need anything. See you later tonight.

嗨，德瑞克。我希望你在學校度過了美好的一天。我去機場接你的爸爸。晚餐在微波爐裡，所以你只需要把它熱一下。一定要先吃飯再做功課。你可以聽音樂，但是記得——作業寫完之前，不能玩電腦遊戲。如果你需要什麼，就打我的手機。今晚晚點見。

Question : What is Derek not allowed to use?

德瑞克不被允許用什麼？

(A) The computer. 電腦。

(B) The microwave. 微波爐。

(C) The cell phone. 手機。

* ***pick up*** *sb.* 接某人　　airport〔'ɛr͵port〕*n.* 機場
microwave〔'maɪkrə͵wev〕*n.* 微波爐
all you need to do is V. 你所需要做的就是…
heat up 把…加熱　　***make sure*** 確定
computer〔kəm'pjutɚ〕*n.* 電腦
computer game 電腦遊戲　　finish〔'fɪnɪʃ〕*v.* 做完；完成
call〔kɔl〕*v.* 打電話給…　　***cell phone*** 手機
see you later 再見；待會見　　allow〔ə'lau〕*v.* 允許；許可

18. (**A**) W : Do you frequently use e-mail?

女：你常使用電子郵件嗎？

M : No, I seldom use it.

男：不，我很少用。

W：How do you communicate with people?

女：你都怎麼跟人聯絡？

M：By talking to them.

男：直接跟他們說話。

W：That's weird. I couldn't imagine life without e-mail.

女：那很奇怪。我無法想像沒有電子郵件的生活。

Question：What does the woman imply?

這位女士暗示什麼？

(A) She relies on e-mail to communicate with people.

她依賴電子郵件來跟人聯繫。

(B) She thinks the Internet is a waste of time.

她覺得網路很浪費時間。

(C) She doesn't have time to use e-mail.

她沒時間使用電子郵件。

* frequently〔'frikwəntlı〕*adv.* 經常
 e-mail〔'i,mel〕*n.* 電子郵件　　seldom〔'sɛldəm〕*adv.* 很少
 communicate〔kə'mjunə,ket〕*v.* 溝通；聯繫
 weird〔wɪrd〕*adj.* 奇怪的　　imagine〔ɪ'mædʒɪn〕*v.* 想像
 imply〔ɪm'plaɪ〕*v.* 暗示　　rely〔rɪ'laɪ〕*v.* 依賴 < *on* >
 Internet〔'ɪntə,nɛt〕*n.* 網際網路
 a waste of time 浪費時間

19. (**B**) M：I'm done for the day, Sharon. I've got to pick up my
 wife from the airport. See you tomorrow.

男：我事情做完了，莎倫。要準備下班了。我必須去機場接我太
太。明天見。

W：Wait, David! Did you finish the progress reports for
 Mr. Wilson?

女：等一下，大衛！你做完威爾森先生要的進度報告了嗎？

M：He said the deadline is Thursday! Today is only Tuesday. I'll have it for him no later than tomorrow afternoon.

男：他說期限是星期四！今天才星期二。我明天下午之前就會做完給他。

Question：What day is tomorrow?

明天是星期幾？

(A) Tuesday. 星期二。

(B) Wednesday. 星期三。

(C) Saturday. 星期六。

* *sb.* ***is done for the day*** 某人完成了一天的工作
progress〔'prɑgrɛs〕*n.* 進步；進度
report〔rɪ'port〕*n.* 報告　　***progress reports*** 進度報告
deadline〔'dɛd,laɪn〕*n.* 截止日期　　***no later than*** 不晚於

20. (**B**) The United States may be a wealthy nation, but when it comes to being an ideal place to raise a family, it ranks well below several European countries. Most of the countries in the top 10 are in Europe, where paid maternity leave is the norm, breastfeeding is widely accepted, and government-backed support programs for new parents abound.

美國也許是一個富裕的國家，但一提到養小孩的理想地方，它的排名遠低於許多歐洲國家。前十名的國家大多在歐洲，在那裡帶薪產假是常態，哺乳非常普遍，而且對於新手爸媽，有很多政府支持的支援計畫。

Question：What does the speaker imply?

說話者暗示什麼？

(A) The U.S. is a great place to raise a family.

美國是個非常適合養小孩的地方。

(B) Europe might be a better place to raise a family.

<u>歐洲可能是一個更適合養小孩的地方。</u>

(C) It doesn't matter where you raise a family.

你在哪裡養小孩都無所謂。

* wealthy〔'wɛlθɪ〕*adj.* 有錢的　　nation〔'neʃən〕*n.* 國家

*** when it comes to*** 一提到　　ideal〔aɪ'diəl〕*adj.* 理想的

raise〔rez〕*v.* 養育

family〔'fæməlɪ〕*n.* 家;(一家的)孩子們

rank〔ræŋk〕*v.* 排名　　well〔wɛl〕*adv.* 大大地;遠遠地

below〔bə'lo〕*prep.* 低於

several〔'sɛvərəl〕*adj.* 好幾個;數個

European〔,jurə'piən〕*adj.* 歐洲的

country〔'kʌntrɪ〕*n.* 國家　　top〔tɑp〕*adj.* 最上面的

*** top ten*** 前十名　　Europe〔'jurəp〕*n.* 歐洲

paid〔ped〕*adj.* 有薪水的

maternity〔mə'tɜnətɪ〕*adj.* 孕婦的　　leave〔liv〕*n.* 休假

*** paid maternity leave*** 帶薪產假

norm〔nɔrm〕*n.* 標準;常態　　breastfeed〔'brɛst,fid〕*v.* 哺乳

widely〔'waɪdlɪ〕*adv.* 廣泛地　　accept〔ək'sɛpt〕*v.* 接受

government〔'gʌvənmənt〕*n.* 政府　　back〔bæk〕*v.* 支持

*** government-backed*** *adj.* 政府支持的

support〔sə'port〕*n.* 支持

program〔'progræm〕*n.* 計畫;節目

*** support program*** 支援計畫　　*** new parents*** 新手爸媽

abound〔ə'baund〕*v.* 大量存在;有許多

matter〔'mætə〕*v.* 有關係;重要

21. (**C**) M : How was the party?

　　男:派對如何?

W：Don't ask.

女：不要問。

M：That bad?

男：有那麼糟喔？

W：Eh, I don't know.

女：呃，我不知道。

M：Come on, tell me about it.

男：快點告訴我啦。

W：First of all, the place was so crowded you couldn't even move. And then the DJ was so loud that I couldn't even talk to my friends. So we left.

女：首先，那個地方擠滿了人，你根本動不了。再來 DJ 太大聲了，我根本無法跟我的朋友聊天。所以我們就離開了。

Question：What does the woman say about the party?

女士說派對如何？

(A) It could have been worse. 原本可能更糟。

(B) It wasn't that bad. 沒那麼糟。

(C) It was too crowded. <u>太擁擠了。</u>

* eh〔ε〕*interj.* 呃；啊　　***come on*** 快點
crowded〔'kraʊdɪd〕*adj.* 擁擠的
DJ〔'di,dʒeɪ〕*n.* 唱片播放員；音樂節目主持人
so…(that) 如此…以致於　　even〔'ivən〕*adv.* 甚至
move〔muv〕*v.* 移動　　loud〔laʊd〕*adj.* 大聲的
leave〔liv〕*v.* 離開
could have been worse 原本可能更糟

 TEST 14 ▶ 詳解

第一部分：辨識句意（第 1-3 題）

1. (**B**) (A) 　(B) 　(C)

The teacher is asking the students to spell the word
"repeat." 老師要求學生們拼出 "repeat" 這個單字。

* spell〔spɛl〕v. 拼（字）　　repeat〔rɪˋpit〕v. 重複

2. (**C**) (A) 　(B) 　(C)

A blind man is riding the bus with his service dog.
有位盲人和他的導盲犬正在搭巴士。

* blind〔blaɪnd〕adj. 失明的；盲的　　ride〔raɪd〕v. 搭乘
service dog 服務犬；導盲犬

3. (**A**) (A) 　(B) 　(C)

A box fell on Tom's shoulder, which is now very sore.

有個箱子掉到湯姆的肩膀上,他的肩膀現在很痛。

* **fall** 〔 fɔl 〕 *v.* 掉落　　**shoulder** 〔ˈʃoldɚ〕 *n.* 肩膀
　sore 〔 sor 〕 *adj.* 疼痛的

第二部分:基本問答(第 4-10 題)

4.(**B**) I got a call from David last night.

我昨晚接到了一通大衛打來的電話。

(A) David lives in Sanchong. 大衛住在三重。

(B) What's David up to these days?

　　大衛最近在忙些什麼?

(C) Yes, I called David. 是的,我打了電話給大衛。

* **call** 〔 kɔl 〕 *n.* 打電話　　***up to*** 忙於⋯的
　these days 最近

5.(**C**) How much did that new MP3 player cost you?

那台新的 MP3 花了你多少錢?

(A) I love listening to music. 我很愛聽音樂。

(B) I can't play. 我不會播放。

(C) It was a gift from my cousin. 這是我表哥送我的禮物。

* ***MP3 player*** MP3 播放器　　**cost** 〔 kɔst 〕 *v.* 花費
　play 〔 ple 〕 *v.* 播放　　**cousin** 〔ˈkʌzn̩〕 *n.* 表(堂)兄弟姐妹

6.(**A**) Mr. Chen is on vacation this week. Would you like to speak with a different agent?

陳先生這個禮拜休假。您要和別的代辦人談嗎?

(A) No, thanks. I'll call back next week.

　　不用了,謝謝。我下禮拜再打來。

(B) How was your vacation? 你的假期如何?

(C) The company is hiring new agents.

公司正在雇用新的代辦人員。

* ***on vacation*** 渡假　　***would like to V***. 想要…
different (ˈdɪfrənt) *adj.* 不同的
agent (ˈedʒənt) *n.* 代理人；代辦人　　***call back*** 再打電話
hire (haɪr) *v.* 雇用

7. (**C**) What time do you get off work on Saturday?

你週六幾點下班？

(A) I'm working. 我正在工作。

(B) I don't know where he gets off.

我不知道他在哪裡下車。

(C) Six o'clock. 六點。

* ***get off work*** 下班　　***get off*** 下車

8. (**A**) Would you prefer to sit next to the window or on the aisle? 您比較想要坐靠窗邊還是靠走道？

(A) I'd like an aisle seat, please.

我想要坐靠走道的位子，謝謝。

(B) Someone needs to wash these windows.

需要有人洗這些窗戶。

(C) He's walking down the aisle. 他走在走道上。

* prefer (prɪˈfɚ) *v.* 比較喜歡　　***next to*** 在…旁邊
aisle (aɪl) *n.* 走道　　down (daʊn) *prep.* 沿著

9. (**B**) Did you see James on the bus this morning?

你今天早上在巴士上有看到詹姆士嗎？

(A) Ask James. 問詹姆士。

(B) No, I didn't see him. 沒有，我沒看見他。

(C) Yes, I can. 是的，我可以。

10. (**B**) How many slices of blueberry pie are left?

還剩幾片藍莓派？

(A) It's too cold. 天氣太冷了。

(B) Only two. 只剩兩片。

(C) On the west side. 在西邊。

* slice〔slaɪs〕*n.* 片　　blueberry〔'blu,bɛrɪ〕*n.* 藍莓
　pie〔paɪ〕*n.* 派；餡餅　　left〔lɛft〕*adj.* 剩下的
　west〔wɛst〕*adj.* 西方的　　side〔saɪd〕*n.* 側；邊；面

第三部分：言談理解（第 11-21 題）

11. (**C**) W : Jensen's Department Store has some great deals on furniture right now.

女：詹森百貨公司的家具現在有一些超棒的優惠。

M : I saw the ads in the newspaper. We can go to the mall after I finish checking my e-mail.

男：我在報紙上有看到廣告。等我檢查完電子郵件，我們可以去一趟購物中心。

W : Great! I'll go get ready. How much longer do you need?

女：太棒了！我去準備一下。你還需要多久？

M : Ten minutes or so.

男：十分鐘左右。

Question : What is the man doing? 那位男士正在做什麼？

(A) Watching television. 看電視。

(B) Reading the newspaper. 看報紙。

(C) Checking his e-mail. 檢查他的電子郵件。

* ***department store*** 百貨公司　　deal〔dil〕*n.* 划算的交易
　furniture〔'fɝnɪtʃɚ〕*n.* 家具　　***right now*** 現在

ad〔æd〕*n.* 廣告 (= *advertisement*)
newspaper〔'nuz,pepɚ〕*n.* 報紙　　mall〔mɔl〕*n.* 購物中心
check〔tʃɛk〕*v.* 查看；檢查　　e-mail〔'i,mel〕*n.* 電子郵件
check** one's **e-mail 檢查某人的電子郵件；收信

12. (**A**)　W：I want to quit my job tomorrow.

女：我明天想要辭掉我的工作。

M：Why? What happened?

男：為什麼？發生了什麼事？

W：I think it's too hard to please my boss, and he never
　　respects me.

女：我覺得很難讓我的老闆滿意，而且他從不尊重我。

M：Do you have any plan if you quit this job?

男：如果你辭職的話，妳有任何計劃嗎？

W：Not yet. Maybe I will run a café or a handmade
　　goods shop.

女：還沒有。也許我會開一間咖啡廳或是手作商店。

Question：Why does the woman want to quit her job?

　　　　　　為什麼女士想要辭掉工作？

(A) She wants to have more respect.

　　她想要得到更多尊重。

(B) She wants to get a higher salary.

　　她想要得到更高的薪水。

(C) She wants to be a boss of a café.

　　她想要成為一家咖啡廳的老闆。

* quit〔kwɪt〕*v.* 辭 (職)　　job〔dʒɑb〕*n.* 工作
please〔pliz〕*v.* 取悅　　boss〔bɔs〕*n.* 老闆
never〔'nɛvɚ〕*adv.* 從不　　respect〔rɪ'spɛkt〕*v. n.* 尊敬；尊重
plan〔plæn〕*n.* 計畫　　***not yet*** 尚未；還沒

run〔rʌn〕*v.* 經營　café〔kəˈfe〕*n.* 咖啡廳
handmade〔͵hændˈmed〕*adj.* 手工做的
goods〔gʊdz〕*n. pl.* 商品
handmade goods shop 手作商店
salary〔ˈsælərɪ〕*n.* 薪水

13. (**C**)　W：Excuse me, but could you tell me which bus goes to the National Palace Museum from here?

女：不好意思，你可以告訴我這裡哪班公車會到國立故宮博物院嗎？

M：There are two, the 15 and the 20, both of which stop here.

男：有兩班，15 和 20 號公車，兩個都會在這站停。

W：Do you know how often they run?

女：你知道它們多久一班嗎？

Question：Where does the woman want to go?

女士想去哪裡？

(A) Taipei 101. 台北 101 大樓。

(B) The airport. 機場。

(C) The National Palace Museum. 國立故宮博物院。

* national〔ˈnæʃən̩〕*adj.* 國家的；國立的
　palace〔ˈpælɪs〕*n.* 宮殿　museum〔mjuˈziəm〕*n.* 博物館
　the National Palace Museum 國立故宮博物院
　how often ～多久一次　run〔rʌn〕*v.* 行駛
　airport〔ˈɛr͵port〕*n.* 機場

14. (**A**)　W：Ben, did you ask you father if it was OK to use his laptop?

女：班，你有問過你爸爸，我們是否可以用他的筆記型電腦？

M：Umm… I forgot.

男：嗯…我忘記了。

W：You know it's polite to ask first before using other people's things.

女：你知道用別人的東西之前，先問一下是一種禮貌吧。

Question：What is Ben probably doing?　班可能在做什麼？

(A) Surfing the Internet. 瀏覽網路。

(B) Eating a sandwich. 吃三明治。

(C) Reading a book. 看一本書。

* laptop〔'læp,tɑp〕*n.* 筆記型電腦　　forget〔fə'gɛt〕*v.* 忘記
  polite〔pə'laɪt〕*adj.* 有禮貌的　　surf〔sɜf〕*v.* 瀏覽
  Internet〔'ɪntə,nɛt〕*n.* 網際網路
  sandwich〔'sændwɪʃ〕*n.* 三明治

15. (**A**) W：Hi, Toby.　How do you like your new school?

女：嗨，托比。你喜歡你的新學校嗎？

M：I love it!

男：我很愛！

W：Wow!　That's great to hear.　What do you like about it?

女：哇！聽你這麼說真是太好了。你喜歡它的什麼呢？

M：Everybody is so friendly, and the cafeteria is awesome.　You can order whatever you want from the menu.　At my old school, there wasn't a selection.

男：大家都很友善，自助餐廳也很棒。你可以點菜單上的任何東西。在我之前的學校，都沒得選擇。

W：Yeah, I hear you.　My high school served the same stuff week after week.　Wait until you get to college, and you can eat whatever you want, wherever you want.

女：是的，我明白你的意思。我的高中也是每個禮拜都供應同樣的東西。等到你上大學了，你就可以隨便吃你想要吃的，隨便選你想去的地方。

Question： What is most likely true about the woman?

關於女士何者最可能是正確的？

(A) She is older than Toby. 她年紀比托比大。

(B) She has graduated from college. 她已經大學畢業了。

(C) She works in a cafeteria. 她在自助餐廳工作。

* wow〔waʊ〕*interj.* 哇　great〔gret〕*adj.* 很棒的
friendly〔'frɛndlɪ〕*adj.* 友善的
cafeteria〔ˌkæfə'tɪrɪə〕*n.* 自助餐廳
awesome〔'ɔsəm〕*adj.* 很棒的　order〔'ɔrdɚ〕*v.* 點餐
whatever〔hwɑt'ɛvɚ〕*pron.* 任何東西
menu〔'mɛnju〕*n.* 菜單　old〔old〕*adj.* 老的；舊的；從前的
selection〔sə'lɛkʃən〕*n.* 選擇　yeah〔jɛ〕*adv.* 是的 (= *yes*)
I hear you 我明白你的意思　serve〔sɝv〕*v.* 供應
same〔sem〕*adj.* 相同的　stuff〔stʌf〕*n.* 東西
week after week 一週又一週；每週
until〔ən'tɪl〕*conj.* 直到　college〔'kɑlɪdʒ〕*n.* 大學
wherever〔hwɛr'ɛvɚ〕*conj.* 無論什麼地方
likely〔'laɪklɪ〕*adv.* 可能　graduate〔'grædʒʊˌet〕*v.* 畢業

16. (**C**) M：Jackson's Department Store. Lost and found. How can I help you?

男：傑克森百貨公司。失物招領處。我可以幫什麼忙嗎？

W：Yes, I was wondering if anyone turned in a cell phone.

女：是的，我想知道是否有人找到一支手機。

M：I've got several cell phones here. Can you give me a description?

男：我這裡有好多支手機。您是否可以形容看看？

W：It's a black Vokia. I'm afraid I don't remember the model.

女：是一支黑色的 Vokia。我恐怕不記得型號了。

M：I've got one of those. Come down to the store and have a look. If you have proof of ownership, that would help, too.

男：我有一支那樣的。您可以來百貨公司看看。如果您有所有權的證明，也會有幫助。

Question：What does the man say? 男士說了什麼？

(A) No one has turned in a cell phone to the lost and found. 沒有人拿手機來失物招領處。

(B) The store will close in half an hour.
百貨公司將在半小時後關門。

(C) It's possible he has the woman's phone.
他可能有女士的手機。

* ***department store*** 百貨公司　　***lost and found*** 失物招領處
wonder〔'wʌndɚ〕*v.* 想知道　　***turn in*** 提交
cell phone 手機　　***have got*** 有
several〔'sɛvərəl〕*adj.* 幾個的
description〔dɪ'skrɪpʃən〕*n.* 描述；形容
model〔'madḷ〕*n.* …型；款式　　***come down to*** 來一趟…
have a look 看一看　　proof〔pruf〕*n.* 證據；證明
ownership〔'onɚˌʃɪp〕*n.* 所有權　　close〔kloz〕*v.* (店) 關門
possible〔'pasəbḷ〕*adj.* 可能的

17. (**C**) Laughter is a universal way to express joy. But as it turns out, your chuckle reveals a lot more than the fact that you are happy. It enables listeners, even those that cannot see

you, to instantly realize whether you are having a good time with a close friend or laughing politely with a complete stranger.

笑是用來表達快樂的一種很普遍的方式。但結果是,你輕聲笑時,除了表示你很快樂以外,還會透露出更多的事。它能使聽到的人,甚至連那些看不到你的人,都能夠立刻知道,你是和一位親密的朋友玩得很愉快,或是正對著完全陌生的人禮貌性地笑。

Question: What does laughter tell another person?

笑聲能夠告訴別人什麼?

(A) That you're angry. 你在生氣。

(B) That you're sad. 你在難過。

(C) Whether you are talking to a friend or a stranger. 你是和朋友還是和陌生人講話。

* laughter〔ˋlæftɚ〕*n.* 笑
  universal〔ˌjunəˋvɝsḷ〕*adj.* 普遍的;全世界的
  way〔we〕*n.* 方式　　express〔ɪkˋsprɛs〕*v.* 表達
  joy〔dʒɔɪ〕*n.* 快樂　　***as it turns out*** 結果
  chuckle〔ˋtʃʌkḷ〕*n.* 低聲輕笑　　reveal〔rɪˋvil〕*v.* 透露
  fact〔fækt〕*n.* 事實　　enable〔ɪnˋebḷ〕*v.* 使能夠
  listener〔ˋlɪsṇɚ〕*n.* 聽的人
  instantly〔ˋɪnstəntlɪ〕*adv.* 立刻;馬上
  realize〔ˋriəˌlaɪz〕*v.* 知道;了解
  have a good time 玩得愉快　　close〔klos〕*adj.* 親密的
  politely〔pəˋlaɪtlɪ〕*adv.* 有禮貌地
  complete〔kəmˋplit〕*adj.* 完全的
  stranger〔ˋstrendʒɚ〕*n.* 陌生人

18. (**A**) W: OK, before I take your case, you have to tell me exactly how the accident happened.

女：好的，在我受理你的案件之前，你必須告訴我，那場意外
　　究竟是如何發生的。

M：Well, I was on my scooter, stopped at a red light,
　　when the car hit me from behind. I went flying over
　　the top of the bike and landed on the pavement.

男：嗯，我在機車上，停下來等紅燈，那時有台車從後面撞了
　　我。我就從機車上飛出去，掉到人行道上。

W：Well, the judge is going to have many questions. For
　　instance, did the driver of the car use his horn?

女：嗯，法官會問很多問題。例如，駕駛人有按喇叭嗎？

M：No, he did not.

男：不，他沒有。

W：Right. So, did you happen to see the car approach in
　　your rearview mirror?

女：好的。那麼，你碰巧有從你的後照鏡看到那輛車接近嗎？

M：No, I was focused on the traffic signal, which was
　　about to turn green.

男：沒有，我那時候很專注的在看紅綠燈，因為快變綠燈了。

Question：Who is the man most likely speaking to?
　　　　　　男士很可能在跟誰說話？

(A) A lawyer. 律師。

(B) A doctor. 醫生。

(C) A banker. 銀行家。

* case〔kes〕*n.* 案件　***take one's case*** 受理某人的案件
　exactly〔ɪgˈzæktlɪ〕*adv.* 確切地
　accident〔ˈæksədənt〕*n.* 意外　scooter〔ˈskutɚ〕*n.* 機車
　from behind 從後面　top〔tɑp〕*n.* 頂端
　bike〔baɪk〕*n.* 腳踏車；機車（= *motorbike*）

land〔lænd〕*v.* 降落　　pavement〔'pevmənt〕*n.* 人行道
judge〔dʒʌdʒ〕*n.* 法官　　***for instance*** 例如（＝ *for example*）
driver〔'draɪvɚ〕*n.* 駕駛人　　horn〔hɔrn〕*n.* 喇叭
happen to V. 碰巧…　　approach〔ə'protʃ〕*v.* 接近
mirror〔'mɪrɚ〕*n.* 鏡子　　***rearview mirror*** 後照鏡
focus〔'fokəs〕*v.* 使集中；使專注　　***be focused on*** 專注於
traffic〔'træfɪk〕*n.* 交通
signal〔'sɪgnḷ〕*n.* 交通號誌；紅綠燈
be about to V. 即將…；快要…　　turn〔tɝn〕*v.* 變成
lawyer〔'lɔjɚ〕*n.* 律師　　banker〔'bæŋkɚ〕*n.* 銀行家

19. (**B**)　M：We need enough snacks and drinks for 10 kids.　Plus,
　　　　　　　we need plates, cups, napkins and plastic silverware.
　　　　　　　I'll stop by the supermarket later today.

　　　　男：我們需要足夠的點心和飲料給十位小朋友。此外，我們還需
　　　　　　要盤子、杯子、餐巾，和塑膠餐具。今天晚一點我會去一趟
　　　　　　超市。

　　　　W：I've ordered a cake from the bakery, so I'll pick that
　　　　　　up tomorrow about an hour before the party.

　　　　女：我向麵包店訂了一個蛋糕，所以明天派對開始前大約一個小
　　　　　　時，我會去拿。

　　　　M：That's cutting it kind of close.　We're going to be
　　　　　　busy setting up then.　Don't forget about the balloons
　　　　　　and decorations.

　　　　男：這樣時間有點趕。我們那時候會忙著佈置。別忘了還有氣球
　　　　　　和裝飾品。

　　　　W：Of course.　I've got everything ready to go.

　　　　女：當然。我一切都準備好了。

　　　　Question：What will take place tomorrow?
　　　　　　　　　明天會舉行什麼？

(A) A funeral. 葬禮。

(B) A birthday party. <u>生日派對。</u>

(C) A wedding. 婚禮。

* enough〔əˋnʌf〕*adj.* 足夠的　　snack〔snæk〕*n.* 點心
　drink〔drɪŋk〕*n.* 飲料　　plus〔plʌs〕*adv.* 此外
　plate〔plet〕*n.* 盤子　　napkin〔ˋnæpkɪn〕*n.* 餐巾
　plastic〔ˋplæstɪk〕*adj.* 塑膠的
　silverware〔ˋsɪlvɚ͵wɛr〕*n.* 餐具　　order〔ˋɔrdɚ〕*v.* 訂購
　bakery〔ˋbekərɪ〕*n.* 麵包店　　***pick up*** 拿
　cut it close （時間）計算得僅僅足夠
　kind of 有點（= *a little*）　　***be busy V-ing*** 忙於～
　set up 設置；安排　　balloon〔bəˋlun〕*n.* 氣球
　decoration〔͵dɛkəˋreʃən〕*n.* 裝飾品　　***of course*** 當然
　ready to go 準備好了　　***take place*** 發生；舉行
　funeral〔ˋfjunərəl〕*n.* 葬禮　　wedding〔ˋwɛdɪŋ〕*n.* 婚禮

20. (**A**) It is Christmas! Have you decided what to buy for your
　　　kids? If not, come and get some surprises for them. Just
　　　make this Christmas the best and unforgettable.
　　　聖誕節到了！你已經決定好要買什麼給你的小孩了嗎？如果還
　　　沒有，來這裡買一些意想不到的禮物給他們吧。要讓這個聖誕
　　　節成為最棒以及最難忘的。

　　　Question：Where might we hear this?
　　　　　　　　我們可能在哪聽到這個？

　　　(A) On the radio. <u>在廣播裡。</u>

　　　(B) On a bike. 在腳踏車上。

　　　(C) On a horse. 在馬上。

　　　* Christmas〔ˋkrɪsməs〕*n.* 聖誕節　　decide〔dɪˋsaɪd〕*v.* 決定
　　　　get〔gɛt〕*v.* 買　　surprise〔səˋpraɪz〕*n.* 意想不到的禮物
　　　　unforgettable〔͵ʌnfɚˋgɛtəbl̩〕*adj.* 難忘的

radio〔'rædɪo〕*n.* 收音機；無線電廣播

bike〔baɪk〕*n.* 腳踏車（= *bicycle*）　　　horse〔hors〕*n.* 馬

21. (**B**)　M : Honey, will you do me a favor?

男：親愛的，妳可以幫我一個忙嗎？

W : Sure, what is it?

女：當然，什麼事？

M : I'm running late for work. Would you call my secretary and let her know?

男：我上班快遲到了。妳可以幫我打電話給我的秘書讓她知道嗎？

W : OK. What's her name again?

女：好。再告訴我一次，她叫什麼名字？

M : Marsha.

男：瑪莎。

Question : What is the man's problem?

男士有什麼問題？

(A) He's feeling ill. 他覺得不舒服。

(B) He's running late. 他快遲到了。

(C) He's out of money. 他快沒錢了。

* favor〔'fevɚ〕*n.* 幫忙　　***do** sb.* ***a favor*** 幫某人一個忙
be running late 快遲到了
secretary〔'sɛkrə,tɛrɪ〕*n.* 秘書
ill〔ɪl〕*adj.* 生病的；不舒服的　　***be out of*** 缺乏；沒有

 TEST 15 ▶ 詳解

第一部分：辨識句意（第 1-3 題）

1. (**A**) (A)　　　　　　　(B)　　　　　　　(C)

Jenny is running on a track at school.
珍妮在學校的跑道上跑步。

 * track〔træk〕*n.* 跑道

2. (**C**) (A)　　　　　　　(B)　　　　　　　(C)

Some students are at an art museum and a woman is
holding up a sign that says, "No cameras." 有些學生正在美
術館，還有一位女士正舉著一個告示牌，上面寫著「請勿拍照。」

 * museum〔mju'ziəm〕*n.* 博物館　　　*art museum* 美術館
 hold up 舉起　　sign〔saɪn〕*n.* 告示牌
 camera〔'kæmərə〕*n.* 照相機　　*No cameras.* 請勿拍照。

3. (**B**) (A)　　　　　　　(B)　　　　　　　(C)

Lucy and Clara are enjoying the sunshine during their hike in the mountains.

露西和克拉拉正在山上健行，享受陽光。

* enjoy〔ɪn'dʒɔɪ〕v. 享受　　sunshine〔'sʌn,ʃaɪn〕n. 陽光
during〔'djʊrɪŋ〕prep. 在…的期間
hike〔haɪk〕n. 健行；徒步旅行　　**in the mountains** 在山上

第二部分：基本問答（第 4-10 題）

4. (**A**) I'd like to sign up for the science contest.
   我想要報名科學競賽。

   (A) OK. Fill out this form and return it to me.
   <u>好的。填寫這張表格再交還給我。</u>

   (B) Sorry. That DVD is sold out.
   抱歉。那個 DVD 已經賣完了。

   (C) Never mind. I'll do it myself. 沒關係。我自己做。

   * **sign up for** 報名參加　　science〔'saɪəns〕n. 科學
   contest〔'kɑntɛst〕n. 比賽　　**fill out** 填寫
   form〔fɔrm〕n. 表格　　return〔rɪ'tɜn〕v. 歸還
   DVD n. 數位影音光碟（= *digital video disk*）
   sold out 賣完了　　**never mind** 沒關係

5. (**A**) Mickey, did anyone call while I was out?
   米奇，我不在的時候有人打電話來嗎？

   (A) No, Mom. Nobody called. <u>沒有，媽。沒人打來。</u>

   (B) Thanks, Mom. I love strawberries.
   謝謝，媽。我最愛草莓了。

   (C) See you then. Have fun. 到時候見。玩得開心。

   * call〔kɔl〕v. 打電話　　out〔aut〕adv. 外出；不在
   strawberry〔'strɔ,bɛrɪ〕n. 草莓　　**see you then** 到時候見
   have fun 玩得愉快

6. (**C**) Why did you close all the windows?　It's like 110 degrees outside!

你爲什麼把所有的窗戶都關起來？外面像是有 110 度！

　　(A) There are ten windows in the house.

　　　　房子裡有十個窗戶。

　　(B) All the doors were closed.　所有的門都關上了。

　　(C) I'm going to turn on the air conditioner.

　　　　<u>我要打開冷氣。</u>

　　* degree〔dɪˋgri〕*n.* 度　　outside〔ˋautˋsaɪd〕*adv.* 在外面
　　　　turn on 打開（電源）　　***air conditioner*** 冷氣

7. (**B**) Are you allergic to any foods?　你對任何食物過敏嗎？

　　(A) My allergies are acting up.　我的過敏正在發作。

　　(B) Yes, shellfish and certain nuts.

　　　　<u>是的，貝類和某些堅果。</u>

　　(C) I put it on the kitchen counter.

　　　　我把它放在廚房的台面上。

　　* allergic〔əˋlɝdʒɪk〕*adj.* 過敏的 < *to* >
　　　　act up 發作；（症狀）惡化　　shellfish〔ˋʃɛlˏfɪʃ〕*n.* 貝類
　　　　certain〔ˋsɝtn〕*adj.* 某些　　nut〔nʌt〕*n.* 堅果
　　　　counter〔ˋkauntɚ〕*n.* 櫃台；（廚房的）長台面

8. (**C**) Will you go to Kaohsiung for the spring holiday?

你春假會去高雄嗎？

　　(A) No, I haven't.　不，我沒有。

　　(B) He was supposed to.　Now he's not sure.

　　　　他應該會去。現在他不確定。

　　(C) Yes.　And I'm really looking forward to it.

　　　　<u>會。而且我非常期待。</u>

　　* ***spring holiday*** 春假　　***be supposed to V.*** 應該…
　　　　sure〔ʃur〕*adj.* 確定的　　***look forward to*** 期待

9. (**C**) Would you care for a glass of water? 你想要一杯水嗎？

    (A) Yes, I love them. 是的，我愛它們。

    (B) Here you go. 拿去吧。

    (C) No, thanks. <u>不用了，謝謝。</u>

    * *care for* 想要   glass〔glæs〕*n.* 玻璃杯的一杯
    Here you go. 拿去吧。(= *Here you are.*)

10. (**A**) How do you like your new teacher? 你喜歡你的新老師嗎？

    (A) She's very nice. <u>她人很好。</u>

    (B) At school. 在學校。

    (C) Several times. 好幾次。

    * nice〔naɪs〕*adj.* 好的   several〔'sɛvərəl〕*adj.* 幾個的
    time〔taɪm〕*n.* 次

第三部分：言談理解（第 11-21 題）

11. (**A**) W：Have you seen this movie before?

    女：你以前看過這部電影嗎？

    M：Yes, I have.

    男：是的，我看過。

    W：OK, well, don't tell me how it ends. I hate when
        people give spoilers.

    女：好吧，嗯，不要告訴我結局。我最討厭人們劇透了。

    M：Don't worry. I won't ruin it for you.

    男：不要擔心。我不會給你破壞的。

    Question：What are the speakers doing?

                說話者正在做什麼？

    (A) Watching a movie. <u>看電影。</u>

    (B) Having a meal. 吃飯。

    (C) Boarding a train. 上火車。

      end〔ɛnd〕*v.* 結束   hate〔het〕*v.* 討厭

spoiler〔'spɔɪlɚ〕*n.* 破壞者；(提前透露結局而) 破壞懸疑的資訊
give spoilers 劇透　　ruin〔'ruɪn〕*v.* 破壞
have〔hæv〕*v.* 吃　　meal〔mil〕*n.* 一餐
board〔bord〕*v.* 上 (車)

12. (**B**) W : How long have you been a smoker?

女：你吸煙已經多久了？

M : Gosh, I started in high school.

男：哎呀，我從高中就開始了。

W : You should really quit. It's bad for you.

女：你眞的應該要戒了。它對你不好。

M : I wish I had a dollar for every time someone said that
to me.

男：我眞希望每次有人對我這麼說，我都可以拿到一美元。

W : Well, it's true. And people only say that because they
care about your health.

女：嗯，這是眞的。人們會這麼說，是因爲他們在乎你的健康。

Question : What does the woman want the man to do?

女士要男士做什麼？

(A) Stop swearing. 不要再咒罵。

(B) Quit smoking. 戒菸。

(C) Start exercising. 開始運動。

* smoker〔'smokɚ〕*n.* 吸煙者　　gosh〔gɑʃ〕*interj.* 哎呀
quit〔kwɪt〕*v.* 停止；戒除
if I had a dollar for (用來諷刺) 如果每次我怎樣…就能有一美元
care about 在乎　　health〔hɛlθ〕*n.* 健康
swear〔swɛr〕*v.* 咒罵　　exercise〔'ɛksɚ‚saɪz〕*v.* 運動

13. (**C**) M : Did you make reservations for dinner?

男：你晚餐有訂位嗎？

W : I tried, but every place is booked solid.

女：我試了，但每個餐廳都被訂滿了。

M : Oh, no. What are we going to do?

男：喔，不。我們要怎麼辦？

W : I guess we could order a pizza.

女：我想我們可以訂披薩。

M : Let's call Mario's. They make the best pizza.

男：我們打給馬里奧吧。他們做的披薩最好吃。

Question : What will the speakers do for dinner?

說話者打算晚餐做什麼？

(A) Cook at home. 在家煮飯。

(B) Go to a restaurant. 去一家餐廳。

(C) Order a pizza. 訂一個披薩。

* reservation〔ˌrɛzɚˈveʃən〕*n.* 預訂　　place〔ples〕*n.* 餐廳
book〔buk〕*v.* 預訂　　solid〔ˈsɑlɪd〕*adv.* 全部地；完全地
be booked solid 被訂滿了　　order〔ˈɔrdɚ〕*v.* 訂（購）
pizza〔ˈpitsə〕*n.* 披薩　　restaurant〔ˈrɛstərənt〕*n.* 餐廳

14. (**C**) W : My steak is undercooked. Look at that. It's
blood-red. How about yours?

女：我的牛排沒有煮熟。你看看。它還血淋淋的。那你的呢？

M : Mine is overcooked and tough. Not rare, for sure.

男：我的過熟而且很老。當然，不是三分熟。

W : Maybe the waiter switched them up. This one is
definitely rare.

女：也許服務生把它們對調了。這個的確是三分熟。

M : I'm going to call the waiter over.

男：我要把服務生叫過來。

W : No, let's just switch plates.

女：不用了，我們互換餐盤吧。

Question : What does the woman think happened?

女士認為發生了什麼事？

(A) The steaks were overcooked. 牛排過熟了。

(B) The steaks were dropped on the floor. 牛排掉在地上。

(C) The waiter made a mistake. <u>服務生弄錯了。</u>

* steak〔stek〕*n.* 牛排

undercooked〔ˌʌndə'kukt〕*adj.* 沒煮熟的

blood-red〔'blʌdˌrɛd〕*adj.* 血紅的

overcooked〔ˌovə'kukt〕*adj.* 煮得過熟的

tough〔tʌf〕*adj.* (肉) 堅韌的　　rare〔rɛr〕*adj.* 三分熟的

for sure 的確　　waiter〔'wetə〕*n.* 服務生

switch sth. up 把某物對調　　definitely〔'dɛfənɪtlɪ〕*adv.* 的確

call sb. over 把某人叫過來　　plate〔plet〕*n.* 盤子

drop〔drɑp〕*v.* 使掉落　　mistake〔mə'stek〕*n.* 錯誤

make a mistake 犯錯

15. (**A**)　M : How many kilometers are there in a mile?

　　　　男：一哩等於多少公里？

　　　　W : I think it's something like one-point-six.

　　　　女：我想好像是 1.6。

　　　　M : You're right. I should have known that. I studied geography for a year.

　　　　男：你說的對。我應該要知道的。我讀地理讀了一年。

　　　　W : Taiwan only uses the metric system. Many Americans get confused. Eventually your country will adopt the metric system like the rest of the world.

　　　　女：台灣只用公制。很多美國人都會搞混。你的國家終究會跟世界上其他的國家一樣，採取公制。

　　　　Question : What do we know about the man?

　　　　　　　　關於男士我們知道什麼？

　　　　(A) He has studied geography. <u>他讀過地理。</u>

　　　　(B) He will be traveling soon. 他不久後將會旅行。

　　　　(C) He is good at math. 他精通數學。

　　　* kilometer〔'kɪləˌmitə〕*n.* 公里　　mile〔maɪl〕*n.* 哩

　　　　something like 有點像；差不多；大約　　point〔pɔɪnt〕*n.* 點

geography〔dʒɪˋɑgrəfɪ〕*n.* 地理學
metric〔ˋmɛtrɪk〕*adj.* 公制的；十進制的
metric system 米制；公制　　confused〔kənˋfjuzd〕*adj.* 困惑的
eventually〔ɪˋvɛntʃuəlɪ〕*adv.* 最後；終究
adopt〔əˋdɑpt〕*v.* 採用　　rest〔rɛst〕*n.* 其餘的人或物
be good at 精通

16. (**B**) When it comes to writing your essay, the best font to use
is a simple font such as Times New Roman, Arial or
Calibri.　Be sure to use a font size that's readable—10 to
12 points works best.

一提到要寫你的文章，最好的字型，就是簡單的字型，像是
Times New Roman、Arial，或 Calibri。字型大小一定要用易讀
的—10 到 12 級的效果最好。

Question：What is this advice mainly about?
　　　　　 這個勸告主要是關於什麼？

(A) Reading. 閱讀。

(B) Writing. 寫作。

(C) Foreign languages. 外語。

* ***when it comes to*** 一提到　　essay〔ˋɛse〕*n.* 短文；論說文
font〔fɑnt〕*n.* 字型　　***such as*** 像是
be sure to V. 一定要…　　size〔saɪz〕*n.* 大小
readable〔ˋridəbḷ〕*adj.* 易讀的　　point〔pɔɪnt〕*n.* 點；度
work〔wɝk〕*v.* 起作用　　***work best*** 效果最好
advice〔ədˋvaɪs〕*n.* 勸告　　mainly〔ˋmenlɪ〕*adv.* 主要地
foreign〔ˋfɔrɪn〕*adj.* 外國的

17. (**A**) Some things really are better the second time around.　In
fact, many used items can be every bit as good as those
purchased new.　Plus, buying used is almost guaranteed
to save you cash.

有些東西真的是二手的比較好。事實上，很多二手的物品可能跟
新買的東西一樣。此外，買二手貨幾乎能保證會讓你省錢。

Question：Which of the following is a benefit of buying
　　　　　used items?　以下何者是買二手物品的好處？

(A) Saves money. <u>省錢。</u>

(B) Better selection. 更好的選擇。

(C) Higher quality. 更高的品質。

* ***the second time around*** 第二次使用　　***in fact*** 事實上
  used〔juzd〕*adj.* 用過的；二手的　　item〔'aɪtəm〕*n.* 物品
  every bit 無論由任何一點看；全然；徹頭徹尾
  as good as 和…一樣；事實上等於　　purchase〔'pɝtʃəs〕*v.* 購買
  new〔nju〕*adv.* 新；新近　　plus〔plʌs〕*adv.* 此外
  buying used 買二手貨（= *buying second hand*）
  guarantee〔ˌgærən'ti〕*v.* 保證　　save〔sev〕*v.* 使節省
  cash〔kæʃ〕*n.* 現金；錢　　benefit〔'bɛnəfɪt〕*n.* 好處
  selection〔sə'lɛkʃən〕*n.* 選擇　　quality〔'kwɑlətɪ〕*n.* 品質

18. (**B**) Possibly the most famous building in the town is the Red
Brick Hotel, built in the 1890s, constructed of bricks from
a nearby quarry, and given the name by Chinese miners
who were reminded of the red brick buildings in China.
可能城裡最著名的建築，就是紅磚酒店，建於 1890 年代，是用
附近採石場的磚頭建造的，而名字是中國礦工取的，因為他們想
起了中國的紅磚建築。

Question：What do we know about the town?
　　　　　關於這個城鎮我們知道什麼？

(A) Many Chinese people live there.
很多中國人住在那裡。

(B) It's more than 100 years old. <u>它有一百年以上的歷史。</u>

(C) The people are very friendly. 那裡的人很友善。

* possibly〔'pɑsəblɪ〕*adv.* 可能　　famous〔'feməs〕*adj.* 有名的
  building〔'bɪldɪŋ〕*n.* 建築物　　town〔taʊn〕*n.* 城鎮
  brick〔brɪk〕*n.* 磚頭　　construct〔kən'strʌkt〕*v.* 建造
  nearby〔'nɪrˌbaɪ〕*adj.* 附近的　　quarry〔'kwɔrɪ〕*n.* 採石場

be given the name 被取了這個名字　　miner〔'maɪnɚ〕 *n.* 礦工
remind〔rɪ'maɪnd〕 *v.* 提醒；使想起 *< of >*

19. (**B**)　W : There is no taxi there. How come? I am in a hurry
　　　　　　　to get to a meeting.

　　女：那裡沒有計程車。怎麼會這樣？我趕著要去一場會議。

　　M : You can try the Uber app.

　　男：你可以試試優步應用程式。

　　W : What is that?

　　女：那是什麼？

　　M : It's a service that can help you call an Uber driver
　　　　with your smartphone. Uber drivers will use their
　　　　own car to get you wherever you want to go, and it is
　　　　cheaper than a taxi.

　　男：它是一種服務，能幫助你用你的智慧型手機叫一位優步司
　　　　機。優步司機會用自己的車載你去任何你想去的地方，而
　　　　且比計程車還便宜。

　　W : It sounds great, but is it safe?

　　女：聽起來很棒，但它安全嗎？

　　M : Well, I am not 100% sure about that.

　　男：嗯，我不是百分之百確定。

　　Question : Why does the man think Uber is a good choice
　　　　　　　 for the woman?

　　　　　　　為什麼男士會認為優步是女士的一個好的選擇？

(A) She doesn't need to use it with her phone.

　　她不需要手機就可以使用。

(B) She can pay less money to travel.

　　她可以付少一點交通費。

(C) She can travel with it very safely.

　　她可以有非常安全的行程。

* hurry〔'hɝɪ〕 *n.* 匆忙　　*in a hurry* 急忙；匆忙　　*get to* 到達

meeting〔'mitɪŋ〕*n.* 會議　　Uber〔'ubɚ〕*n.* 優步
app〔æp〕*n.* 應用程式 (= *application*)
service〔'sɝvɪs〕*n.* 服務
smartphone〔'smɑrt,fon〕*n.* 智慧型手機
own〔on〕*adj.* 自己的　　cheap〔tʃip〕*adj.* 便宜的
great〔gret〕*adj.* 很棒的　　safe〔sef〕*adj.* 安全的
sure〔ʃur〕*adj.* 確定的　　choice〔tʃɔɪs〕*n.* 選擇
pay〔pe〕*v.* 支付　　travel〔'trævḷ〕*v.* 旅行；行進

20. (**B**) M : Michelle, would you like to play softball with us on
　　　　　　Sunday afternoon?
　　　男：蜜雪兒，妳週日下午想跟我們一起打壘球嗎？
　　　W : It sounds like fun, Chester, but I'm really out of
　　　　　shape. Besides, I haven't swung a bat or thrown a
　　　　　ball in years.
　　　女：聽起來很好玩，契斯特，但我的身體狀況很差。而且，我已
　　　　　經好多年沒有揮球棒或是投球了。
　　　M : That's all right. We just play to socialize, have some
　　　　　fun, and get a little exercise. Don't worry about it.
　　　　　Nobody takes it seriously.
　　　男：沒關係。我們打球也只是為了社交、好玩，而且稍微運動一
　　　　　下而已。不用擔心。沒有人在認真的。
　　　W : Well, in that case, I don't have any plans. OK, I'm in.
　　　女：嗯，那樣的話，我沒任何計畫。好的，我加入。
　　　M : Great! We'd love to have you on the team, and we
　　　　　could really use you on Sunday. Three of our players
　　　　　are out sick.
　　　男：太棒了！我們很樂意有妳加入我們這一隊，而且我們週日真
　　　　　的很需要妳。我們有三位隊員請病假。
　　　Question : What is true about the softball team?
　　　　　　　　關於壘球隊，以下何者正確？
　　　(A) They play to win. 他們打球是為了要贏。

(B) They play for fun. 他們打球是爲了好玩。

(C) They don't allow women to play.

他們不允許女人打球。

* softball〔'sɔft,bɔl〕*n.* 壘球　　***out of shape*** 身體狀況差

socialize〔'soʃə,laɪz〕*v.* 社交；交際

take *sth.* ***seriously*** 認眞看待某事　　team〔tim〕*n.* 隊伍

be out sick （因生病）無法出席；請病假

allow〔ə'laʊ〕*v.* 允許

21. (**C**) M：It's freezing in here! Why don't you turn on the heat?

男：這裡面好冷！妳爲什麼不開暖氣？

W：I'm trying to conserve energy. Besides, I'm used to it.

女：我要節約能源。而且，我已經習慣了。

M：You're going to wind up catching pneumonia.

男：妳這樣下去會得肺炎的。

W：Put on a sweater and quit complaining.

女：穿上一件毛衣，不要再抱怨了。

Question：Why won't the woman turn on the heat?

爲何女士不開暖氣？

(A) She wants to get sick. 她想要生病。

(B) She prefers cold weather to hot.

她喜歡寒冷的天氣甚於炎熱的天氣。

(C) She is trying to save energy. 她想要節約能源。

* freezing〔'frizɪŋ〕*adj.* 極冷的　　***turn on*** 打開（電源）

heat〔hit〕*n.* 暖氣　　conserve〔kən's₃v〕*v.* 節省

energy〔'ɛnədʒɪ〕*n.* 能源　　***be used to*** 習慣於

wind〔waɪnd〕*v.* 蜿蜒；曲折　　***wind up*** 結果（以⋯）收場

pneumonia〔nu'monjə〕*n.* 肺炎　　***put on*** 穿上

sweater〔'swɛtə〕*n.* 毛衣　　quit〔kwɪt〕*v.* 停止

complain〔kəm'plen〕*v.* 抱怨　　***prefer*** *A* ***to*** *B* 喜歡 A 甚於 B

weather〔'wɛðə〕*n.* 天氣　　save〔sev〕*v.* 節省

 **TEST 16 ▶ 詳解**

第一部分：辨識句意（第 1-3 題）

1. (**C**) (A)  (B)  (C)

Bob is a new student at school and is introducing himself to his new classmates.

鮑勃是學校新來的學生，正在向他的新同學們自我介紹。

* introduce〔ˌɪntrəˋdjus〕 *v.* 介紹

2. (**C**) (A)  (B)  (C)

A group of men are going to beat Kenneth with a baseball bat and take his money.

一群男人要用一支棒球棍打肯尼斯，並拿走他的錢。

* beat〔bit〕 *v.* 打　　bat〔bæt〕 *n.* 球棒

3. (**B**) (A)  (B)  (C)

Edgar and Louis are studying in a library, where the use of cell phones is not permitted.

愛德格和路易斯正在圖書館讀書，那裡不允許用手機。

* library (ˈlaɪˌbrɛrɪ) *n.* 圖書館　　*cell phone* 手機
permit (pɚˈmɪt) *v.* 允許

第二部分：基本問答（第 4-10 題）

4. (**A**) It's dark out there, Stevie.　You better bring a flashlight.

外面很暗，史提夫。你最好帶個手電筒。

(A) I can't find mine.　Can I borrow yours?

我找不到我的。我可以借你的嗎？

(B) I hope you understand.　I'm sorry.

我希望你能了解。我很抱歉。

(C) I think you should go.　It will be fun.

我認為你應該去。會很好玩的。

* dark (dɑrk) *adj.* 暗的　　*out there* 在外面
you better 你最好（ = *you had better* ）
flashlight (ˈflæʃˌlaɪt) *n.* 手電筒　　borrow (ˈbɑro) *v.* 借（入）
fun (fʌn) *adj.* 有趣的

5. (**A**) How many of his paintings are in the museum?

他的畫有幾幅在博物館？

(A) Several dozen. 好幾十幅。

(B) In an hour. 一個小時內。

(C) On the second page. 在第二頁。

* painting (ˈpentɪŋ) *n.* 畫
museum (mjuˈziəm) *n.* 博物館
dozen (ˈdʌzn) *n.* 一打；十二個　　page (pedʒ) *n.* 頁

6. (**C**) How was your trip to the zoo over the weekend?
你週末的動物園之旅如何？

(A) They talked the whole way, so I didn't say anything.
他們全程都在講話，所以我什麼都沒說。

(B) He seemed to be enjoying himself, I think.
我覺得他似乎玩得很愉快。

(C) It rained the whole time, so we didn't get to see all
the animals. 一直在下雨，所以我們沒看到所有的動物。

* trip〔trɪp〕*n.* 旅行；行程　　zoo〔zu〕*n.* 動物園
weekend〔'wik'ɛnd〕*n.* 週末　　whole〔hol〕*adj.* 整個的
way〔we〕*n.* 路程　　seem〔sim〕*v.* 似乎
enjoy *oneself* 玩得愉快　　***get to*** *V.* 得以…
animal〔'ænəml̩〕*n.* 動物

7. (**C**) Where do you want me to put your suitcases?
你想要我把你的行李箱放在哪裡？

(A) You are welcome. 不客氣。

(B) On the phone. 電話中。

(C) In the bedroom. 房間裡。

* suitcase〔'sut,kes〕*n.* 行李箱　　bedroom〔'bɛd,rum〕*n.* 臥室

8. (**A**) Did you book your flight to Orlando yet?
你已經訂了去奧蘭多的機票嗎？

(A) Not yet. 還沒。

(B) Sometimes. 有時候。

(C) Every time. 每次。

* book〔buk〕*v.* 預訂　　flight〔flaɪt〕*n.* 班機
Orlando〔ɔr'lændo〕*n.* 奧蘭多　　yet〔jɛt〕*adv.* 已經
not yet 尚未；還沒　　sometimes〔'sʌm,taɪmz〕*adv.* 有時候
time〔taɪm〕*n.* 次

9. (**A**) Was the market crowded this morning?

今天早上市場有很擁擠嗎？

(A) <u>No. Maybe because of the holiday.</u>

沒有。可能因為是假日吧。

(B) Take your time. Don't rush. 慢慢來。別急。

(C) Absolutely not. I won't accept any money.

絕對不行。我不會接受任何錢。

* market ('markɪt) *n.* 市場
crowded ('kraʊdɪd) *adj.* 擁擠的
holiday ('halə,de) *n.* 假日　　***Take your time.*** 慢慢來。
rush (rʌʃ) *v.* 匆忙；急
absolutely ('æbsə,lutlɪ) *adv.* 絕對地
accept (ək'sɛpt) *v.* 接受

10. (**B**) Did Roger tell you about his fishing trip in Alaska?

羅傑有告訴你他在阿拉斯加的釣魚之旅嗎？

(A) Yes, at the bottom. 有，在底部。

(B) Yes, last time I saw him. <u>有，上次我看到他的時候。</u>

(C) Yes, you can use it. 有，你可以用它。

* fishing ('fɪʃɪŋ) *n.* 釣魚　　Alaska (ə'læskə) *n.* 阿拉斯加
bottom ('batəm) *n.* 底部

第三部分：言談理解（第 11-21 題）

11. (**B**) Overcooking rice might be a rookie mistake, but it
happens to the best of us, much more often than we'd like
to admit. Fortunately there are several ways to rework
overdone rice that can save you from throwing it out and
starting all over again.

把米飯煮過熟可能是新手會犯的錯，但誰都有可能發生這種事，而且比我們想要承認的還要多次。幸好，有好幾個方式可以彌補煮得太久的米飯，能夠使你不必把它丟掉或重新來過。

Question : Who is the speaker most likely talking to?

說話者很可能在跟誰講話？

(A) People who work outdoors. 在戶外工作的人。

(B) People who cook at home. 在家煮飯的人。

(C) People who make a lot of money. 賺很多錢的人。

　　overcook〔ˏovəˈkʊk〕*v.* 把…煮得過熟　　rice〔raɪs〕*n.* 米飯
　　rookie〔ˈrʊkɪ〕*n.* 新人；新手　　***the best*** 佼佼者
　　it happens to the best of us 誰都有可能發生這種事
　　admit〔ədˈmɪt〕*v.* 承認
　　fortunately〔ˈfɔrtʃənɪtlɪ〕*adv.* 幸好；幸運的是
　　several〔ˈsɛvərəl〕*adj.* 幾個的　　way〔we〕*n.* 方法
　　rework〔riˈwɝk〕*v.* 修改；修正
　　overdone〔ˏovəˈdʌn〕*adj.* 煮得太久的
　　save sb. from 挽救某人免於
　　throw out 扔掉；丟棄 (= ***throw away***)
　　start all over again 從頭再來
　　outdoors〔ˏaʊtˈdorz〕*adv.* 在戶外
　　make money 賺錢

12. (**C**)　M : Are you ready to order?

　　男：妳準備好要點餐了嗎？

　　W : Any specials today?

　　女：今天有特餐嗎？

　　M : We have a roast beef dinner set for $7.99.

　　男：我們有個烤牛肉晚間套餐，只要 7.99 元。

　　W : What does it come with?

　　女：有附什麼？

M：Soup, salad, mashed potatoes, steamed vegetables, dinner rolls, and choice of coffee, tea, or beer.

男：湯、沙拉、馬鈴薯泥、蒸蔬菜、餐包，還有特選的咖啡、茶，或啤酒。

W：All right, then I'll have the special. And bring me a cold beer. That sounds good.

女：好，那我要一個特餐。給我一杯冰啤酒。那聽起來很不錯。

Question：Which of the following does not come with the special? 下列哪一個不附在特餐裡？

(A) Soup. 湯。

(B) Vegetables. 蔬菜。

(C) Apple pie. 蘋果派。

* order〔'ɔrdɚ〕*v.* 點餐   special〔'spɛʃəl〕*n.* 特餐
roast〔rost〕*adj.* 烤過的   beef〔bif〕*n.* 牛肉
set〔sɛt〕*n.* 一套；一組   *dinner set* 晚間套餐
come with 附有   soup〔sup〕*n.* 湯
salad〔'sæləd〕*n.* 沙拉   mash〔mæʃ〕*v.* 把⋯搗碎
mashed potato 馬鈴薯泥   steam〔stim〕*v.* 蒸
roll〔rol〕*n.* 麵包捲；圓形小麵包   *dinner roll* 餐包
choice〔tʃɔɪs〕*n.* 精選的東西   beer〔bɪr〕*n.* 啤酒
sound〔saʊnd〕*v.* 聽起來

13. (**B**) W：Would you mind lending me some cash until we get back to the hotel?

女：你介意在我們回到飯店之前，借我一點錢嗎？

M：How much? I might need to hit an ATM as well.

男：多少？我可能也需要去找一台提款機。

W：Fifty bucks, if you have that much, but twenty should cover me.

女：五十美元，如果你有那麼多的話，但二十應該夠我用。

Question：What does the woman want? 女士想要什麼？

(A) She wants to go back to the hotel. 她想要回飯店。

(B) She wants to borrow money from the man.
　　她想要跟男士借錢。

(C) She wants to find an ATM. 她想要找一台提款機。

* mind〔maɪnd〕*v.* 介意　　lend〔lɛnd〕*v.* 借（出）
  cash〔kæʃ〕*n.* 現金；錢　　until〔ən'tɪl〕*prep.* 直到…爲止
  hotel〔ho'tɛl〕*n.* 飯店　　hit〔hɪt〕*v.* 到達；找到
  ATM 自動提款機（= *automated-teller machine*）
  as well 也（= *too*）　　buck〔bʌk〕*n.* 一美元
  cover〔'kʌvɚ〕*v.* 對…夠用　　borrow〔'baro〕*v.* 借（入）

14. (**C**)　W：Hi, Oscar. It's Serena. Look, I'm on my way to the
　　　　　　　airport. Could you do me a huge favor?
　　　　　女：嗨，奧斯卡。我是賽琳娜。喂，我正在前往機場的路上。
　　　　　　　你可以幫我一個大忙嗎？

　　　　　M：I'll try my best, Serena. What can I do for you?
　　　　　男：我會盡力的，賽琳娜。我可以幫妳什麼？

　　　　　Question：What does Serena want Oscar to do?
　　　　　　　　　　賽琳娜想要奧斯卡做什麼？

　　　(A) Pick her up from the airport. 去機場接她。

　　　(B) Take her to the airport. 載她去機場。

　　　(C) It's impossible to say. 很難說。

　　* look〔luk〕*interj.* 哎；喂；注意
　　　on one's ***way to*** 在某人去…的路上
　　　airport〔'ɛr,port〕*n.* 機場　　huge〔hjudʒ〕*adj.* 巨大的
　　　favor〔'fevɚ〕*n.* 幫忙　　***do*** sb. ***a favor*** 幫某人的忙
　　　try one's ***best*** 盡力　　***pick*** sb. ***up*** 接某人
　　　impossible〔ɪm'pasəbl̩〕*adj.* 不可能的

15. (**A**) M : Hi, Ellen.　What are you doing?

男：嗨，艾倫。妳在做什麼？

W : I'm trying to figure out how to use my new camera.

女：我想了解怎麼使用我的新的照相機。

M : Don't you have the instruction manual?

男：妳沒有說明書嗎？

W : I do, but it's entirely in Japanese!

女：我有，但它全是日語！

Question : What problem does the woman have with her camera?　女士的相機有什麼問題？

(A) She can't read the instruction manual.

　　她看不懂說明書。

(B) There are too many buttons.　有太多按鈕了。

(C) The battery is dead.　電池沒電了。

* *figure out* 了解　　camera〔'kæmərə〕*n.* 照相機
instruction〔ɪn'strʌkʃən〕*n.* 說明
manual〔'mænjuəl〕*n.* 手冊
instruction manual 說明書
entirely〔ɪn'taɪrlɪ〕*adv.* 完全地
Japanese〔ˌdʒæpə'niz〕*n.* 日語
button〔'bʌtn̩〕*n.* 按鈕　　battery〔'bætərɪ〕*n.* 電池
dead〔dɛd〕*adj.* 沒電的

16. (**C**) W : How do you like Emma's new winter coat?

女：你喜歡艾瑪的新大衣嗎？

M : It's nice and it's the brightest red I've seen.

男：還不錯，而且是我看過最亮的紅色。

Question : What did the man say about Emma's coat?

　　　　　關於艾瑪的大衣，那位男士說了什麼？

(A) It's warm. 它很暖和。

(B) It's wool. 它是毛料的。

(C) It's red. 它是紅色的。

* ***winter coat*** （冬天的）大衣　　bright〔braɪt〕*adj.* 明亮的
  warm〔wɔrm〕*adj.* 溫暖的　　wool〔wʊl〕*adj.* 毛料的

17. (**B**) M : Maria, I can't find my address book. Did you take it?

　　　　男：瑪莉亞，我找不到我的通訊錄。妳有拿嗎？

　　　　W : No, why would I do that?

　　　　女：沒有，我爲什麼要那麼做？

　　　　Question : What is the man looking for?

　　　　　　　　　這位男士正在找什麼？

(A) Maria. 瑪莉亞。

(B) An address book. 通訊錄。

(C) His cell phone. 他的手機。

* address〔ə'drɛs, 'ædrɛs〕*n.* 地址　　***address book*** 通訊錄
  look for 尋找　　***cell phone*** 手機

18. (**B**) W : Did you call a plumber?

　　　　女：你有叫水管工人嗎？

　　　　M : Yes. He'll be here at 5:00 p.m.

　　　　男：有。他下午五點會來。

　　　　W : But that's too late! I have to leave for work at 4:00.

　　　　女：但那太晚了！我四點必須去上班。

　　　　M : No problem. I'll cut out of work early to be here.

　　　　男：沒問題。我會提早下班來這裡。

　　　　Question : What problem do the speakers most likely
　　　　　　　　　have? 說話者很可能遇到了什麼問題？

(A) Their roof is leaking. 他們的屋頂在漏水。

(B) Their pipes are clogged. 他們的水管塞住了。

(C) Their walls need painting. 他們的牆壁需要油漆。

* plumber〔'plʌmɚ〕n. 水管工人
leave for 動身前往　　work〔wɜk〕n. 工作地點
cut out of work early 提早下班（= *cut out early*）
leak〔lik〕v. 漏水　　pipe〔paɪp〕n.（水）管
clog〔klɑg〕v. 使阻塞　　paint〔pent〕v. 油漆
need painting 需要油漆（= *need to be painted*）

19. (**A**)　M：Helen, I know it's your day off tomorrow, but I have
　　　　　　a big favor to ask.

　　　男：海倫，我知道妳明天休假，但我需要妳幫一個大忙。

　　　W：You want me to work, don't you?

　　　女：你想要我來上班，是嗎？

　　　M：Mike is sick and he won't be able to open the shop
　　　　　in the morning.

　　　男：麥可生病了，所以他明天早上沒辦法開店。

　　　W：I see.

　　　女：我知道了。

　　　M：You would only need to be here for an hour or so.
　　　　　I'll get here at nine.

　　　男：妳只需要在這待一個小時左右。我九點就會到。

　　　Question：Why will Helen have to work tomorrow?

　　　　　　　　為什麼海倫明天必須要上班？

　　　(A) A co-worker is ill. 有位同事生病了。

　　　(B) The manager is out of town. 經理在城外。

　　　(C) It's a holiday. 明天是假日。

　　　* ***day off*** 休假　　favor〔'fevɚ〕n. 恩惠；幫忙

ask sb. a favor 請某人幫忙　　co-worker〔͵ko'wɝkɚ〕*n.* 同事
ill〔ɪl〕*adj.* 生病的　　manager〔'mænɪdʒɚ〕*n.* 經理
out of town 在城外　　holiday〔'hɑlə͵de〕*n.* 假日

20. (**B**) The Peace Corps is a volunteer program run by the United
States government. The stated mission of the Peace Corps
includes providing technical assistance, helping people
outside the United States to understand American culture,
and helping Americans to understand the cultures of other
countries.

和平部隊是美國政府經營的一個志願服務計劃。和平部隊規定的
任務，包括提供技術援助、協助外國人了解美國文化，以及協助
美國人民了解其他國家的文化。

Question：What is the Peace Corps?　和平工作團是什麼？

(A) A military unit. 一個軍事單位。

(B) A volunteer program. <u>一個志願服務組織。</u>

(C) A school. 一所學校。

* peace〔pis〕*n.* 和平　　corps〔kor〕*n.* 軍團；兵團；…隊
Peace Corps（由美國甘迺迪總統發起的）和平部隊
volunteer〔͵vɑlən'tɪr〕*adj.* 志願的
program〔'progræm〕*n.* 計畫；方案；活動
volunteer program 志願服務計畫　　run〔rʌn〕*v.* 經營；管理
government〔'gʌvənmənt〕*n.* 政府
stated〔'stetɪd〕*adj.* 規定的；指定的
mission〔'mɪʃən〕*n.* 任務　　include〔ɪn'klud〕*v.* 包括
provide〔prə'vaɪd〕*v.* 提供　　technical〔'tɛknɪkl̩〕*adj.* 技術的
assistance〔ə'sɪstəns〕*n.* 協助
outside〔aʊt'saɪd〕*prep.* 在…之外　　culture〔'kʌltʃɚ〕*n.* 文化
country〔'kʌntrɪ〕*n.* 國家　　military〔'mɪlə͵tɛrɪ〕*adj.* 軍事的
unit〔'junɪt〕*n.* 單位

21. (**A**) M : Do you think we should take Jimmy for a grooming?
His coat is looking really shaggy.

男：妳認為我們該帶吉米去修毛了嗎？牠的毛看起來很蓬亂。

W : With the hot summer months coming, it would
probably be a good idea.

女：由於炎熱的夏季即將來臨，這可能是個不錯的主意。

Question : What is implied about Jimmy?

關於吉米，本文暗示什麼？

(A) He is a dog. 牠是一隻狗。

(B) He is very energetic. 牠非常有活力。

(C) He is lazy in the summer. 牠在夏天都很懶散。

* groom〔grum〕*v.* 給…梳理毛髮
coat〔kot〕*n.*（獸類的）毛；毛皮
shaggy〔'ʃægɪ〕*adj.*（毛、髮）蓬亂的
with〔wɪθ〕*prep.* 因為；由於　　month〔mʌnθ〕*n.* 月
imply〔ɪm'plaɪ〕*v.* 暗示
energetic〔ˌɛnɚ'dʒɛtɪk〕*adj.* 充滿活力的
lazy〔'lezɪ〕*adj.* 懶惰的；懶散的；懶洋洋的

【劉毅老師的話】

聽力、口說是未來的趨勢。學英文要從「說」開始，會「說」自然會「聽」，也會「讀」和「寫」。可參照「學習出版公司」出版的「一口氣英語」系列和「英文一字金」系列。

第一部分：辨識句意（第 1-3 題）

1. (**B**) (A)　　　　　(B)　　　　　(C)

Hank and his dog Rex are playing with a ball in front of Rex's house.

漢克和他的狗雷克斯正在雷克斯的房子前面玩球。

* ***in front of*** 在…前面

2. (**C**) (A)　　　　　(B)　　　　　(C)

Today is December 25, 2040. 今天是 2040 年 12 月 25 日。

* December〔dɪˋsɛmbɚ〕*n.* 十二月

3. (**C**) (A)　　　　　(B)　　　　　(C)

One student is cleaning the window, another is sweeping the floor, and another is erasing the blackboard.

一位學生在清理窗戶，另一位在掃地板，還有一位在擦黑板。

* clean〔klin〕*v.* 清理　　sweep〔swip〕*v.* 掃
  floor〔flor〕*n.* 地板　　erase〔ɪˋres〕*v.* 擦
  blackboard〔ˋblækˌbord〕*n.* 黑板

第二部分：基本問答（第 4-10 題）

4.（**B**）What would you like for breakfast this morning?
　　你今天早上想吃什麼早餐？

　　(A) I'll stay home from school today.
　　　　我今天要留在家裡，不去上學。

　　(B) I'd like to have some cereal. <u>我想要吃一些麥片。</u>

　　(C) I usually eat breakfast at 7:30. 我通常在七點半吃早餐。

　　* stay〔ste〕*v.* 停留　　***would like to V.*** 想要…
　　　have〔hæv〕*v.* 吃　　cereal〔ˋsɪrɪəl〕*n.* 麥片
　　　usually〔ˋjuʒʊəlɪ〕*adv.* 通常

5.（**C**）Here's that CD by Rain I've been telling you about.
　　這是我一直跟你說的那個 Rain 的 CD。

　　(A) It's due on Monday. 星期一到期。

　　(B) You can't tell him anything. 你不能告訴他任何事。

　　(C) Thanks, I'll listen to it this weekend.
　　　　<u>謝謝，我這個週末會聽聽看。</u>

　　* ***CD*** 光碟　　***Rain*** 韓國男歌手
　　　due〔du〕*adj.* 到期的；應付的
　　　weekend〔ˋwikˋɛnd〕*n.* 週末

6.（**A**）The escalator is out of order. You'll have to take the stairs. 電扶梯故障了。你必須爬樓梯。

(A) Thanks for the tip. 謝謝你的提醒。

(B) On the second floor. 在二樓。

(C) At the end of the hall. 在走廊的盡頭。

* escalator (ˈɛskə,letɚ) *n.* 電扶梯　　***out of order***　故障
stair (stɛr) *n.* 樓梯　　***take the stairs***　爬樓梯
tip (tɪp) *n.* 提醒；建議　　floor (flor) *n.* 樓層
end (ɛnd) *n.* 末端；盡頭　　hall (hɔl) *n.* 走廊 (= *hallway*)

7. (**B**) Do you practice or follow any type of religion?
你有信仰任何類型的宗教嗎?

(A) I'm a vegetarian. 我是素食者。

(B) I don't. 我沒有。

(C) I've been practicing. 我一直都在練習。

* practice (ˈpræktɪs) *v.* 練習；實踐
follow (ˈfɑlo) *v.* 追隨；擁護；信 (教)　　type (taɪp) *n.* 類型
religion (rɪˈlɪdʒən) *n.* 宗教　　***practice religion***　信仰宗教
vegetarian (ˌvɛdʒəˈtɛrɪən) *n.* 素食者

8. (**A**) I've never seen it so empty. We have the whole place to
ourselves! 我從來沒見過它這麼空。整個地方都是我們的了!

(A) Well, it's a weekday, so everybody is at school or
work. 嗯,今天是平日,所以大家都在上學或上班。

(B) They're all here to see the movie star, I guess.
我猜他們都是來看電影明星的。

(C) If you want, the other side is a little more
comfortable.
如果你想要的話,另外一邊會比較舒服一點。

* never (ˈnɛvɚ) *adv.* 從未　　empty (ˈɛmptɪ) *adj.* 空的
whole (hol) *adj.* 整個的　　***have sth. to oneself***　獨自享用某物
weekday (ˈwik,de) *n.* 平日　　guess (gɛs) *v.* 猜
comfortable (ˈkʌmfɚtəbḷ) *adj.* 舒服的

9. (**B**) How long has the city had a light rail system?

這個城市有輕軌系統已經多久了？

(A) No, it doesn't go to the airport. Take the bus.

不，它不會去機場。要搭巴士。

(B) Not that long. It just opened last year.

沒有很久。去年才開通的。

(C) Sorry. I didn't see you there.

抱歉。我沒看到你在那裡。

* light〔laɪt〕*adj.* 輕的　　rail〔rel〕*n.* 鐵軌
  system〔'sɪstəm〕*n.* 系統　　airport〔'ɛr͵port〕*n.* 機場
  open〔'opən〕*v.* 開放；開始

10. (**C**) It's almost noon and time for lunch, Doris. What would you like to eat?

快要中午了，該吃午餐了，桃麗絲。妳想吃什麼？

(A) Greetings. 大家好。

(B) I feel so fortunate. 我覺得很幸運。

(C) I'm in the mood for beef noodles. 我想吃牛肉麵。

* almost〔'ɔl͵most〕*adv.* 幾乎　　noon〔nun〕*n.* 中午
  greetings〔'gritɪŋ〕*n. pl.* 問候語
  fortunate〔'fɔrtʃənɪt〕*adj.* 幸運的　　mood〔mud〕*n.* 心情
  be in the mood for 想要做某事；有心情做某事
  beef〔bif〕*n.* 牛肉　　noodle〔'nudl〕*n.* 麵

第三部分：言談理解（第 11-21 題）

11. (**C**) M : How late does the café stay open?

男：咖啡廳開到多晚？

W : We're open until ten on weeknights, midnight on weekends.

女：平日晚上我們開到十點，週末到十二點。

M : Is Friday considered a weeknight or a weekend?

男：那星期五算平日晚上還是週末？

W : We consider it part of the weekend.

女：我們把它視爲週末。

Question : What time does the café close on Friday night?

咖啡廳週五晚上幾點關門？

(A) 10:00 p.m.　晚上十點。

(B) 11:00 p.m.　晚上十一點。

(C) 12:00 a.m.　<u>凌晨十二點。</u>

* café〔kəˈfe〕*n.* 咖啡廳　　open〔ˈopən〕*adj.* 開著的
until〔ənˈtɪl〕*prep.* 直到　　weeknight〔ˈwikˌnaɪt〕*n.* 平日晚上
midnight〔ˈmɪdˌnaɪt〕*n.* 午夜；半夜十二點
weekend〔ˈwikˌɛnd〕*n.* 週末　　consider〔kənˈsɪdɚ〕*v.* 認爲
consider A (to be) B　認爲 A 是 B

12. (**C**) W : How much do I owe you?

女：我該給你多少錢？

M : Let's see. It's six hundred on the meter, plus fifty
each for your bags. Call it seven hundred.

男：我們來看看。跳錶是六百，加上每件行李五十元。就算作
七百吧。

W : Can you break a thousand dollar bill?

女：你可以找一千元的紙鈔嗎？

M : No problem.

男：沒問題。

W : Just give me back two hundred and keep a hundred
for yourself.

女：只要找我兩百，另外一百你自己留著。

Question：What did the woman give the man?

女士給了男士什麼？

(A) A kiss on the cheek. 一個臉頰上的吻。

(B) A business card. 一張名片。

(C) A tip. 小費。

* owe〔o〕*v.* 欠　　meter〔'mitə〕*n.* 錶
plus〔plʌs〕*prep.* 加上　　call〔kɔl〕*v.* 把…算作
break〔brek〕*v.* 將（大鈔）換零　　bill〔bɪl〕*n.* 紙鈔
give…back 歸還　　cheek〔tʃik〕*n.* 臉頰
business〔'bɪznɪs〕*n.* 商業　　card〔kɑrd〕*n.* 卡片
business card 名片　　tip〔tɪp〕*n.* 小費

13. (**A**) W：Look at the line. Let's go somewhere else.

女：你看這個隊伍。我們去其他地方吧。

M：I think it's going to be more of the same no matter where we go. It's the lunchtime rush.

男：我覺得不管我們去哪裡都一樣。現在是午餐尖峰時間。

W：Which is why I wanted to make reservations.

女：這就是為什麼我原本想要預約的。

M：Well, I wasn't sure I would be able to join you today. I didn't want you to go to any extra trouble, just in case I couldn't make it.

男：嗯，我原本不確定我今天可以和妳一起吃。萬一我真的不能來，我不希望給妳添額外的麻煩。

Question：Where is this conversation most likely taking place? 這個對話很有可能是在哪裡發生？

(A) Outside a restaurant. 在餐廳外面。

(B) In a theater. 在電影院。

(C) Behind a bank. 在銀行後面。

* line〔laɪn〕 *n.* 隊伍　　somewhere〔'sʌm,hwɛr〕 *adv.* 在某處
else〔ɛls〕 *adj.* 其他的；別的　　***go somewhere else*** 去其他地方
more of the same 都一樣　　***no matter*** 不論
lunchtime〔'lʌntʃ,taɪm〕 *n.* 午餐時間　　rush〔rʌʃ〕 *n.* 尖峰時間
reservation〔,rɛzə'veʃən〕 *n.* 預訂　　***be able to V.*** 能夠…
join〔dʒɔɪn〕 *v.* 加入；和…一起做同樣的事
trouble〔'trʌbl̩〕 *n.* 麻煩　　***go to…trouble*** 花…心思
extra〔'ɛkstrə〕 *adj.* 額外的　　***in case*** 以防萬一
make it 成功；辦到；能來　　***take place*** 發生
outside〔aʊt'saɪd〕 *prep.* 在…的外面
theater〔'θiətɚ〕 *n.* 電影院　　bank〔bæŋk〕 *n.* 銀行

14. (**B**) In an effort to increase ticket sales, the Cleveland Indians
decided to hold a "Ten-Cent Beer Night," allowing fans
to buy cups of beer for just 10 cents each, during a home
game against the Texas Rangers. The promotion did
boost attendance; however, it also created a stadium full
of drunken spectators who disrupted early innings of the
game with streaking and flashing.

為了要增加門票銷售量，克里夫蘭印第安人隊在一場與德州遊騎
兵隊的主場比賽中，決定舉辦「十元啤酒之夜」，讓球迷能買到
一杯只要十分錢的啤酒。這個促銷活動的確增加了出席人數；可
是也造成體育場充滿了喝醉的觀眾，因為他們裸奔和暴露，所以
打斷了最初幾局的比賽。

Question：Why did the Cleveland Indians hold a
　　　　　"Ten-Cent Beer Night"? 為什麼克里夫蘭印第
　　　　　安人隊會舉辦「十元啤酒之夜」？

(A) To see more beer. 為了看見更多啤酒。

(B) To sell more tickets. 為了賣更多的門票。

(C) To confuse the Rangers. 為了擾亂德州遊騎兵隊。

effort〔'ɛfət〕*n.* 努力　***in an effort to V.*** 努力…

increase〔ɪn'kris〕*v.* 增加　ticket〔'tɪkɪt〕*n.* 門票

sales〔selz〕*n. pl.* 銷售量

Cleveland Indians 克里夫蘭印第安人隊【棒球隊】

decide〔dɪ'saɪd〕*v.* 決定　hold〔hold〕*v.* 舉辦

cent〔sɛnt〕*n.* 一分錢　beer〔bɪr〕*n.* 啤酒

allow〔ə'laʊ〕*v.* 允許；讓　fan〔fæn〕*n.* 球迷

home game 主場比賽　against〔ə'gɛnst〕*prep.* 對抗

ranger〔'rendʒə〕*n.* 騎兵巡邏隊員

Texas Rangers 德州遊騎兵隊

promotion〔prə'moʃən〕*n.* 促銷

boost〔bust〕*v.* 提高；增加

attendance〔ə'tɛndəns〕*n.* 參加人數；出席人數

create〔krɪ'et〕*v.* 創造　stadium〔'stedɪəm〕*n.* 體育場

be full of 充滿了　drunken〔'drʌŋkən〕*adj.* 酒醉的

spectator〔'spɛktetə〕*n.* 觀衆

disrupt〔dɪs'rʌpt〕*v.* 使中斷　inning〔'ɪnɪŋ〕*n.* 局

streak〔strik〕*v.* 裸奔　flash〔flæʃ〕*v.* 暴露

confuse〔kən'fjuz〕*v.* 使困惑；擾亂

15. (**C**) M：Anne, your cousin is so cool!

男：安，妳的表妹好酷喔！

W：You mean Lucy? Actually, she's not my cousin.

女：妳是說露西嗎？事實上，她不是我的表妹。

M：Really? I thought you were related. You guys look similar.

男：眞的嗎？我以爲妳們是親戚。妳們長得很像。

W：A lot of people say that.

女：很多人都這麼說。

M：But you are very close to Lucy, aren't you?

男：但妳跟露西很親近，不是嗎？

W : Yes. Our moms went to college together and they've been best friends ever since.

女：是的。我們的媽媽一起唸大學，她們從那時起，一直都是最好的朋友。

Question : How does Anne know Lucy?

安是怎麼認識露西的？

(A) They are co-workers. 她們是同事。

(B) They are cousins. 她們是表姐妹。

(C) Their moms are best friends.

她們的媽媽是最好的朋友。

* cousin〔'kʌzn̩〕*n.* 堂（表）兄弟姐妹

cool〔kul〕*adj.* 很酷的　　mean〔min〕*v.* 意思是；意指

actually〔'æktʃuəlɪ〕*adv.* 事實上

related〔rɪ'letɪd〕*adj.* 親戚的　　guy〔gaɪ〕*n.* 人；傢伙

you guys 你們　　similar〔'sɪmələ〕*adj.* 相似的

close〔klos〕*adj.* 親近的　　college〔'kɑlɪdʒ〕*n.* 大學

ever since 其後；從那以後（一直）

co-worker〔ˌko'wɝkə〕*n.* 同事

16. (**B**) Charlotte and Ella, both 12, have been making movies together since they were in the fifth grade. The girls, who live in San Francisco, California, meet up with other kids in their neighborhood after school and on weekends to film together.

夏綠蒂和艾拉，兩位都十二歲，自從五年級開始，就一起拍電影。這兩個女孩住在加州舊金山，她們會在放學後或是週末，和鄰近地區的其他孩子們碰面，一起拍電影。

Question : What do we know about Charlotte and Ella?

關於夏綠蒂和艾拉，我們知道什麼？

(A) They are in the fifth grade. 她們唸五年級。

(B) They live in San Francisco. <u>她們住在舊金山。</u>

(C) They only work together. 她們只有一起工作。

* **_make a movie_** 拍電影　　together〔tə'gɛðɚ〕 *adv.* 一起
fifth〔fɪfθ〕 *adj.* 第五的　　grade〔gred〕 *n.* 年級
San Francisco〔ˌsænfrən'sɪsko〕 *n.* 舊金山
California〔ˌkælə'fɔrnjə〕 *n.* 加州　　**_meet up_** 碰面
neighborhood〔'nebɚˌhʊd〕 *n.* 鄰近地區
after school 放學後　　film〔fɪlm〕 *v.* 拍電影

17. (**B**) M : Who is handling the preparations for this year's science fair?

男：誰負責準備今年的科展？

W : Frank Smith and Julie Lawrence are heading the committee. That's all I know.

女：法蘭克史密斯和茱莉勞倫斯是委員會的負責人。我只知道這些。

M : There hasn't been much communication among the faculty. I think it's safe to assume we'll be asked to pitch in at some point.

男：教職員之間都沒什麼溝通。我想我們可以假定，在某個時刻，我們會被叫去幫忙，這樣比較保險。

Question : What does the man imply?

男士在暗示什麼？

(A) He is eager to participate in the science fair.
他渴望想參加科展。

(B) He will probably help out at the science fair.
<u>他可能會協助科展。</u>

(C) He is disappointed with the science fair.

他對科展很失望。

* handle〔'hændḷ〕 *v.* 處理
  preparation〔,prɛpə'reʃən〕 *n.* 準備；籌備
  fair〔fɛr〕 *n.* 展覽會　　***science fair*** 科學展覽會；科展
  head〔hɛd〕 *v.* 領導　　committee〔kə'mɪtɪ〕 *n.* 委員會
  communication〔kə,mjunə'keʃən〕 *n.* 溝通
  among〔ə'mʌŋ〕 *prep.* 在…之間
  faculty〔'fækḷtɪ〕 *n.* 全體教職員
  assume〔ə'sum〕 *v.* 假定；認為　　***pitch in*** 投入；參與；支援
  some〔sʌm〕 *adj.* 某個　　point〔pɔɪnt〕 *n.* 時刻
  imply〔ɪm'plaɪ〕 *v.* 暗示　　eager〔'igɚ〕 *adj.* 渴望的
  participate〔par'tɪsə,pet〕 *v.* 參加 < *in* >
  probably〔'prɑbəblɪ〕 *adv.* 可能　　***help out*** 幫忙
  disappointed〔,dɪsə'pɔɪntɪd〕 *adj.* 失望的 < *with* >

18. (**B**) Well, I read your essay, Kim, and here are my thoughts. First, it's very well-written, but some of the sentences are too long. You need to shorten some of the longer ones. Second, the intro and body support your thesis, but I think the conclusion needs to be tighter.

嗯，我看過妳的論文了，金，以下是我的想法。首先，妳寫得很好，但是有些句子太長了。妳必須把一些比較長的句子縮短。其次，前言和主文能支持妳的論點，但是我覺得結論需要更簡潔一點。

Question：What did Kim ask the speaker to do?

金要求說話者做什麼？

(A) Write her essay. 寫她的論文。
(B) Read her essay. 看她的論文。
(C) Shorten her essay. 縮短她的論文。

* essay〔'ɛse〕*n.* 短文；論文　　thought〔θɔt〕*n.* 想法
  well-written〔'wɛl'rɪtn̩〕*adj.* 寫得很好的
  sentence〔'sɛntəns〕*n.* 句子　　shorten〔'ʃɔrtn̩〕*v.* 縮短
  intro〔'ɪntro〕*n.* 介紹；前言（= *introduction*）
  body〔'badɪ〕*n.* (作文)主文；主要部份
  support〔sə'port〕*v.* 支持；確認
  thesis〔'θisɪs〕*n.* 論點；論文
  conclusion〔kən'kluʒən〕*n.* 結論
  tight〔taɪt〕*adj.* (文字)簡潔的；精練的

19. (**C**) W：Are they ever going to finish construction on that office building?

女：他們到底會不會完成那棟辦公大廈的建築工程？

M：I don't know.　It's been like that for almost a year.

男：我不知道。它這個狀態已經快一年了。

W：It looks like they gave up on it.

女：看來他們似乎放棄它了。

M：What an awful waste of resources.

男：真是太浪費資源了。

Question：What are they talking about?

他們正在談論什麼？

(A) Whether or not to rent an office.

是否要租一間辦公室。

(B) The lack of natural resources. 天然資源的缺乏。

(C) A puzzling situation. 一個令人困惑的情況。

* ever〔'ɛvɚ〕*adv.* 究竟；到底　　finish〔'fɪnɪʃ〕*v.* 完成
  construction〔kən'strʌkʃən〕*n.* 建造；建築工程
  building〔'bɪldɪŋ〕*n.* 大樓　　almost〔'ɔl,most〕*adv.* 幾乎
  give up on 放棄對⋯的希望
  awful〔'ɔful〕*adj.* 可怕的；非常的　　waste〔west〕*n.* 浪費

resource〔rɪˈsors〕*n.* 資源　***whether or not*** 是否

rent〔rɛnt〕*v.* 租　　office〔ˈɔfɪs〕*n.* 辦公室

lack〔læk〕*n.* 缺乏　　***natural resources*** 天然資源

puzzling〔ˈpʌzl̩ɪŋ〕*adj.* 令人困惑的

situation〔͵sɪtʃʊˈeʃən〕*n.* 情況

20. (**C**)　M：Have you seen the new Star Wars movie yet?

　　　男：妳去看了最新的星際大戰電影了嗎？

　　　W：No, thanks.

　　　女：不要，謝謝。

　　　M：What do you mean?

　　　男：妳這是什麼意思？

　　　W：I don't want to see it with you.

　　　女：我不想跟你一起看。

　　　M：I was just making conversation.

　　　男：我只是想找話題聊。

　　　W：I thought you were asking me out.

　　　女：我以爲你在約我出去。

　　　Question：What did the man ask the woman?

　　　　　　　男士問女士什麼？

　　　(A) If she wanted to see a movie. 她想不想看電影。

　　　(B) If she wanted to go on a date. 她想不想去約會。

　　　(C) If she had seen a particular movie.

　　　　　她是否看過某一部電影。

　　* ***Star Wars*** 星際大戰　　yet〔jɛt〕*adv.* 已經

　　　mean〔min〕*v.* 意思是

　　　make conversation 找話題聊；聊天

　　　ask sb. out 約某人出去　　***go on a date*** 去約會

　　　particular〔pɚˈtɪkjələ〕*adj.* 特定的；某一的

21. (**B**) M : You're not eating your chicken burger. Is there something wrong with it?

　　　男：妳沒有在吃妳的雞肉漢堡。它有什麼不對勁嗎？

　　　W : No, it's fine. I'm just waiting for it to cool down. Then I'll eat it.

　　　女：不，它很好。我只是想要等它冷卻一點。然後再吃。

　　　M : Well, you're in for a treat. This place does the best chicken burgers in town.

　　　男：嗯，妳一定會喜歡的。這家餐廳做的雞肉漢堡是城裡最棒的。

　　　Question : How does the woman feel about her burger?

　　　　　　　　女士覺得她的漢堡如何？

　　　(A) It's overcooked. 煮得過熟。

　　　(B) It's too hot. 太燙了。

　　　(C) It's the best in town. 是城裡最棒的。

　　　* burger〔′bɜgə〕*n.* 漢堡　　***cool down*** 冷卻
　　　　be in for 肯定會經歷
　　　　treat〔trit〕*n.* 快樂；喜悅；非常好的事物
　　　　you're in for a treat 你一定會喜歡的
　　　　place〔ples〕*n.* 餐館　　　town〔taun〕*n.* 城鎮
　　　　overcooked〔͵ovə′kukt〕*adj.* 煮得過熟的

> ── 【劉毅老師的話】 ──
>
> 　　什麼都要練習，聽越多遍越好。訓練自己先看選項，再聽題目，熟能生巧。題目做得越多，越有信心。

🎧 TEST 18 ▶ 詳解

第一部分：辨識句意（第 1-3 題）

1. (**A**) (A)　　　　　　(B)　　　　　　(C)

Ms. Watson opened a box and a large and beautiful butterfly flew out.
華生小姐打開箱子，然後一隻又大又美麗的蝴蝶就飛了出來。
* butterfly〔ˋbʌtɚ͵flaɪ〕*n.* 蝴蝶

2. (**C**) (A)　　　　　　(B)　　　　　　(C)

Tina is at school, but she's thinking about her friend Beth who is home sick with the flu. 蒂娜在學校，但她正想著她的朋友貝絲，她得了流行性感冒，待在家裡。
* sick〔sɪk〕*adj.* 生病的　　flu〔flu〕*n.* 流行性感冒（= *influenza*）

3. (**B**) (A)　　　　　　(B)　　　　　　(C)

A group of farmers have gathered in a circle to pray for rain to water their crops.

一群農夫聚在一起圍成圓圈，祈求下雨，以灌溉他們的農作物。

* farmer〔'fɑrmɚ〕*n.* 農夫　　gather〔'gæðɚ〕*v.* 聚集
circle〔'sɝkl̩〕*n.* 圓圈　　***in a circle*** 圍成圓圈
pray〔pre〕*v.* 祈禱　　water〔'wɔtɚ〕*v.* 給…澆水
crop〔krɑp〕*n.* 農作物

第二部分：基本問答（第 4-10 題）

4. (**C**) Who are those kids? I've never seen them around here before. 那些小孩是誰？我以前從沒在附近看過他們。

(A) That's too bad. 那太糟了。

(B) My brother. 我的兄弟。

(C) I don't know. I've never seen them before, either.
<u>我不知道。我以前也從沒看過他們。</u>

* kid〔kɪd〕*n.* 小孩　　never〔'nɛvɚ〕*adv.* 從未
around〔ə'raund〕*prep.* 在…附近
either〔'iðɚ〕*adv.* 也（不）

5. (**C**) What do you do for a living? 你以什麼維生？

(A) I'm a vegetarian. 我吃素。

(B) I'm Chinese and French. 我是中法混血兒。

(C) I'm a teacher. <u>我是個老師。</u>

* living〔'lɪvɪŋ〕*n.* 生計
do sth. for a living 做某事維生
vegetarian〔,vɛdʒə'tɛrɪən〕*n.* 素食者；吃素的人
French〔frɛntʃ〕*adj.* 法國人的
I'm Chinese and French. 我是中法混血兒。
（= *I'm a mix of Chinese and French.*）

6. (**B**) Do you know how to play the drums?　你知道怎麼打鼓嗎？

　　(A) No.　I'm not hungry.　不。我不餓。

　　(B) No.　I never learned how.　<u>不。我從沒學過。</u>

　　(C) Let me get you a towel.　讓我幫你拿一條毛巾。

　　* play〔ple〕*v.* 演奏（樂器）　　drum〔drʌm〕*n.* 鼓
　　　hungry〔'hʌŋgrɪ〕*adj.* 飢餓的　　towel〔'tauəl〕*n.* 毛巾

7. (**A**) Hi, Jane.　Why are you so cheerful today?

　　嗨，珍。妳今天怎麼這麼高興？

　　(A) It's my birthday!　<u>今天是我的生日！</u>

　　(B) I don't feel very well.　我覺得不太舒服。

　　(C) They were absent yesterday.　他們昨天缺席。

　　* cheerful〔'tʃɪrfəl〕*adj.* 快樂的　　birthday〔'bɝθ,de〕*n.* 生日
　　　well〔wɛl〕*adj.* 健康的　　absent〔'æbsn̩t〕*adj.* 缺席的

8. (**A**) Do you remember where we parked our bicycles?　I
　　totally forgot!　你記得我們把腳踏車停在哪裡嗎？我完全忘了！

　　(A) Don't worry.　I remember.　<u>別擔心。我記得。</u>

　　(B) Close the door.　It's cold.　把門關上。好冷。

　　(C) It's OK.　They can't hear us.
　　　沒關係。他們聽不見我們的聲音。

　　* remember〔rɪ'mɛmbɚ〕*v.* 記得　　park〔pɑrk〕*v.* 停（車）
　　　totally〔'totl̩ɪ〕*adv.* 完全地　　forget〔fɚ'gɛt〕*v.* 忘記
　　　worry〔'wɝɪ〕*v.* 擔心　　close〔kloz〕*v.* 關上

9. (**A**) That was quite a party last night.　What time did you
　　leave?　昨晚的派對相當不錯。你幾點離開的？

　　(A) I left around midnight.　<u>我大概半夜十二點離開的。</u>

　　(B) He was the host.　他是主人。

　　(C) I went to a party.　我參加了一場派對。

* ***quite a*** 相當不尋常或有趣的　　leave〔liv〕*v.* 離開
around〔ə'raʊnd〕*adv.* 大約
midnight〔'mɪd͵naɪt〕*n.* 半夜十二點　　host〔host〕*n.* 主人

10. (**B**) Would you mind if I joined you? The cafeteria is so crowded today.

你介意我跟你一起坐嗎？今天自助餐廳擠滿了人。

(A) Yes, let's join them. 是的，我們去和他們一起坐吧。

(B) No, I wouldn't mind at all. <u>不，我完全不介意。</u>

(C) My friend won't be coming. 我的朋友不會來。

* mind〔maɪnd〕*v.* 介意　　join〔dʒɔɪn〕*v.* 加入；和⋯一起
cafeteria〔͵kæfə'tɪrɪə〕*n.* 自助餐廳
crowded〔'kraʊdɪd〕*adj.* 擁擠的；擠滿人的
not⋯at all 一點也不⋯

第三部分：言談理解（第 11-21 題）

11. (**C**) M：How's your essay coming along?

男：妳的文章進展得如何？

W：Pretty good. My teacher was very pleased with the revisions I made.

女：還不錯。我的老師對我做的修改很滿意。

M：So is it finished now?

男：所以現在寫完了嗎？

W：Not quite. I've still got to type up a final draft and then I'll turn it in.

女：還差一點。我還需要把最後的草稿打出來，然後再交出去。

Question：What did the woman do? 女士做了什麼？

(A) She typed her essay. 她打了她的文章。

(B) She turned in her essay. 她交她的文章。

(C) She made changes to her essay.

她將文章做了一些變更。

* essay〔'ɛse〕*n.* 文章　　***come along*** 進展
pretty〔'prɪtɪ〕*adv.* 相當　　pleased〔plizd〕*adj.* 滿意的
revision〔rɪ'vɪʒən〕*n.* 修改　　finished〔'fɪnɪʃt〕*adj.* 完成的
not quite 還差一點　　type〔taɪp〕*v.* 打（字）
type up 把（手寫稿）打出來　　final〔'faɪnḷ〕*adj.* 最後的
draft〔dræft〕*n.* 草稿　　***turn in*** 繳交
change〔tʃendʒ〕*n.* 改變；變更

12. (**C**)　Why do you think our kids want to play sports? What is it that inspires them to sign up and play on a team? Well, after 30-some years of coaching youth sports programs, I think I can tell you. The number one reason? FUN! I hate to sound trite, but this is the main reason. Kids are kids, which means they want to have fun.

你覺得我們的孩子爲什麼想要運動？是什麼激勵他們去報名，要在球隊裡打球？嗯，在當了三十多年青少年運動課程的敎練後，我覺得我能告訴你。第一個原因？好玩！我討厭聽起來很老套，但這是主要的原因。孩子就是孩子，這代表他們只是想要好玩而已。

Question：What do we know about the speaker?

關於說話者，我們知道什麼？

(A) He likes to have fun.　他喜歡玩得愉快。

(B) He has been a teacher for 30 years.

他當老師當了三十年。

(C) He is a coach.　他是一位敎練。

* ***play sports*** 運動　　inspire〔ɪn'spaɪr〕*v.* 激勵
sign up 報名　　***play on a team*** 在球隊裡打球

30-some *adj.* 三十幾的

coach〔kotʃ〕*v.* 指導；當…的教練 *n.* 教練

youth〔juθ〕*n.* 年輕人；青少年 sports〔sports〕*adj.* 運動的

program〔'progræm〕*n.* 計畫；課程

reason〔'rizn̩〕*n.* 原因 fun〔fʌn〕*n.* 有趣

hate〔het〕*v.* 討厭；不願意 sound〔saʊnd〕*v.* 聽起來

trite〔traɪt〕*adj.* 老套的 main〔men〕*adj.* 主要的

mean〔min〕*v.* 意思是 ***have fun*** 玩得愉快

13. (**A**) W：I'm going to try out for the volleyball team.

女：我要參加排球隊的甄選。

M：Really? Have you ever played before?

男：真的嗎？妳之前有打過嗎？

W：No, never. But it looks like so much fun. I've always wanted to try.

女：不，從來沒有。但是看起來很好玩。我一直都很想試試看。

M：I hate to rain on your parade, but there are a lot of talented girls trying to make the team this year.

男：我不想潑妳冷水，但是今年有很多有才能的女孩，都想進入球隊。

W：I know. That's OK. I might as well give it a shot.

女：我知道。沒關係。我還是不妨試一試。

Question：What does the man mean when he says, "I hate to rain on your parade"?

當男士說「我不想潑妳冷水」時，他是什麼意思？

(A) He doesn't want to discourage the woman.

他不想使女士氣餒。

(B) He has high expectations of the woman.

他對女士有很高的期望。

(C) He will also join the volleyball team.

他也會加入排球隊。

* ***try out*** 角逐…的選拔；參加 (選手的) 甄試
  volleyball ('vɑlɪ,bɔl) *n.* 排球　　team (tim) *n.* 隊
  play (ple) *v.* 打 (球)　　parade (pə'red) *n.* 遊行
  rain on one's parade 使某人掃興；潑某人冷水
  talented ('tæləntɪd) *adj.* 有才能的
  make the team 加入團隊　　***give it a shot*** 試一試
  discourage (dɪs'kɝɪdʒ) *v.* 使氣餒
  expectation (,ɛkspɛk'teʃən) *n.* 期待
  join (dʒɔɪn) *v.* 加入

14. (**B**) W : Last night I had Japanese food for the first time in
　　　　my life. It was incredible!

女：昨晚是我人生中第一次吃日本料理。眞是棒極了！

M : Really? Where?

男：眞的嗎？在哪裡吃的？

W : Sakana Bune in Richmond. Sakana Bune means
　　"blue boat."

女：在里奇蒙的 Sakana Bune。Sakana Bune 的意思是「藍色的
　　船」。

M : You're kidding, right? You must not know anything
　　about Japanese food, because Sakana Bune is
　　garbage. The chef isn't even Japanese.

男：妳在開玩笑，對吧？妳一定對日本料理一無所知，因爲
　　Sakana Bune 根本就沒那價值。連廚師都不是日本人。

Question : What does the man think of Sakana Bune?
　　　　　　男士對於 Sakana Bune 有什麼想法？

(A) It's the best he's ever tasted. 那是他吃過最好吃的。

(B) It's not very good. 不是很好吃。

(C) It's fine if you know Japanese food.

如果你懂日本料理的話，它其實還可以。

* Japanese〔͵dʒæpə'niz〕*adj.* 日本（人）的　*n.* 日本人
incredible〔ɪn'krɛdəbḷ〕*adj.* 令人難以置信的；很棒的
Richmond〔'rɪtʃmənd〕*n.* 里奇蒙
kid〔kɪd〕*v.* 開玩笑　　must〔mʌst〕*aux.* 一定
garbage〔'gɑrbɪdʒ〕*n.* 垃圾；剩菜；無價值的東西
chef〔ʃɛf〕*n.* 主廚；廚師　　ever〔'ɛvɚ〕*adv.* 曾經
taste〔test〕*v.* 品嚐　　fine〔faɪn〕*adj.* 好的

15.（**A**）China has about 30 million more young adult men than young adult women because of a one-child policy in a society that prefers boys. As a result, many men worry they won't find a mate.

因為一胎化的政策，在中國這個比較喜歡男孩子的社會中，年輕的成年男子比年輕的成年女子多大約三千萬人。因此，許多男士擔心自己會找不到對象。

Question：What are Chinese men worried about finding?

中國男士擔心找不到什麼？

(A) A wife. 妻子。

(B) Success. 成功。

(C) Company. 同伴。

* million〔'mɪljən〕*n.* 百萬　　adult〔ə'dʌlt〕*adj.* 成年的
policy〔'pɑləsɪ〕*n.* 政策　　***one-child policy*** 一胎化政策
society〔sə'saɪətɪ〕*n.* 社會　　prefer〔prɪ'fɝ〕*v.* 比較喜歡
as a result 因此　　worry〔'wɝɪ〕*v.* 擔心
mate〔met〕*n.* 對象　　wife〔waɪf〕*n.* 妻子
success〔sək'sɛs〕*n.* 成功
company〔'kʌmpənɪ〕*n.* 同伴；公司

16. (**A**) W : I think I'm lost. I'm looking for the Circle J Ranch.

女： 我想我迷路了。我正在找 Circle J Ranch。

M : What you want to do is turn around and go back to Route 10 and make a right. Make a left at Santa Maria Road. Stay on that for about three miles, and you'll start seeing signs for the Circle K.

男： 妳要做的就是迴轉，回到 10 號公路然後右轉。在聖塔瑪麗亞路左轉。沿著那條路走大約三英里，妳就會開始看到前往 Circle K 的路標。

W : Thanks. You've been a great help.

女： 謝謝。你幫了我一個大忙。

Question : What should the woman do at Route 10?

在 10 號公路時，女士該做什麼？

(A) Turn right. 右轉。

(B) Turn left. 左轉。

(C) Go straight. 直走。

* lost〔lɔst〕*adj.* 迷路的　　***look for*** 尋找
turn around 迴轉　　route〔rut〕*n.* 路；路線
make a right 右轉 (= *turn right*)
make a left 左轉 (= *turn left*)　　stay〔ste〕*v.* 停留
mile〔maɪl〕*n.* 英里　　sign〔saɪn〕*n.* 告示；標誌
straight〔stret〕*adv.* 直直地

17. (**C**) M : Look, Hogan's Department Store is having a big sale. Why don't we go see if there are any good deals?

男： 喂，霍根百貨公司現在正舉行大拍賣。我們何不去看看有沒有什麼買了很划算的東西？

W : We don't really need anything, Randy. We just bought a new washing machine and dryer.

女：我們其實並不需要任何東西，蘭迪。我們才剛買了一台新的
洗衣機和烘乾機。

M：I didn't say I wanted to buy anything. I just want to
check it out.

男：我沒有說我想要買任何東西。我只是想要看看。

Question：What does Randy want to do at Hogan's
Department Store?

蘭迪想要去霍根百貨公司做什麼？

(A) Return an item. 退貨。

(B) Buy something. 買東西。

(C) Look around. 到處看看。

* *department store* 百貨公司　　sale〔sel〕*n.* 拍賣
deal〔dil〕*n.* 交易　　*good deal* 划算的交易
washing machine 洗衣機　　dryer〔'draɪɚ〕*n.* 烘乾機
check it out 看看　　return〔rɪ'tɝn〕*v.* 退還
item〔'aɪtəm〕*n.* 物品　　around〔ə'raʊnd〕*adv.* 到處

18. (**B**) W：What's wrong, Cameron? What happened?

女：怎麼了，卡麥隆？發生什麼事了？

M：I spilled red wine on Amanda's new couch. She's
going to kill me.

男：我把紅酒灑在阿曼達新的長沙發上。她會殺了我。

W：You mean that little spot? She'll never notice that.

女：你是說那個小斑點嗎？她絕不會注意到的。

M：You don't know Amanda. She doesn't miss a thing,
and that couch is her prized possession.

男：妳不了解阿曼達。她不會錯過任何事，而那個長沙發是她珍
貴的寶物。

Question：What did the man do? 男士做了什麼？

(A) He broke up with Amanda. 他跟阿曼達分手了。

(B) He spilled wine on Amanda's new couch.

他把紅酒灑在阿曼達新的長沙發上。

(C) He came home late last night. 他昨晚很晚回家。

* wrong〔rɔŋ〕*adj.* 不對勁的　　spill〔spɪl〕*v.* 灑出
wine〔waɪn〕*n.* 葡萄酒　　couch〔kautʃ〕*n.* 長沙發
kill〔kɪl〕*v.* 殺死　　spot〔spɑt〕*n.* 斑點
notice〔'notɪs〕*v.* 注意到　　miss〔mɪs〕*v.* 錯過；沒看到
prized〔praɪzd〕*adj.* 非常重要的；珍貴的
possession〔pə'zɛʃən〕*n.* 所有物；財產
break up 分手　　late〔let〕*adv.* 晚

19. (**B**) W：How are you doing, Marvin?

女：你好嗎，馬文？

M：I'm good. What's up?

男：我很好。妳好嗎？

W：Listen, I was wondering. Have you decided whether
you're going to stay with us another year?

女：聽著，我很想知道這件事。你已經決定是否要跟我們一起再
住一年嗎？

M：Yes. I mean, no, I'm not. I found a studio apartment
near the park.

男：是的。我的意思是，不，我不會。我在公園附近找到了一間
套房。

W：So that means we should start looking for somebody
to take your room?

女：所以這代表我們應該要開始找人來租你的房間？

M：Probably.

男：也許吧。

W：But… I thought you liked it here.

女：但…我以為你喜歡這裡。

M：It's OK. But I'm ready to live on my own.

男：是還不錯。但我準備要一個人住。

Question：Who are the speakers? 說話者是什麼關係？

(A) Co-workers. 同事。

(B) Roommates. 室友。

(C) Classmates. 同學。

* ***How are you doing?*** 你好嗎？（= *What's up?*）
  wonder〔'wʌndə〕*v.* 想知道　　decide〔dɪ'saɪd〕*v.* 決定
  whether〔'hwɛðə〕*conj.* 是否　　stay〔ste〕*v.* 暫住
  studio apartment 套房　　near〔nɪr〕*prep.* 靠近
  probably〔'prɑbəblɪ〕*adv.* 可能；或許
  like it here 喜歡這裡　　ready〔'rɛdɪ〕*adj.* 準備好的
  on one's ***own*** 自己；獨自
  co-worker〔,ko'wɜkə〕*n.* 同事
  roommate〔'rum,met〕*n.* 室友

20. (**A**) W：Hey, Robert, before you go… did you happen to see Tanya last weekend?

女：嘿，羅伯特，在你走之前…你是否有在上個週末見到譚雅？

M：No, I didn't. Why?

男：不，我沒有。怎麼了？

W：She was supposed to stop by and pay back the money I loaned her, but she never showed.

女：她原本應該來一趟，還我借她的錢，但她都沒出現。

M：Have you tried calling her?

男：妳有試著打給她嗎？

W：She's not picking up.

女：她都沒接。

Question：What does the woman mean by "She's not picking up"?

女士說的「她都沒接」是什麼意思？

(A) Tanya isn't answering her phone. 譚雅不接電話。

(B) Tanya isn't doing her work. 譚雅沒在做她的工作。

(C) Tanya isn't home. 譚雅不在家。

* ***happen to*** *V.* 碰巧… weekend〔'wik'ɛnd〕*n.* 週末
be supposed to *V.* 應該要… ***stop by*** 順道拜訪
pay back 償還 loan〔lon〕*v.* 借給
show〔ʃo〕*v.* 出現（= *show up*） ***pick up*** 接電話
answer〔'ænsɚ〕*v.* 接（電話）

21. (**C**) A swarm of angry bees killed two dogs in Midland and injured the dogs' owner, stinging the man more than 50 times in the attack. James Roy of Midland went outside to check on his dogs on Thursday and thought the two dogs were fighting, but they were in fact being attacked by a swarm of bees. The two dogs, Susie and Sammy, were stung more than 1,000 times, according to News West 9, and the dogs later died at a veterinarian's office in Midland.

在米德蘭，有一群憤怒的蜜蜂殺死了兩隻狗，也傷了狗的主人，在攻擊時螫了那個男子五十幾下。米德蘭的詹姆斯・羅伊，在星期四的時候去外面察看他的狗，他以為兩隻狗正在打架，但其實牠們正被一群蜜蜂攻擊。根據 News West 9 的報導，這兩隻狗，蘇西和薩米，被螫了一千多下，後來在米德蘭的一間獸醫診所去世了。

Question : Who survived the bee-sting attack?
誰被蜜蜂螫傷攻擊後存活下來？

(A) Susie. 蘇西。

(B) Sammy. 薩米。

(C) James Roy. 詹姆斯‧羅伊。

* swarm〔swɔrm〕*n.*（昆蟲）群　　bee〔bi〕*n.* 蜜蜂
Midland〔ˈmɪdlənd〕*n.* 米德蘭【位於美國中部】
injure〔ˈɪndʒɚ〕*v.* 傷害　　owner〔ˈonɚ〕*n.* 主人
sting〔stɪŋ〕*v.* 螫；叮　　time〔taɪm〕*n.* 次
attack〔əˈtæk〕*n. v.* 攻擊　　outside〔ˈaʊtˈsaɪd〕*adv.* 到外面
check on 檢查；察看　　fight〔faɪt〕*v.* 打架
in fact 事實上　　**according to** 根據
news〔njuz〕*n.* 新聞　　later〔ˈletɚ〕*adv.* 後來
veterinarian〔ˌvɛtrəˈnɛrɪən〕*n.* 獸醫
office〔ˈɔfɪs〕*n.* 辦公室；診所
survive〔sɚˈvaɪv〕*v.* 自…中生還

【劉毅老師的話】

　　會說英文，就像一件漂亮的衣服穿在身上，人人喜歡和你做朋友，可以交到全世界的朋友，有更寬闊的視野。趁年輕記憶力好的時候，多背我們出版的「一口氣英語」系列，和「**英文一字金**」系列。

 TEST 19 ▶ 詳解

第一部分：辨識句意（第 1-3 題）

1. (**C**) (A)　　　　　(B)　　　　　(C)

Mr. Sanchez is wondering if his wife remembered to buy him a cake for his birthday.

桑切斯先生很想知道，他的太太是否記得給他買個生日蛋糕。

* wonder〔'wʌndɚ〕*v.* 想知道　　wife〔waɪf〕*n.* 太太
　remember〔rɪ'mɛmbɚ〕*v.* 記得　　birthday〔'bɝθ,de〕*n.* 生日

2. (**C**) (A)　　　　　(B)　　　　　(C)

Jason went to see a movie but he didn't get in because he isn't 18 years old yet.

傑森去看了一部電影，但他沒有進去，因為他還沒滿十八歲。

* *not…yet* 還沒…

3. (**A**) (A)　　　　　(B)　　　　　(C)

A cat and a mouse swim happily in the river while a cow watches from the riverbank. 一隻貓和一隻老鼠快樂地在河裡游泳，同時一頭母牛正在河邊看。

* mouse〔maʊs〕*n.* 老鼠　　while〔hwaɪl〕*conj.* 當…時候；同時
cow〔kaʊ〕*n.* 母牛　　riverbank〔'rɪvə,bæŋk〕*n.* 河岸；河邊

第二部分：基本問答（第 4-10 題）

4. (**A**) Are you still planning to drop out of school?
你還是打算要休學嗎？

(A) No, I've had second thoughts. 不，我重新考慮了。

(B) No, they will give you a second chance.
不，他們會再給你一次機會。

(C) No, I wouldn't give her a second look.
不，我不會再看她一眼。

* still〔stɪl〕*adv.* 仍然　　plan〔plæn〕*v.* 打算
drop out of school 退學；休學
have second thoughts 重新考慮
a second 另一個（= *another*）　　chance〔tʃæns〕*n.* 機會
give *sb.* ***a second look*** 再看某人一眼

5. (**A**) Today's special is spaghetti with tomato sauce and garlic bread. 今天的特餐是茄汁義大利麵和大蒜麵包。

(A) Sounds delicious. I'll have that.
聽起來很好吃。我要那個。

(B) It's making a strange sound. 它在發出奇怪的聲音。

(C) Thanks, but I don't drink. 謝謝，但我不喝酒。

* special〔'spɛʃəl〕*n.* 特餐　　spaghetti〔spə'gɛtɪ〕*n.* 義大利麵
tomato〔tə'meto〕*n.* 蕃茄　　sauce〔sɔs〕*n.* 醬
garlic〔'gɑrlɪk〕*n.* 大蒜　　sound〔saʊnd〕*v.* 聽起來 *n.* 聲音
delicious〔dɪ'lɪʃəs〕*adj.* 美味的
strange〔strendʒ〕*adj.* 奇怪的　　drink〔drɪŋk〕*v.* 喝酒

6. (**C**)　Have you ever been to the top of Taipei 101?

你有去過台北 101 的頂樓嗎？

(A)　I have never been to the zoo.　我從未去過那個動物園。

(B)　I came out top in the test.　我考試得第一名。

(C)　Sure! It's got a great view, huh?

　　　當然！它有很棒的風景，是吧？

* ever (ˈɛvɚ) *adv.* 曾經　　top (tɑp) *n.* 頂端　*adj.* 第一名的
　zoo (zu) *n.* 動物園
　come out （在考試中）獲得（…的）成績；結果變成
　sure (ʃur) *adv.* 當然　　***It's got*** 它有（= *It has*）
　view (vju) *n.* 景色；風景　　huh (hʌ) *interj.* 嗯；啊

7. (**B**)　In what part of town do you live?　你住在城裡的哪一區？

(A)　My apartment.　我的公寓。

(B)　I live on the north side.　我住在北邊。

(C)　The rent is too high.　租金太高了。

* part (pɑrt) *n.* 部份；區域　　town (taun) *n.* 城鎮
　apartment (əˈpɑrtmənt) *n.* 公寓　　north (nɔrθ) *adj.* 北方的
　side (saɪd) *n.* 邊　　rent (rɛnt) *n.* 租金

8. (**C**)　Maggie is always checking herself in the mirror.

瑪姬總是在照鏡子。

(A)　That's a good quality in a friend.

　　　那是一個很好的朋友特質。

(B)　You should have a check-up.　你應該接受健康檢查。

(C)　She must be very vain.　她一定很自戀。

* check (tʃɛk) *v.* 檢查；察看　　mirror (ˈmɪrɚ) *n.* 鏡子
　quality (ˈkwɑlətɪ) *n.* 特質
　check-up (ˈtʃɛkˌʌp) *n.* 健康檢查
　vain (ven) *adj.* 虛榮的；自負的；自戀的

9. (**A**) How did you sleep last night?　你昨晚睡得好嗎？

　　(A) Not very well.　不是很好。

　　(B) We won't know for a while.　我們暫時不會知道。

　　(C) I was sleeping when you called last night.
　　　　你昨晚打來的時候我正在睡覺。

　　* while〔hwaɪl〕*n.* 一段時間

10. (**A**) Do your friends want to stay for dinner?
　　　你的朋友們會想要留下來吃晚餐嗎？

　　(A) Let me ask them.　讓我去問他們。

　　(B) I'll take you to dinner.　我會帶你去吃晚餐。

　　(C) Yes, that's my watch.　是的，那是我的手錶。

　　* stay〔ste〕*v.* 停留

第三部分：言談理解（第 11-21 題）

11. (**C**) M：Aren't you running for charity this weekend?

　　　　男：妳這個週末不是要去慈善路跑嗎？

　　　　W：Yes, as a matter of fact I'm running a 5K on Saturday.
　　　　　　It's a benefit for breast cancer research.

　　　　女：是的，其實我星期六要跑五千公尺。是一個為了乳癌研究的
　　　　　　慈善活動。

　　　　M：Oh, cool.　Where will the race be held?

　　　　男：喔，很酷。賽跑會在哪裡舉行？

　　　　W：It starts at Stow Lake in Golden Gate Park, and the
　　　　　　finish line is at Ocean Beach, up at the Cliff House.
　　　　　　They'll have a big tent and several bands are
　　　　　　supposed to play.

　　　　女：從金門公園的斯托湖開始，終點線在海洋沙灘，在上面懸崖
　　　　　　屋那裡。他們會有大帳篷，應該會有好幾個樂團演奏。

Question : What will take place on Saturday?

星期六會舉行什麼活動？

(A) An award ceremony. 頒獎典禮。

(B) A sales promotion. 促銷活動。

(C) A charity event. 慈善活動。

* charity〔'tʃærətɪ〕*n.* 慈善　　weekend〔'wik'ɛnd〕*n.* 週末

as a matter of fact 事實上（ = *in fact* ）

5K 五千公尺（ = *5,000 meters* ）；五公里

benefit〔'bɛnəfɪt〕*n.* 利益；慈善活動

breast〔brɛst〕*n.* 胸部　　cancer〔'kænsə〕*n.* 癌症

breast cancer 乳癌　　research〔'risɝtʃ〕*n.* 研究

cool〔kul〕*adj.* 很酷的　　race〔res〕*n.* 賽跑

hold〔hold〕*v.* 舉辦　　lake〔lek〕*n.* 湖

golden〔'goldn̩〕*adj.* 金色的　　gate〔get〕*n.* 大門

finish line 終點線　　cliff〔klɪf〕*n.* 懸崖

tent〔tɛnt〕*n.* 帳篷　　several〔'sɛvərəl〕*adj.* 幾個的

band〔bænd〕*n.* 樂團　　***be supposed to*** 應該

play〔ple〕*v.* 演奏　　***take place*** 舉行；舉辦

award〔ə'wɔrd〕*n.* 獎　　ceremony〔'sɛrə,monɪ〕*n.* 典禮

sales〔selz〕*adj.* 銷售的

promotion〔prə'moʃən〕*n.* 促銷

event〔ɪ'vɛnt〕*n.* 事件；活動

12. (**A**) M : Hi, Maggie.

男：嗨，瑪姬。

W : Oh, hello, Peter. It's nice to see you again.

女：喔，哈囉，彼得。很高興再次見到你。

M : Long time no see. How long has it been since we took that chemistry class together?

男：好久不見。自從我們一起上化學課以來，已經多久了？

W : Three years? Maybe four.

女：三年？可能四年。

M : Wow, I can't believe how time flies.

男：哇，我無法相信時間過得這麼快。

Question : Who are the speakers? 說話者是什麼關係？

(A) Former classmates. 以前的同學。

(B) Former co-workers. 以前的同事。

(C) Current roommates. 目前的室友。

> ***Long time no see***. 好久不見。
> chemistry〔ˋkɛmɪstrɪ〕*n.* 化學　　together〔təˋgɛðɚ〕*adv.* 一起
> maybe〔ˋmebɪ〕*adv.* 可能　　believe〔bəˋliv〕*v.* 相信
> ***time flies*** 時光飛逝　　former〔ˋfɔrmɚ〕*adj.* 以前的
> co-worker〔͵koˋwɝkɚ〕*n.* 同事　　current〔ˋkɝənt〕*adj.* 目前的
> roommate〔ˋrum͵met〕*n.* 室友

13. (**B**)　M : Were you able to register for all the classes you
　　　　　　　 wanted this semester?

男：妳有登記到妳這學期想要的所有課程嗎？

W : Everything but biology.

女：除了生物學其他都有。

M : Well, that's pretty good. Most people I've talked to
　　 said they got about half the classes they wanted.

男：嗯，還蠻不錯的。大部份我問過的人都說，他們只拿到一半
　　他們想要的課程。

W : Yes, except I need that biology class. I can't graduate
　　 without it.

女：嗯，只是我需要那堂生物課。我沒有它沒辦法畢業。

M : Oh, that's not good. What are you going to do?

男：喔，那就不好了。妳打算怎麼做？

W : I'm going to see my academic advisor this afternoon. Maybe he can <u>pull some strings</u> and get me in.

女：我今天下午要去見我的學術指導老師。說不定他可以靠關係讓我進去。

Question : What does it mean to "pull some strings"?

「靠關係」是什麼意思？

(A) Operate a puppet. 操作木偶。

(B) Use personal influence. <u>利用個人的影響力。</u>

(C) Make a decision. 做決定。

* **be able to V.** 能夠…

register〔'rɛdʒɪstɚ〕v. 登記；報名 < for >

semester〔sə'mɛstɚ〕n. 學期

but〔bʌt〕prep. 除了（= except）

biology〔baɪ'ɑlədʒɪ〕n. 生物學　　pretty〔'prɪtɪ〕adv. 相當

except〔ɪk'sɛpt〕prep. 除了　　graduate〔'grædʒu,et〕v. 畢業

academic〔,ækə'dɛmɪk〕adj. 學院的；學術的

advisor〔əd'vaɪzɚ〕n. 指導老師

pull〔pʊl〕v. 拉　　string〔strɪŋ〕n.（操縱木偶的）線

pull strings 幕後操縱；通過私人關係；暗中運用影響力

operate〔'ɑpə,ret〕v. 操作　　puppet〔'pʌpɪt〕n. 木偶

personal〔'pɝsn̩l〕adj. 個人的

influence〔'ɪnfluəns〕n. 影響力　　decision〔dɪ'sɪʒən〕n. 決定

14. (**C**) W : Good afternoon, Mr. Gordon. How was your trip?

女：午安，戈登先生。您的旅途如何？

M : It was fine, Sue, thanks. Any messages while I was away?

男：很好，蘇，謝謝。我不在的時候有任何留言嗎？

W : Yes, quite a few of them. I put them on your desk.

女：有，相當多。我把它們放在您的辦公桌上了。

Question： Where did Sue put Mr. Gordon's messages?
　　　　　 蘇將戈登先生的留言放在哪裡？

(A) In a computer file. 在電腦的檔案裡。

(B) On the bulletin board. 在佈告欄上。

(C) On his desk. 在他的辦公桌上。

* message〔ˈmɛsɪdʒ〕*n.* 訊息；留言
away〔əˈwe〕*adj.* 不在的；離開的 　*quite a few* 很多
desk〔dɛsk〕*n.* 書桌；辦公桌 　　file〔faɪl〕*n.* 檔案
bulletin〔ˈbʊlətn̩〕*n.* 佈告
board〔bord〕*n.* 木板；布告牌 　*bulletin board* 佈告欄

15. (**A**) A seven-year-old Japanese boy abandoned by his parents in a forest, Yamato Tanooka, told the authorities he walked several kilometers to an empty hut in a military drill area. He said the door was unlocked and water from a faucet outside the hut was his only source of nourishment. He kept warm, he said, by sleeping between mattresses in the hut.

七歲的日本小男孩田野岡大和，被他的父母遺棄在森林裡，他告訴當局，他走了幾公里後，才到達軍事演習區內的一個空的小木屋。他說門沒鎖，而小木屋外的水龍頭的水，是他唯一的食物來源。他說為了保暖，他睡在小木屋裡的床墊中間。

Question： What do we know about Yamato Tanooka?
　　　　　 關於田野岡大和，我們知道什麼？

(A) He's still alive. 他還活著。

(B) He's still missing. 他仍然失蹤。

(C) He's still living in a hut. 他還住在小木屋裡。

* Japanese〔͵dʒæpəˈniz〕*adj.* 日本的

abandon〔ə'bændən〕*v.* 拋棄　　forest〔'fɔrɪst〕*n.* 森林
Yamato Tanooka 田野岡大和
authorities〔ə'θɔrətɪz〕*n. pl.* 當局
kilometer〔'kɪlə,mitə〕*n.* 公里　　empty〔'ɛmptɪ〕*adj.* 空的
hut〔hʌt〕*n.* 小木屋　　military〔'mɪlə,tɛrɪ〕*adj.* 軍事的
drill〔drɪl〕*n.* 演習　　area〔'ɛrɪə〕*n.* 地區
unlocked〔ʌn'lɑkt〕*adj.* 沒鎖的　　faucet〔'fɔsɪt〕*n.* 水龍頭
outside〔'aʊt,saɪd〕*prep.* 在…的外面　　source〔sɔrs〕*n.* 來源
nourishment〔'nɝɪʃmənt〕*n.* 滋養物；食物
warm〔wɔrm〕*adj.* 溫暖的
between〔bə'twin〕*prep.* 在…之間
mattress〔'mætrɪs〕*n.* 床墊　　still〔stɪl〕*adv.* 仍然；還
alive〔ə'laɪv〕*adj.* 活的　　missing〔'mɪsɪŋ〕*adj.* 失蹤的

16. (**A**) W : There's a free concert in the park tonight. Would you like to go?

女：今晚公園裡會有一場免費的演唱會。你想要去嗎？

M : Sure. Who will be performing?

男：當然。有誰會來表演？

W : Two heavy metal bands from Sweden and a famous punk group from Taiwan.

女：兩個來自瑞典的重金屬樂團，和一個台灣知名的龐克樂團。

M : Count me in.

男：算我一個。

Question : What does the man mean by "count me in"?

男士說「算我一個」的意思是什麼？

(A) He will go to the concert.　他會去演唱會。

(B) He will not go to the concert.　他不會去演唱會。

(C) He will be performing at the concert.

他將在演唱會上表演。

* free〔fri〕*adj.* 免費的　concert〔'kɑnsɜt〕*n.* 演唱會
perform〔pɚ'fɔrm〕*v.* 表演　heavy〔'hɛvɪ〕*adj.* 重的
metal〔'mɛtḷ〕*n.* 金屬　band〔bænd〕*n.* 樂團
Sweden〔'swidn̩〕*n.* 瑞典　famous〔'feməs〕*adj.* 有名的
punk〔pʌŋk〕*adj.* 龐克風格的
group〔grup〕*n.* 團體；小演奏樂團　count〔kaʊnt〕*v.* 數；算
count me in 算我一個；我也要加入　mean〔min〕*v.* 意思是

17. (**A**)　W：My school's social club is sponsoring a trip to
Disneyland this summer.

女：今年夏天，我學校的社團會贊助一趟去迪士尼樂園之旅。

M：Are you going?

男：妳會去嗎？

W：No. My schedule this summer is crazy. I've got so
much going on.

女：不會。我今年暑期的行程已經爆滿了。我有太多事要做了。

M：That's too bad. Have you ever been to Disneyland?

男：好可惜。妳去過迪士尼樂園嗎？

W：Yes. That's why I'm not very disappointed about
missing the trip.

女：去過。這就是為什麼我不會因為錯過這趟旅行，而非常失望
的原因。

Question：What does the woman imply? 女士暗示什麼？

(A) She is too busy to go on the trip.

　　她太忙，無法去旅行。

(B) She has never been to Disneyland.

　　她從未去過迪士尼樂園。

(C) She has a fear of flying.　她害怕搭飛機。

* social〔'soʃəl〕*adj.* 社交的　club〔klʌb〕*n.* 社團

social club 社團　　sponsor〔'spɑnsə〕*v.* 贊助
Disneyland〔'dɪznɪ,lænd〕*n.* 迪士尼樂園
schedule〔'skɛdʒul〕*n.* 時間表；行程
crazy〔'krezɪ〕*adj.* 瘋狂的　　***I've got*** 我有（= *I have*）
go on 進行　　***That's too bad.*** 太糟糕了；太可惜了。
disappointed〔,dɪsə'pɔɪntɪd〕*adj.* 失望的
miss〔mɪs〕*v.* 錯過　　imply〔ɪm'plaɪ〕*v.* 暗示
too···to~ 太···以致於不~　　busy〔'bɪzɪ〕*adj.* 忙碌的
go on a trip 去旅行　　fear〔fɪr〕*n.* 恐懼
fly〔flaɪ〕*v.* 飛；搭飛機

18. (**C**) W：What is that sound and where is it coming from?

　　女：那是什麼聲音，是從哪裡傳來的？

　　M：It's the kid upstairs. Apparently, he now plays electric guitar.

　　男：是樓上的孩子。他現在似乎在彈電吉他。

　　W：I'm calling the landlord. This has got to stop.

　　女：我要打給房東。這必須得停止。

　　M：Oh, come on now. He's just a kid. Besides, at least he's doing something productive.

　　男：喔，別這樣啦。他只是個孩子。再說，他至少在做有意義的事。

　　W：I don't see how making all that racket is considered productive.

　　女：我不懂製造這樣的噪音，怎麼可以被認為是有意義的。

　　Question：What does the woman threaten to do?

　　　　　　女士威脅要做什麼？

　　(A) Go upstairs and talk to the boy's parents.

　　　　上樓去跟男孩的父母談一談。

(B) Play the electric guitar. 彈電吉他。

(C) Complain to the building owner about the noise.
    跟這棟大樓的擁有者抱怨這個噪音。

* sound〔saʊnd〕*n.* 聲音　　kid〔kɪd〕*n.* 孩子
  upstairs〔ˈʌpˈstɛrz〕*adv.* 在樓上
  apparently〔əˈpærəntlɪ〕*adv.* 似乎
  play〔ple〕*v.* 彈奏　　electric〔ɪˈlɛktrɪk〕*adj.* 電動的
  guitar〔gɪˈtɑr〕*n.* 吉他　　*electric guitar* 電吉他
  landlord〔ˈlændˌlɔrd〕*n.* 房東　　*have got to V.* 必須…
  come on 別這樣　　just〔dʒʌst〕*adv.* 只是
  besides〔bɪˈsaɪdz〕*adv.* 此外　　*at least* 至少
  productive〔prəˈdʌktɪv〕*adj.* 有生產力的；有意義的
  see〔si〕*v.* 理解　　racket〔ˈrækɪt〕*n.* 喧嘩；吵鬧
  consider〔kənˈsɪdɚ〕*v.* 認為　　threaten〔ˈθrɛtn̩〕*v.* 威脅
  complain〔kəmˈplen〕*v.* 抱怨　　building〔ˈbɪldɪŋ〕*n.* 大樓
  owner〔ˈonɚ〕*n.* 擁有者　　noise〔nɔɪz〕*n.* 噪音

19. (**C**) For most men, this is a chore. It is something we could
    do without. Most of us rush through this task as the last
    thing we do before getting dressed and running out the
    door in the morning. Now, if you're like me and not a
    morning person (and you have a fairly light beard), I
    suggest moving the ritual from morning to night. I've
    found I'm much more likely to slow down and enjoy the
    process at night.

    對大部份的男人來說,這是一件雜事。它是一件我們可以不去做
    的事。我們大部份的人都是在早上穿好衣服,急著跑出門之前,
    會匆忙做好的最後一件事。那麼,如果你跟我一樣,不習慣早起
    (而且你也有相當少的鬍子),我建議你,把這個儀式從早上移
    到晚上。我發現,我晚上更可能放慢速度,享受這個過程。

Question : What is the speaker most likely talking about?

　　　　　說話者很有可能是在談論什麼？

(A) Bathing. 洗澡。

(B) Exercising. 運動。

(C) Shaving. 刮鬍子。

* chore〔tʃor〕*n.* 雜事　　***can do without*** 可以沒有
rush〔rʌʃ〕*v.* 匆促行事　　***rush through*** 匆忙做完
task〔tæsk〕*n.* 任務；工作　　***get dressed*** 穿好衣服
morning person 習慣早起的人　　fairly〔'fɛrlɪ〕*adv.* 相當地
light〔laɪt〕*adj.* 稀少的　　beard〔bɪrd〕*n.* 鬍子
suggest〔səg'dʒɛst〕*v.* 建議　　move〔muv〕*v.* 使移動
ritual〔'rɪtʃuəl〕*n.* 儀式　　likely〔'laɪklɪ〕*adj.* 有可能的
slow down 減低速度　　enjoy〔ɪn'dʒɔɪ〕*v.* 享受
process〔'prɑsɛs〕*n.* 過程　　bathe〔beð〕*v.* 洗澡
exercise〔'ɛksɚ͵saɪz〕*v.* 運動　　shave〔ʃev〕*v.* 刮鬍子

20. (**B**)　W : You're home early. What's going on?

　　　　女：你今天很早回家。怎麼了嗎？

　　　　M : I'm not feeling very well.

　　　　男：我覺得不太舒服。

　　　　W : Do you need to see a doctor?

　　　　女：你需要去看醫生嗎？

　　　　M : No, I don't think so. I just need to get some rest.

　　　　男：不，我覺得應該不用。我只需要休息一下。

　　　　Question : Why is the man home early?

　　　　　　　　　為什麼男士這麼早回家？

　　　(A) The boss sent everyone home. 老闆要所有人回家。

　　　(B) He doesn't feel well. 他覺得不舒服。

　　　(C) He has a doctor's appointment. 他有跟醫生預約門診。

* early 〔'ɜlɪ〕 *adv.* 早　　***go on*** 發生
　well 〔wɛl〕 *adj.* 健康的；安好的　　rest 〔rɛst〕 *n.* 休息
　boss 〔bɔs〕 *n.* 老闆　　send 〔sɛnd〕 *v.* 派遣；安排去
　appointment 〔ə'pɔɪntmənt〕 *n.* 預約（門診）

21. (**C**)　I consider myself lucky to have had Walt Walker as my basketball coach. From Coach Walker, I learned that the phrase "I can't" needed to be removed from my language. He taught me that the way you play basketball is the way you live your life. If you play hard and give everything you have on the basketball court, then you should do the same in life.

　　我認為自己很幸運，有華特沃克當我的籃球教練。從沃克教練那裡，我學到了「我沒辦法」這個片語，必須從我的語言中除去。他教導我，你打籃球的方式，就是你的生活方式。如果你在籃球場上努力打球，付出一切，那麼你在生活中，同樣也要這麼做。

　　Question : What phrase needed to be removed from the woman's language?
　　　　　　　什麼片語需要從女士的語言中除去？

(A) I will. 我會。

(B) I won't. 我不會。

(C) I can't. 我沒辦法。

* consider 〔kən'sɪdə〕 *v.* 認為　　lucky 〔'lʌkɪ〕 *adj.* 幸運的
　Walt Walker 〔'wɔlt'wɔlkə〕 *n.* 華特沃克
　basketball 〔'bæskɪt,bɔl〕 *n.* 籃球　　coach 〔kotʃ〕 *n.* 教練
　phrase 〔frez〕 *n.* 片語　　remove 〔rɪ'muv〕 *v.* 除去
　language 〔'læŋgwɪdʒ〕 *n.* 語言　　way 〔we〕 *n.* 方式
　play 〔ple〕 *v.* 打（球）　　***live~life*** 過~生活
　hard 〔hɑrd〕 *adv.* 努力地　　court 〔kort〕 *n.* 球場
　same 〔sem〕 *adj.* 同樣的　　***the same*** 同樣的人、事、物

TEST 20 ▸ 詳解

第一部分：辨識句意（第 1-3 題）

1. (**C**) (A) (B) (C)

Mike is sitting at his desk and writing a thank-you note to his teacher. 麥克正坐在書桌前，寫一封感謝函給他的老師。

* note〔not〕*n.* 短信　　***thank-you note*** 感謝函

2. (**A**) (A) (B) (C)

Tom is taking a picture of his dog as it drinks from a bowl of milk. 湯姆正在拍他的狗喝一碗牛奶的照片。

* ***taking a picture*** 拍照　　bowl〔bol〕*n.* 碗

3. (**A**) (A) (B) (C)

The teacher has called upon a student to answer a question. 老師叫了一位同學回答問題。

* **call upon** 叫   question〔'kwɛstʃən〕*n.* 問題

第二部分：基本問答（第 4-10 題）

4. (**B**) With so many universities to choose from, why do you want to attend Harvard?

有這麼多大學可以選，你為什麼想要唸哈佛？

(A) They offer retirement benefits. 他們提供退休福利。

(B) It has an excellent reputation. 它有很棒的名聲。

(C) I've been unemployed for a year. 我已經失業一年了。

* university〔,junə'vɝsətɪ〕*n.* 大學
choose〔tʃuz〕*v.* 選擇；挑選   attend〔ə'tɛnd〕*v.* 上（學）
Harvard〔'hɑrvəd〕*n.* 哈佛   offer〔'ɔfɚ〕*v.* 提供
retirement〔rɪ'taɪrmənt〕*n.* 退休
benefits〔'bɛnəfɪts〕*n. pl.* 津貼；福利
excellent〔'ɛkslənt〕*adj.* 優秀的；極好的
reputation〔,rɛpjə'teʃən〕*n.* 名聲
unemployed〔,ʌnɪm'plɔɪd〕*adj.* 失業的

5. (**A**) Listen! They're playing our favorite song.

你聽！他們正在播放我們最喜愛的歌。

(A) No, you must be thinking of someone else. I hate that song. 不，你一定搞錯人了。我討厭那首歌。

(B) Yes, we can play all your favorites. Name a few.
是的，我們可以播放所有你最喜愛的歌。你就說個幾首吧。

(C) Maybe they're free. Ask someone.
也許他們有空。去問問看。

* play〔ple〕*v.* 播放
favorite〔'fevərɪt〕*adj.* 最喜愛的   *n.* 最喜愛的人或物

else〔εls〕*adj.* 別的；其他的　　must〔mʌst〕*aux.* 一定
think of 想到　　hate〔het〕*v.* 討厭
name〔nem〕*v.* 說出⋯的名字　　***a few*** 一些
free〔fri〕*adj.* 有空的

6. (**A**) Excuse me, I think this is yours. It fell out of your purse.
不好意思，我想這應該是你的。它是從你的皮包裡掉出來的。

(A) Oh, thank you so much! 喔，非常感謝你！

(B) Wow, that's a lot! 哇，那很多耶！

(C) See, I told you! 你看吧，我告訴過你！

* fall〔fɔl〕*v.* 掉落　　purse〔pɝs〕*n.* 皮包
wow〔waʊ〕*interj.* 哇　　***a lot*** 很多

7. (**B**) What is the Tasty? 西堤牛排是什麼？

(A) It is on my way home. 它就在我回家的路上。

(B) It is a big restaurant. 它是一間很大的餐廳。

(C) It is excellent. 它很棒。

* Tasty〔'testɪ〕*n.* 西堤牛排【餐廳名】
on *one's* ***way home*** 在某人回家的路上

8. (**A**) Would you mind helping me with this box?
你介意幫我搬這個箱子嗎？

(A) Sorry. I didn't notice you were having a hard time
with it. 抱歉。我沒發現你搬得這麼辛苦。

(B) That's OK. Put it in the box.
沒關係。把它放進箱子裡。

(C) No. We don't need it any more.
不。我們不再需要它了。

* mind〔maɪnd〕*v.* 介意　　notice〔'notɪs〕*v.* 注意到
having a hard time 很辛苦　　***not⋯any more*** 不再⋯

9. (**B**) What did you have for lunch? 你午餐吃了什麼？

   (A) Twelve. 十二。

   (B) Sushi. 壽司。

   (C) Wednesday. 星期三。

   * have〔hæv〕*v.* 吃　　sushi〔'susɪ〕*n.* 壽司

10. (**C**) How was baseball practice? 棒球練習得如何？

   (A) We lost. 我們輸了。

   (B) Nine players on each team. 每隊有九個球員。

   (C) It was a lot of fun. 很有趣。

   * baseball〔'bes,bɔl〕*n.* 棒球　　practice〔'præktɪs〕*n.* 練習
   lose〔luz〕*v.* 輸　　player〔'pleɚ〕*n.* 選手；球員
   each〔itʃ〕*adj.* 每個　　team〔tim〕*n.* 隊
   fun〔fʌn〕*n.* 樂趣；有趣

第三部分：言談理解（第 11-21 題）

11. (**B**) Since the mid-2000s, mate-finding and courtship have seen changes due to online dating services. Computer technologies have developed rapidly since around 1995, allowing daters the use of mobile phones and web-based systems to find partners.

   自從 2004、2005 年以來，找伴侶和追求對象，已經因為網路交友的服務而產生了一些變化。大約自 1995 年以來，電腦科技迅速發展，讓約會的人能使用行動電話和網路系統來尋找對象。

   Question：According to the speaker, where are many people finding their partners?

   根據說話者的說法，很多人都在哪裡找對象？

   (A) At social events. 在社交活動。

(B) On the Internet. 在網路上。

(C) At work. 在工作場所。

* since〔sɪns〕*prep.* 自從　　mid〔mɪd〕*adj.* 中間的
   the mid-2000s 2004 年或 2005 年【the 2000s 是指 2000 年～2009 年
   的十年期間】　　mate〔met〕*n.* 配偶
   courtship〔'kortˌʃɪp〕*n.* 追求　　see〔si〕*v.* 經歷
   change〔tʃendʒ〕*v.* 改變；變化　　***due to*** 由於
   online〔'ɑnˌlaɪn〕*adj.* 線上的；網路上的
   date〔det〕*v.* 約會　　service〔'sɝvɪs〕*n.* 服務
   online dating service 線上交友軟體；網路交友的服務
   technology〔tɛk'nɑlədʒɪ〕*n.* 科技
   develop〔dɪ'vɛləp〕*v.* 發展　　rapidly〔'ræpɪdlɪ〕*adv.* 快速地
   around〔ə'raʊnd〕*adv.* 大約；…左右
   allow〔ə'laʊ〕*v.* 允許；給予；提供　　dater〔'detɚ〕*n.* 約會者
   mobile〔'mobḷ〕*adj.* 移動的
   mobile phone 行動電話；手機 (= *cell phone*)
   web〔wɛb〕*n.* 網路　　based〔best〕*adj.* 以…為根據地的
   web-based *adj.* 網路的　　system〔'sɪstəm〕*n.* 系統
   partner〔'pɑrtnɚ〕*n.* 配偶；伴侶；對象
   according to 根據　　social〔'soʃəl〕*adj.* 社交的
   event〔ɪ'vɛnt〕*n.* 活動　　Internet〔'ɪntɚˌnɛt〕*n.* 網際網路

12. (**A**) W : What are you doing, Mike? Stretching before a run?

　　　女：你在做什麼，麥可？做跑步前的伸展嗎？

　　　M : No, I'm doing yoga.

　　　男：不是，我是在做瑜伽。

　　　W : Yoga?

　　　女：瑜伽？

　　　M : Yes, yoga. I'm learning it in my PE class. It's kind
　　　　　of like stretching, except you hold certain poses for a
　　　　　period of time. What I'm doing now is called
　　　　　Monkey Steals the Peach.

男：是的，瑜伽。我在上體育課時學的。有點像伸展，只是某些姿勢需要維持一段時間。我現在做的叫作「猴子偷桃」。

Question：What are the speakers discussing?
說話者正在討論什麼？

(A) A type of exercise. 一種運動。

(B) A species of animal. 一種動物。

(C) A place of business. 一個營業場所。

* stretch〔strɛtʃ〕v. 伸展手腳　　run〔rʌn〕n. 跑
yoga〔'jogə〕n. 瑜伽　　**PE** 體育課（= *physical education*）
kind of 有點　　except〔ɪk'sɛpt〕prep. 除了；只是
hold〔hold〕v. 保持；維持　　certain〔'sɜtn̩〕adj. 某些
pose〔poz〕n. 姿勢　　period〔'pɪrɪəd〕n. 期間
a period of time 一段時間　　peach〔pitʃ〕n. 桃子
Monkey Steals the Peach 猴子偷桃【一種武術的姿勢】
discuss〔dɪ'skʌs〕v. 討論　　type〔taɪp〕n. 類型
exercise〔'ɛksə,saɪz〕n. 運動
species〔'spiʃɪz〕n.（動植物分類上的）種【單複數同形】
business〔'bɪznɪs〕n. 商業；營業

13. (**A**) The relation between older and younger generations can be compared to that of a freshman and a senior in high school. The senior has just experienced all there is to high school. The freshman is new to the system and unaware of what is to be expected in the coming years. As the older individual in the situation, the senior is responsible for teaching the freshman; in return, the freshman shows appreciation.
較年長與較年輕世代之間的關係，可以比喻成高中的高一生和高三生之間的關係。高三已經經歷過所有的高中生活。高一生對於

高中很陌生，不知道要對未來的幾年有什麼樣的期待。在這種情況下，較年長的高三生，有責任要敎導高一生；而高一生則要表示感謝，作爲回報。

Question : What is the senior expected to do?

高三生必須要做什麼？

(A) Teach the freshman.　敎導高一生。

(B) Compare the freshman.　比較高一生。

(C) Bully the freshman.　欺負高一生。

* relation〔rɪ'leʃən〕*n.* 關係

　generation〔͵dʒɛnə'reʃən〕*n.* 世代

　compare〔kəm'pɛr〕*v.* 比較；比喻

　freshman〔'frɛʃmən〕*n.* 高一學生

　senior〔'sinjɚ〕*n.* 高三學生

　experience〔ɪk'spɪrɪəns〕*v.* 經歷　　system〔'sɪstəm〕*n.* 制度

　unaware〔͵ʌnə'wɛr〕*adj.* 不知道的 < *of* >

　expect〔ɪk'spɛkt〕*v.* 期待

　coming〔'kʌmɪŋ〕*adj.* 即將來臨的

　individual〔͵ɪndə'vɪdʒʊəl〕*n.* 個人

　situation〔͵sɪtʃu'eʃən〕*n.* 情況

　responsible〔rɪ'spɑnsəbl̩〕*adj.* 有責任的 < *for* >

　in return　作爲回報　　show〔ʃo〕*v.* 表示

　appreciation〔ə͵priʃɪ'eʃən〕*n.* 感激

　bully〔'bʊlɪ〕*v.* 霸凌；欺負

14. (**C**) M : I'm back, Janice. I got the stuff you wanted from the store.

男：我回來了，珍妮絲。我去商店買了妳要的東西。

W : Wonderful! But I noticed you didn't bring the list with you.

女：太棒了！但我發現你沒把購物清單帶去。

M : No, I didn't need it.

男：沒有，我不需要它。

Question : What does the man imply? 男士在暗示什麼？

(A) He is handy with tools. 他對使用工具很在行。

(B) He is good with money. 他善於理財。

(C) He has a good memory. <u>他有很好的記憶力。</u>

* stuff〔stʌf〕*n.* 東西　　wonderful〔'wʌndəfəl〕*adj.* 很棒的
　notice〔'notɪs〕*v.* 注意到　　bring〔brɪŋ〕*v.* 帶
　list〔lɪst〕*n.*（購物）清單　　imply〔ɪm'plaɪ〕*v.* 暗示
　handy〔'hændɪ〕*adj.* 手巧的；在行的　　tool〔tul〕*n.* 工具
　good〔gʊd〕*adj.* 擅長的　　*be good with money* 善於理財
　memory〔'mɛmərɪ〕*n.* 記憶力

15. (**B**) M : Did you hear about John?

　　男：妳有聽說關於約翰的事嗎？

　　W : Yes, he had a terrible accident. Do you know if he's
　　　　going to be OK?

　　女：有，他發生了一場很嚴重的意外。你知道他是否會康復嗎？

　　M : I think he's going to pull through.

　　男：我覺得他會恢復健康的。

　　Question : What does the man imply? 男士在暗示什麼？

　　(A) John had it coming. 這是約翰自找的。

　　(B) John will probably survive. <u>約翰可能會活下來。</u>

　　(C) John is a poor driver. 約翰的開車技術很差。

　　* *hear about* 聽說關於⋯的事
　　　terrible〔'tɛrəbḷ〕*adj.* 可怕的；嚴重的
　　　accident〔'æksədənt〕*n.* 意外
　　　OK〔'o'ke〕*adj.* 好的；沒問題的　　*pull through* 恢復健康
　　　sb. had it coming 某人自找的；某人罪有應得

probably〔'prɑbəblɪ〕*adv.* 可能
survive〔sə'vaɪv〕*v.* 生還；存活　　poor〔pur〕*adj.* 差勁的
driver〔'draɪvə〕*n.* 駕駛人

16. (**A**) I've been trying to go through life the last year and a half
without a cell phone. I tell you... that's hard in this day
and age. People expect you to have a phone. I miss
school calls telling me my kids are sick. I miss doctors
calling back with important information. Cell phones are
an important piece of technology if you are to live in this
world today.

我在過去的一年半，嘗試過著沒有手機的生活。我告訴你…在今
天這個時代，那很困難。人們預期你會有手機。我錯過學校打來
通知說我的孩子生病了。我錯過醫生回電告訴我重要的資訊。如
果你要活在現今的世界裡，手機真的是一個很重要的科技產品。

Question：What do we know about the man?

關於男士我們知道什麼？

(A) He has kids. 他有孩子。

(B) He works full-time. 他有全職工作。

(C) He lives in the city. 他住在城市裡。

* ***go through*** 經歷　　***cell phone*** 手機
hard〔hɑrd〕*adj.* 困難的
in this day and age 在今天這個時代；當今
expect〔ɪk'spɛkt〕*v.* 預期　　miss〔mɪs〕*v.* 錯過
sick〔sɪk〕*adj.* 生病的　　***call back*** 再打電話；以電話回覆
important〔ɪm'pɔrtn̩t〕*adj.* 重要的
information〔ˌɪnfə'meʃən〕*n.* 資訊
piece〔pis〕*n.* 一件　　technology〔tɛk'nɑlədʒɪ〕*n.* 科技
be to V. 預定要…；必須要…
full-time〔'fʊl'taɪm〕*adv.* 全職地　　city〔'sɪtɪ〕*n.* 城市

17. (**B**) M : Can you recommend a decent restaurant in the area?

男：妳可以推薦這一區一家不錯的餐廳嗎？

W : That depends on what you'd like to eat.

女：那要看你想吃什麼。

M : I'm open to just about anything, as long as it's good.

男：只要是好吃的，我幾乎什麼都吃。

W : There's an Indian place just up the street called New Delhi Palace. That's where I would go if I were you.

女：在這條街上有家印度餐廳叫新德里宮。如果我是你，我會去那裡。

Question : What does the man want to do?

男士想做什麼？

(A) Get some rest. 休息一下。

(B) Get something to eat. 吃點東西。

(C) Open a new restaurant. 開一家新的餐廳。

* recommend (ˌrɛkəˈmɛnd) v. 推薦
  decent (ˈdisn̩t) adj. 高尚的；不錯的   area (ˈɛrɪə) n. 地區
  depend on 視…而定   *would like* 想要
  be open to 願意接受   *just about* 幾乎
  as long as 只要   Indian (ˈɪndɪən) adj. 印度的
  place (ples) n. 地方；餐廳
  up (ʌp) prep. 沿…而去   street (strit) n. 街
  New Delhi (njuˈdɛlɪ) n. 新德里
  palace (ˈpælɪs) n. 宮殿   rest (rɛst) n. 休息

18. (**C**) M : Do you ever watch NBA basketball?

男：妳曾經看過 NBA 籃球嗎？

W : Sometimes. Why?

女：有時候。爲什麼這麼問？

M : There's an incredible player named Jeremy Lin. He's the first Taiwanese to play in the NBA.

男：有一位很棒的球員叫作林書豪。他是第一位在 NBA 打球的台灣人。

W : Yes, I think I've heard of him. "Linsanity" and all that. He's been around for a while, right?

女：是的，我想我聽說過他。「林來瘋」什麼的。他已經出名一陣子了，對吧？

Question : What is special about Jeremy Lin?

林書豪有什麼特別的？

(A) He's better than Kobe Bryant.

他比柯比・布萊恩厲害。

(B) He's taller than Yao Ming.　他比姚明高。

(C) He's the first Taiwanese to play in the NBA.

他是第一位在 NBA 打球的台灣人。

* ever〔ˋɛvɚ〕*adv.* 曾經

NBA 國家籃球協會 (*= National Basketball Association*)

basketball〔ˋbæskɪt͵bɔl〕*n.* 籃球

sometimes〔ˋsʌm͵taɪmz〕*adv.* 有時候

incredible〔ɪnˋkrɛdəbḷ〕*adj.* 令人無法置信的；很棒的

player〔ˋpleɚ〕*n.* 球員　　***named*** ~ 名叫~

Jeremy Lin 林書豪　　Taiwanese〔͵taɪwɑˋniz〕*n.* 台灣人

hear of 聽說　　Linsanity〔lɪnˋsænətɪ〕*n.* 林來瘋

and all that …等等；諸如此類的；什麼的

around〔əˋraʊnd〕*adj.* 存在著的；活躍的；被見到的

a while （短暫的）時間　　special〔ˋspɛʃəl〕*adj.* 特別的

Kobe Bryant 柯比・布萊恩　　***Yao Ming*** 姚明

19. (**C**) W : How was your date with Kim last night?

女：你昨天跟金的約會如何？

M : It wasn't a date. We're just friends.

男：那不是約會。我們只是朋友。

W : Since when do you take your "friends" to dinner and a movie?

女：你從什麼時候開始會帶你的「朋友」去吃飯還有看電影？

M : Look, it's not what you think. We went Dutch on everything.

男：妳聽我說，不是妳想的那樣。我們全部都是各付各的。

Question : What happened on the man's date with Kim?

男士與金的約會發生了什麼事？

(A) They split the bill at dinner. 他們晚餐各付各的。

(B) The shared the cost of the movie.

他們分擔了電影的費用。

(C) Both of the above. <u>以上兩者皆是。</u>

* date〔det〕 *n.* 約會   look〔lʊk〕 *interj.* 你看；聽我說
Dutch〔dʌtʃ〕 *adj.* 荷蘭的   ***go Dutch*** 各付各的
split〔splɪt〕 *v.* 分攤   bill〔bɪl〕 *n.* 帳單
share〔ʃɛr〕 *v.* 分擔   cost〔kɔst〕 *n.* 費用
above〔ə'bʌv〕 *adj.* 上面的；上述的
the above 上述；以上

20. (**B**) M : Why is Mona wearing a mask? Is she ill?

男：為什麼蒙娜戴著口罩？她生病了嗎？

W : No. But a couple of her classmates are sick and she's afraid she'll catch something.

女：不是。但是她有幾個同學生病了，所以她怕會被傳染。

M : Well, it is the cold and flu season. But that mask isn't going to help her. The key to staying healthy is washing your hands frequently.

男：嗯，現在正是感冒和流感的季節。但是那個口罩無法幫助
　　她。保持健康的關鍵就是勤洗手。

Question：What do we know about Mona?
　　　　　關於蒙娜我們知道什麼？

(A) She is ill. 她生病了。

(B) She is a student. 她是個學生。

(C) She is careless. 她很粗心。

* wear〔wɛr〕v. 戴著　　mask〔mæsk〕n. 面具；口罩
　ill〔ɪl〕adj. 生病的　　*a couple of* 幾個的
　sick〔sɪk〕adj. 生病的　　afraid〔ə'fred〕adj. 害怕的
　catch〔kætʃ〕v. 感染　　cold〔kold〕n. 感冒
　flu〔flu〕n. 流行性感冒　　season〔'sizn̩〕n. 活躍季節；旺季
　key〔ki〕n. 關鍵　　*the key to N./V-ing* …的關鍵
　stay〔ste〕v. 保持　　healthy〔'hɛlθɪ〕adj. 健康的
　frequently〔'frikwəntlɪ〕adv. 經常地
　careless〔'kɛrlɪs〕adj. 粗心的

21. (**B**) W：Would you mind sharing your notes with me?
　　　　　女：你介意跟我分享你的筆記嗎？
　　　　　M：Not at all.　I'll e-mail them to you.　What's your
　　　　　　　address?
　　　　　男：一點也不。我會用電子郵件把它們寄給妳。妳的地址是什麼？
　　　　　W：Which would you prefer?　TSN, Baboo! or MOL?
　　　　　女：你比較喜歡用哪一個？TSN、Baboo! 還是 MOL？
　　　　　M：Geez, why so many?
　　　　　男：天啊，怎麼會這麼多？
　　　　　W：Well, I use TSN for my friends, Baboo! for my
　　　　　　　family, and MOL for school.

女：嗯，我通常用 TSN 跟朋友聯絡，Baboo! 跟家人，MOL 跟同學。

M : Then I guess I fall in the MOL category?

男：那我猜我是屬於 MOL 的類別？

W : No, silly! Send it to butterfly sixty-nine at TSN.

女：不是啦，傻瓜！你寄到 TSN 的 butterfly sixty-nine。

Question : What does the woman imply?

女士在暗示什麼？

(A) She considers the man part of the family.

她認為男士是家人的一部份。

(B) She considers the man to be a friend.

她認為男士是朋友。

(C) She considers the man to be nothing more than a classmate. 她認為男士只是同班同學。

* mind〔maɪnd〕v. 介意　　share〔ʃɛr〕v. 分享
note〔not〕n. 筆記　　***not at all*** 一點也不
e-mail〔'i‚mel〕v. 用電子郵件寄　　address〔ə'drɛs〕n. 地址
prefer〔prɪ'fɝ〕v. 比較喜歡
geez〔dʒiz〕*interj.* 哎呀；天啊（ = *jeez*）
guess〔gɛs〕v. 猜　　***fall in*** 屬於
category〔'kætə‚gorɪ〕n. 類別；範疇　　silly〔'sɪlɪ〕n. 傻瓜
send〔sɛnd〕v. 寄　　imply〔ɪm'plaɪ〕v. 暗示
consider〔kən'sɪdɚ〕v. 認為
consider *A* (***to be***) *B* 認為 A 是 B　　part〔pɑrt〕n. 部份
nothing more than 只是（ = *only*）

第一部分：辨識句意（第 1-3 題）

1. (**C**) (A) (B) (C)

Hank met a blind man on the street and gave him some money. 漢克在街上遇見一位盲人，並給了他一些錢。

　　* meet〔mit〕v. 遇見　　blind〔blaınd〕adj. 盲的

2. (**C**) (A) (B) (C)

Suzie saw a turtle, which made her angry for some reason. 蘇西看到了一隻烏龜，但因為某個原因使她很生氣。

　　* turtle〔'tɝtl̩〕n. 烏龜　　angry〔'æŋgrı〕adj. 生氣的
　　some〔sʌm〕adj. 某個　　reason〔'rizn̩〕n. 原因；理由

3. (**A**) (A) (B) (C)

Ken is sitting in front of the TV, playing video games.

肯正坐在電視前面打電動。

* *in front of* 在…前面　　*video game* 電動玩具；電動遊戲

第二部分：基本問答（第 4-10 題）

4. (**C**) Jerry is the most charming and handsome man I've ever met. 傑瑞是我見過最迷人而且帥氣的男人。

   (A) She should lose a few pounds. 她應該再瘦個幾磅。

   (B) She is a charming young lady. 她是一位迷人的小姐。

   (C) I don't find him attractive at all.

      <u>我完全不覺得他吸引人。</u>

   * charming (ˈtʃɑrmɪŋ) *adj.* 迷人的
     handsome (ˈhænsəm) *adj.* 英俊的
     lose (luz) *v.* 失去；瘦　　pound (paund) *n.* 磅
     lady (ˈledɪ) *n.* 女士；小姐　　*not…at all* 一點也不…
     find (faɪnd) *v.* 覺得　　attractive (əˈtræktɪv) *adj.* 吸引人的

5. (**C**) When will we be taking off? Why are we still sitting on the runway? 我們什麼時候起飛？為什麼我們還在跑道上？

   (A) Relax. Take your time. 放輕鬆。慢慢來。

   (B) Not now. I need to sit down.

      現在不要。我需要先坐下。

   (C) Calm down. The captain said there will be a brief delay. <u>冷靜下來。機長說會稍微延遲。</u>

   * *take off* 起飛　　sit (sɪt) *v.* 坐；位於
     runway (ˈrʌnˌwe) *n.* 跑道　　relax (rɪˈlæks) *v.* 放鬆
     take one's time 慢慢來　　*calm down* 冷靜
     captain (ˈkæptən) *n.* 機長　　brief (brif) *adj.* 短暫的
     delay (dɪˈle) *n.* 延遲

6. (**C**) Do you enjoy visiting museums and art galleries?

你喜歡參觀博物館和美術館嗎?

(A) Art and science. 藝術與科學。

(B) It was sold out. 它已經賣完了。

(C) Sometimes. 有時候。

* enjoy〔ɪn'dʒɔɪ〕v. 喜歡　　visit〔'vɪzɪt〕v. 參觀
museum〔mju'ziəm〕n. 博物館　　art〔art〕n. 藝術
gallery〔'gælərɪ〕n. 畫廊;美術館
science〔'saɪəns〕n. 科學　　*sold out* 賣完了

7. (**B**) Were you surprised that the exam was cancelled?

考試被取消時你有很驚訝嗎?

(A) One at a time. 一次一個。

(B) Shocked is more like it. 震驚還差不多。

(C) You should work hard and play hard.

你應該努力工作,並且拼命玩樂。

* surprised〔sə'praɪzd〕adj. 驚訝的
exam〔ɪg'zæm〕n. 考試　　cancel〔'kænsl〕v. 取消
at a time 一次　　shocked〔ʃɑkt〕adj. 震驚的
…is more like it …還差不多
hard〔hard〕adv. 努力地;拼命地

8. (**A**) Henry, would you please turn down your radio?

亨利,可以請你把收音機關小聲一點嗎?

(A) Sorry, Mom. There, is that better?

對不起,媽。這樣,有好一點嗎?

(B) But I finished my homework, Mom.

但是我做完功課了,媽。

(C) Aren't you going to help me, Mom?

妳不打算來幫我嗎,媽?

* ***turn down*** 關小聲　　radio〔'redɪ,o〕*n.* 收音機
there〔ðɛr〕*interj.* 你瞧；好啦；怎麼樣
finish〔'fɪnɪʃ〕*v.* 做完

9. (**B**) What happened to the ice cream? I just brought home a
half gallon of Frazier's Choco-chunk last night.
冰淇淋發生了什麼事？昨晚我才剛把半加侖的 Frazier's Choco-
chunk 巧克力脆片口味的冰淇淋帶回家。

(A) Jimmy drank it all. 吉米把它喝完了。

(B) Jimmy ate it all. <u>吉米把它吃完了。</u>

(C) Jimmy cooked it all. 吉米把它煮完了。

* happen〔'hæpən〕*v.* 發生　　***ice cream*** 冰淇淋
gallon〔'gælən〕*n.* 加侖【容量單位】
Frazier's Choco-chunk 巧克力脆片牌子的冰淇淋

10. (**B**) How come your hair always looks perfect?
為什麼你的頭髮總是看起來這麼完美？

(A) I spend a lot of time there. 我花很多時間在那裡。

(B) Actually, this is a wig. <u>事實上，這是一頂假髮。</u>

(C) Thanks. I just made it. 謝謝。我剛剛做的。

* ***How come*** + *S.* + *V.?* 為什麼～？　　look〔luk〕*v.* 看起來
perfect〔'pɝfɪkt〕*adj.* 完美的　　spend〔spɛnd〕*v.* 花（時間）
actually〔'æktʃuəlɪ〕*adv.* 事實上　　wig〔wɪg〕*n.* 假髮

第三部分：言談理解（第 11-21 題）

11. (**A**) M：Hi, Carol. I was surprised you didn't attend the
company picnic.
男：嗨，卡蘿。我很驚訝妳沒參加公司的野餐。

W：Yes, I'm sorry to have missed it. Freddie had a
terrible cold and I couldn't leave him alone.

女：是的，我很遺憾就這樣錯過了。弗雷迪得了重感冒，我不能不管他。

M：Oh, that's too bad. Is he feeling better now?

男：喔，那真糟糕。他現在有沒有好一點？

W：I think so. The doctor said he can go back to school next week.

女：我想應該有。醫生說他下禮拜就可以回去上學了。

Question：Who are the speakers? 說話者是什麼關係？

(A) Co-workers. 同事。

(B) Classmates. 同學。

(C) Neighbors. 鄰居。

* attend〔ə'tɛnd〕*v.* 參加　　company〔'kʌmpənɪ〕*n.* 公司
  picnic〔'pɪknɪk〕*n.* 野餐　　miss〔mɪs〕*v.* 錯過
  terrible〔'tɛrəbl̩〕*adj.* 可怕的；嚴重的
  cold〔kold〕*n.* 感冒　　alone〔ə'lon〕*adj.* 單獨的；獨自的
  have…alone 不理會…；不管…
  co-worker〔ˌko'wɝkɚ〕*n.* 同事　　neighbor〔'nebɚ〕*n.* 鄰居

12. (**A**) M：In Taiwan, is it considered impolite to ask someone how much they make?

男：在台灣，問一個人賺多少錢會被認為很沒禮貌嗎？

W：Um, I don't know. I mean, I think people talk about it all the time, don't they?

女：嗯，我不知道。我的意思是，我想人們隨時都在談論它，不是嗎？

M：Back home, it's not something you should ask a complete stranger.

男：在我的家鄉，這不是一件應該問陌生人的事。

W：Well, no, of course. You wouldn't want to do that here, either. Why do you ask?

女：嗯，當然不是。你在這裡也不會想要這麼做。你怎麼會這麼問？

M : I'm just trying to figure out the culture. I met a woman the other day and it was one of the first things she asked me.

男：我只是想要了解這裡的文化。我前幾天認識一位女士，而這是她最先問我的問題之一。

W : How queer! That's definitely not normal.

女：真奇怪！那的確不太正常。

Question : What is the man interested in?

男士對什麼感興趣？

(A) Taiwanese culture. 台灣的文化。

(B) Taiwanese food. 台灣的食物。

(C) Taiwanese women. 台灣的女人。

* consider〔kən'sɪdɚ〕*v.* 認為
  impolite〔,ɪmpə'laɪt〕*adj.* 無禮的　　make〔mek〕*v.* 賺（錢）
  um〔ʌm〕*interj.* 啊；嗯　　mean〔min〕*v.* 意思是
  talk about 談論　　**all the time** 一直
  back home 在家鄉　　complete〔kəm'plit〕*adj.* 完全的
  stranger〔'strendʒɚ〕*n.* 陌生人　　**of course** 當然
  either〔'iðɚ〕*adv.* 也（不）　　**figure out** 了解
  culture〔'kʌltʃɚ〕*n.* 文化　　**the other day** 前幾天
  meet〔mit〕*v.* 認識　　queer〔kwɪr〕*adj.* 奇怪的
  definitely〔'dɛfənɪtlɪ〕*adv.* 的確
  normal〔'nɔrml̩〕*adj.* 正常的
  interested〔'ɪntərɪstɪd〕*adj.* 感興趣的＜*in*＞
  Taiwanese〔,taɪwɑ'niz〕*adj.* 台灣的

13. (**C**) M : Do you remember the first time you ever kissed a boy?

男：妳記得妳生平第一次跟男生接吻嗎？

W : Yes, I was 16. His name was Jacob Fuller. What about you? Do you remember the first time you kissed a girl?

女：是的，我當時十六歲。他的名字叫作雅各‧富勒。那你呢？你記得你跟女生的第一次接吻嗎？

M : I didn't even hold hands with a girl until I was 18. My first kiss came sometime after that, while I was in college. I couldn't tell you her name, though.

男：我直到十八歲才跟女孩子牽手。沒多久後我就有了我的初吻，當時我在唸大學。不過我不能告訴妳她的名字。

Question : When did the man get his first kiss?
男士什麼時候有了他的初吻？

(A) At 16. 十六歲。

(B) At 18. 十八歲。

(C) At some point in college. 在上大學的某個時刻。

* time〔taɪm〕*n.* 次　　ever〔'ɛvɚ〕*adv.* 曾經；有史以來
kiss〔kɪs〕*v. n.* 接吻　　*What about~?* ～如何？
not…until 直到～才…　　*hold hands* 牽手
come〔kʌm〕*v.* 出現；發生
sometime〔'sʌm,taɪm〕*adv.* 某時　　college〔'kɑlɪdʒ〕*n.* 大學
though〔ðo〕*adv.* 不過【置於句尾】
some〔sʌm〕*adj.* 某個　　point〔pɔɪnt〕*n.* 時刻

14. (**B**) For any parent who has looked with pity upon their teenage children as they drag themselves out of bed at 6:00 a.m. each day, there is a way to help. Be pro-active and approach your school board with pleas for a later start to the high school day. Not only will our students be healthier and more successful at tasks in school, they will become nicer individuals.

對於任何用憐憫的眼光，看著自己十幾歲的小孩，每天早上六點就要起床的父母而言，其實有一種改善的方式。只要積極主動去接近學校董事會，請求讓高中生晚點上課。那樣我們的學生不僅會更健康，而且學業會更傑出，也會成爲更好的人。

Question：What is the speaker's main point?

　　　　　說話者的要點是什麼？

(A) Students have too much homework.

　　學生有太多功課。

(B) Students have to get up too early in the morning.

　　學生早上必須很早起床。

(C) Teachers need to be more understanding.

　　老師需要更體諒一點。

* pity〔'pɪtɪ〕*n.* 憐憫　　***look upon*** 看著
teenage〔'tin,edʒ〕*adj.* 青少年的；十幾歲的
drag〔dræg〕*v.* 拖；拉　　***drag*** *oneself* ***out of bed*** 從床上起來
pro-active〔pro'æktɪv〕*adj.* 積極主動的
approach〔ə'protʃ〕*v.* 接近　　***school board*** 學校董事會
plea〔pli〕*n.* 懇求　　healthy〔'hɛlθɪ〕*adj.* 健康的
successful〔sək'sɛsfəl〕*adj.* 成功的
task〔tæsk〕*n.* 工作；任務；課業　　nice〔naɪs〕*adj.* 好的
individual〔,ɪndə'vɪdʒuəl〕*n.* 個人　　main〔men〕*adj.* 主要的
main point 要點　　***get up*** 起床
understanding〔,ʌndə'stændɪŋ〕*adj.* 體諒的

15. (**A**) M：Do you want to hang out on Saturday?

　　男：妳週六想不想出去玩？

W：My next-door neighbor is getting married this
　　Saturday.　I have to go.

　　女：我隔壁鄰居這個週六要結婚。我必須去。

M：You don't sound too excited about it.

　　男：對於這件事，妳聽起來不太興奮。

W : Eh, why do people have to make such a big deal about getting married? It should be a personal thing, you know. Why do they have to drag everybody else into their business? Just to get some money and gifts? I don't care if she's getting married. Good for her. Just don't ask me to help pay for it. I don't even like the girl! She lives next door. That's it. I tell you, when I get married, it's going be a simple ceremony with only my family and closest friends.

女： 嗯，爲什麼人們結婚都要這麼小題大作？它應該是一件很私人的事，你知道的。爲什麼他們非要把所有的人都扯進去呢？就爲了拿到一些錢和禮物？我才不在乎她是否要結婚。恭喜她。就是不要叫我付錢。我甚至不喜歡那個女生！她住在隔壁。就這樣。我告訴你，當我結婚時，將會是一個簡單的儀式，只會有家人和最親近的朋友。

Question : Which description best matches the woman's attitude? 哪一項敘述最適合形容女士的態度？

(A) Bitter. 極爲不滿的。

(B) Amused. 感到有趣的。

(C) Grateful. 感激的。

* ***hang out*** 出去玩　　next-door *adj.* 隔壁的
neighbor〔'nebɚ〕*n.* 鄰居　　marry〔'mærɪ〕*v.* 結婚
sound〔saʊnd〕*v.* 聽起來　　excited〔ɪk'saɪtɪd〕*adj.* 興奮的
eh〔ɛ, e〕*interj.* 呃；嗯　　***make a big deal*** 小題大作
personal〔'pɝsn̩l〕*adj.* 私人的　　drag〔dræg〕*v.* 把…捲入
business〔'bɪznɪs〕*n.* 事情　　care〔kɛr〕*v.* 在乎
Good for her. 做得好。　　***pay for*** 支付…的錢
That's it. 就這樣。　　simple〔'sɪmpl̩〕*adj.* 簡單的
ceremony〔'sɛrə,monɪ〕*n.* 儀式；典禮
close〔klos〕*adj.* 親近的　　description〔dɪ'skrɪpʃən〕*n.* 敘述
match〔mætʃ〕*v.* 符合　　attitude〔'ætə,tjud〕*n.* 態度

bitter〔'bɪtɚ〕*adj.* 苦的;極為不滿的
amused〔ə'mjuzd〕*adj.* 感到有趣的
grateful〔'gretfəl〕*adj.* 感激的

16. (**B**) M : I always see you at this café. Don't you have a job?

男:我總是在這間咖啡廳見到妳。妳沒有在工作嗎?

W : I work nights in a factory. My shift starts at 7:00 p.m.

女:我在工廠上夜班。我的輪班時間是晚上七點開始。

M : What time do you get off?

男:妳幾點下班?

W : 4:00 a.m.

女:凌晨四點。

M : Hmm, almost the exact opposite of my schedule.
How do you like working nights?

男:嗯,幾乎跟我的時間表恰好相反。妳喜歡上夜班嗎?

Question : Where are the speakers? 說話者在哪裡?

(A) In a factory. 在工廠。

(B) In a café. 在咖啡廳。

(C) In a night club. 在夜店。

* café〔kə'fe〕*n.* 咖啡廳　　***work nights*** 上夜班
factory〔'fæktrɪ〕*n.* 工廠　　shift〔ʃɪft〕*n.* 輪班
get off 下班　　exact〔ɪg'zækt〕*adj.* 恰好的
opposite〔'ɑpəzɪt〕*n.* 相反的事物
schedule〔'skɛdʒul〕*n.* 時間表　　***night club*** 夜店

17. (**B**) If you're a bird lover, then there's no question that you've
seen some of the adorable videos both online and on
television of parrots and other types of pet birds dancing
their tails off to popular music. If you'd like to teach
your bird how to dance, I can teach you how to encourage
your pet to try out a few moves. Not only will teaching

your bird to dance be entertaining, but it will offer your pet some extra exercise, which can improve its overall health.

如果你很喜歡鳥，那你一定看過一些網路或電視上，很可愛的鸚鵡和其他的寵物鳥，隨著流行音樂忘情地跳舞的影片。如果你想要教你的鳥跳舞，我可以教你如何鼓勵你的寵物，嘗試一些動作。教你的鳥跳舞不只很有趣，也會給你的寵物額外的運動，可以改善牠整體的健康。

Question : What does the speaker say he can do?

說話者說他可以做什麼？

(A) Teach your bird to speak. 教你的鳥說話。

(B) Teach your bird to dance. 教你的鳥跳舞。

(C) Teach your bird to fly. 教你的鳥飛。

* lover (ˈlʌvɚ) *n.* 愛好者　　***there is no question*** 毫無疑問
adorable (əˈdorəbḷ) *adj.* 可愛的　　video (ˈvɪdɪ,o) *n.* 影片
online (ˈɑn,laɪn) *adv.* 在網路上　　parrot (ˈpærət) *n.* 鸚鵡
type (taɪp) *n.* 種類　　pet (pɛt) *adj.* 作為寵物的　　*n.* 寵物
dance one's tail off 跳舞跳得忘形
to (tə) *prep.* 配合著（音樂）　　popular (ˈpɑpjələ) *adj.* 流行的
encourage (ɪnˈkɝɪdʒ) *v.* 鼓勵　　***try out*** 試試看
move (muv) *n.* 跳舞的動作
not only…but (also) 不僅…而且
entertaining (ˌɛntɚˈtenɪŋ) *adj.* 有趣的　　offer (ˈɔfɚ) *v.* 提供
extra (ˈɛkstrə) *adj.* 額外的　　exercise (ˈɛksɚ,saɪz) *n.* 運動
improve (ɪmˈpruv) *v.* 改善　　overall (ˈovɚ,ɔl) *adj.* 整體的
health (hɛlθ) *n.* 健康

18. (**C**) W : You've been to Taipei before, haven't you?

女：你以前去過台北，對吧？

M : You bet. Many times.

男：沒錯。很多次。

W : What are some of your favorite spots?

女：你最喜歡的景點有哪些？

M : Oh, there are so many. I never miss a chance to visit the Tonghua Night Market, though. They have so many great snacks!

男：喔，有很多。不過我從不會錯過去通化夜市的機會。他們有很多很棒的小吃！

Question : What do we know about the man?

關於男士我們知道什麼？

(A) He's been to every night market in Taipei.

他去過台北的所有夜市。

(B) He usually avoids night markets in Taipei.

他在台北通常會避開夜市。

(C) He enjoys eating snacks at the night market.

他喜歡吃夜市的小吃。

* ***you bet*** 當然　　spot〔spɑt〕*n.* 地點　　miss〔mɪs〕*v.* 錯過
chance〔tʃæns〕*n.* 機會　　visit〔'vɪzɪt〕*v.* 拜訪；遊覽；去
night market 夜市　　snack〔snæk〕*n.* 小吃
avoid〔ə'vɔɪd〕*v.* 避開　　enjoy〔ɪn'dʒɔɪ〕*v.* 喜歡；享受

19. (**B**) W : What is that pin on your jacket?

女：你夾克上的那個別針是什麼？

M : Oh, it's an American flag.

男：喔，它是個美國國旗。

W : Why are you wearing it?

女：你為什麼要佩戴它？

M : To show my support for the troops overseas, fighting the enemy.

男：為了表示我對海外軍隊的支持，他們正在跟敵人打仗。

Question : What is the man wearing? 男士正佩戴著什麼？

(A) An Army flag. 一個軍旗。

(B) A pin that looks like an American flag.

一個看起來像美國國旗的別針。

(C) A funny hat. 一頂滑稽的帽子。

* pin〔pɪn〕*n.* 別針　　jacket〔'dʒækɪt〕*n.* 夾克
  flag〔flæg〕*n.* 旗子；國旗（ = *national flag* ）
  wear〔wɛr〕*v.* 佩戴著　　show〔ʃo〕*v.* 表示
  support〔sə'port〕*n.* 支持　　troops〔trups〕*n. pl.* 軍隊
  overseas〔'ovɚ'siz〕*adv.* 在海外　　fight〔faɪt〕*v.* 與…打仗
  enemy〔'ɛnəmɪ〕*n.* 敵人　　army〔'ɑrmɪ〕*n.* 軍隊
  funny〔'fʌnɪ〕*adj.* 好笑的；滑稽的

20. (**B**) Music is a powerful thing. It creates feelings and has the
power to bring people together. Music is also a way for
people to express themselves and share ideas. But today,
artists are not known for their music, but for how flashy
their outfits are and how many times their wealthy
relatives can get them out of jail.

音樂是很有力量的東西。它可以創造感情，而且具有能使人們凝
聚在一起的力量。音樂也是一種讓人們表達和分享自己想法的方
式。但現在，藝術家已不再因為他們的音樂而有名，而是因為他
們的服裝有多麼華麗，或是他們富裕的親戚能夠幫他們出獄多少
次。

Question：According to the speaker, what does music
have the power to do?

根據說話者，音樂擁有做什麼的力量？

(A) Get people out of jail. 使人們出獄。

(B) Bring people together. 使人們凝聚在一起。

(C) Drive people apart. 使人們分開。

* powerful〔'pauɚfəl〕*adj.* 強有力的
  create〔krɪ'et〕*v.* 創造　　power〔'pauɚ〕*n.* 力量；能力

bring〔brɪŋ〕v. 使　　together〔tə'gɛðɚ〕adv. 一起
express〔ɪk'sprɛs〕v. 表達　　share〔ʃɛr〕v. 分享
idea〔aɪ'diə〕n. 想法　　today〔tə'de〕adv. 現在
artist〔'ɑrtɪst〕n. 藝術家　　**not** A **but** B 不是 A，而是 B
be known for 以~而有名　　flashy〔'flæʃɪ〕adj. 華麗的
outfit〔'aʊt,fɪt〕n. 服裝　　wealthy〔'wɛlθɪ〕adj. 有錢的
relative〔'rɛlətɪv〕n. 親戚　　jail〔dʒel〕n. 監獄
drive〔draɪv〕v. 使　　apart〔ə'pɑrt〕adj. 分開的

21. (**A**) M：Are you an animal lover?

男：妳喜歡動物嗎？

W：Sure! I wish I could have a pet, but we can't have them. My sister has really bad allergies.

女：當然！我希望我可以養寵物，但我們不能。我妹妹有很嚴重的過敏。

M：That's too bad. Do you prefer dogs or cats?

男：真可惜。妳比較喜歡貓還是狗？

W：If I had a choice, I'd have a cat.

女：如果我可以選擇的話，我會養貓。

M：Me, too. They're so lovable.

男：我也是。牠們很可愛。

Question：Why can't the woman have a pet?

為什麼女士不能養寵物？

(A) Her sister can't be around them.

她的妹妹不能接近牠們。

(B) Her parents don't want one. 她的父母不想要寵物。

(C) Her preference is for a dog. 她比較喜歡狗。

* **have a pet** 養寵物　　bad〔bæd〕adj. 嚴重的
allergy〔'ælədʒɪ〕n. 過敏症　　prefer〔prɪ'fɝ〕v. 比較喜歡
choice〔tʃɔɪs〕n. 選擇　　lovable〔'lʌvəbl̩〕adj. 可愛的
preference〔'prɛfərəns〕n. 偏愛 <for>

TEST 22 ▶ 詳解

第一部分：辨識句意（第 1-3 題）

1. (**B**) (A)　　　　　　(B)　　　　　　(C)

Tom is a very good swimmer and he thinks about it often.
湯姆很會游泳，而他也時常想到這件事。

2. (**C**) (A)　　　　　　(B)　　　　　　(C)

Mona was shocked to hear that Nick and Fiona were married last month.
蒙娜聽說尼克和菲歐娜上個月結婚了，覺得很震驚。

* shocked〔ʃɑkt〕*adj.* 震驚的　　married〔ˈmærɪd〕*adj.* 已婚的

3. (**C**) (A)　　　　　　(B)　　　　　　(C)

At the seashore, Alvin collected trash from the beach
while Polly sunbathed in a lounge chair. 阿爾文在岸邊
收集海灘的垃圾，而波莉則是在躺椅上做日光浴。

* seashore〔'si,ʃor〕*n.* 海岸　　collect〔kə'lɛkt〕*v.* 收集
trash〔træʃ〕*n.* 垃圾　　beach〔bitʃ〕*n.* 海灘
sunbathe〔'sʌn,beð〕*v.* 做日光浴
lounge〔laʊndʒ〕*n.* 交誼廳；躺椅　　***lounge chair*** 躺椅

第二部分：基本問答（第 4-10 題）

4. (**C**) What's the best pizza place in town?
城裡最棒的披薩店是哪一家？

(A) Kleenex. 可麗舒。

(B) McDonald's. 麥當勞。

(C) Pizza Hut. <u>必勝客。</u>

* pizza〔'pitsə〕*n.* 披薩　　place〔ples〕*n.* 餐館
town〔taʊn〕*n.* 城鎮
Kleenex〔'klinɛks〕*n.* 可麗舒【紙巾品牌】
McDonald's〔mək'danḷdz〕麥當勞　　hut〔hʌt〕*n.* 小木屋

5. (**A**) Where should we hold our social committee meeting?
我們的社交委員會會議應該要在哪裡舉行？

(A) How about my office? It shouldn't be too crowded.
<u>在我的辦公室如何？應該不會太擁擠。</u>

(B) We can blame it on Barry. He's so lazy.
我們可以把這件事怪到貝瑞頭上。他太懶惰了。

(C) How about two o'clock? We can avoid the rush.
兩點如何？我們可以避開尖峰時間。

* hold〔hold〕*v.* 舉行　　social〔'soʃəl〕*adj.* 社交的
committee〔kə'mɪtɪ〕*n.* 委員會　　meeting〔'mitɪŋ〕*n.* 會議

office〔'ɔfɪs〕 *n.* 辦公室
crowded〔'kraʊdɪd〕 *adj.* 擁擠的
blame〔blem〕 *v.* 責怪；將…歸因於 < *on* >
lazy〔'lezɪ〕 *adj.* 懶惰的   avoid〔ə'vɔɪd〕 *v.* 避開
rush〔rʌʃ〕 *n.* 交通尖峰時間

6. (**C**) Excuse me, sir. Which way to city hall?

不好意思，先生。市政府怎麼走？

(A) Keep going up. It's in the city.

持續往前走。它在城市裡。

(B) Take the elevator. Room 301. 搭電梯。301 室。

(C) Make a left at Main Street. You can't miss it.

在主街左轉。你不可能錯過的。

* city〔'sɪtɪ〕 *n.* 城市   *city hall* 市政府
keep〔kip〕 *v.* 持續   up〔ʌp〕 *adv.* 向前
take〔tek〕 *v.* 搭乘   elevator〔'ɛlə,vetɚ〕 *n.* 電梯
room〔rum〕 *n.* 室   *make a left* 左轉
main〔men〕 *adj.* 主要的   miss〔mɪs〕 *v.* 錯過

7. (**C**) Hi, Brian. I thought you were leaving for Germany this afternoon. 嗨，布萊恩。我以為你今天下午會動身前往德國。

(A) Nice to meet you. 很高興認識你。

(B) No, I've never been to Germany.

不，我從未去過德國。

(C) No, I'm leaving tomorrow afternoon.

不是，我明天下午離開。

* leave〔liv〕 *v.* 離開   *leave for* 動身前往
Germany〔'dʒɝmənɪ〕 *n.* 德國
meet〔mit〕 *v.* 認識   *not anymore* 不再

8. (**A**) Why is your arm in a cast? 為什麼你的手臂打上石膏？

    (A) I broke it. 我骨折了。

    (B) I lost it. 我把它丟了。

    (C) I found it. 我找到它了。

    * cast〔kæst〕*n.* 石膏繃紮　　break〔brek〕*v.* 折斷
    lose〔luz〕*v.* 失去；遺失

9. (**C**) Can you perform any popular songs on your guitar?
你能用你的吉他演奏任何流行歌曲嗎？

    (A) I can make your smile disappear.

        我可以讓你的微笑消失。

    (B) Yes, I came here yesterday. 是的，我昨天才來這裡。

    (C) No, I'm just a beginner. 不，我只是個初學者。

    * perform〔pɚˋfɔrm〕*v.* 演奏　　popular〔ˋpɑpjələ〕*adj.* 流行的
    guitar〔gɪˋtɑr〕*n.* 吉他　　disappear〔͵dɪsəˋpɪr〕*v.* 消失
    beginner〔bɪˋgɪnɚ〕*n.* 初學者

10. (**B**) What did you wear to the annual Christmas party?
妳穿什麼去參加年度聖誕派對？

    (A) It was great. 它很棒。

    (B) A black dress. 一件黑色洋裝。

    (C) He was smiling at me. 他正在對我微笑。

    * wear〔wɛr〕*v.* 穿　　annual〔ˋænjʊəl〕*adj.* 年度的
    Christmas〔ˋkrɪsməs〕*n.* 聖誕節
    great〔gret〕*adj.* 很棒的　　dress〔drɛs〕*n.* 洋裝

第三部分：言談理解（第 11-21 題）

11. (**C**) W : How long were you in Paris?
女：你在巴黎待了多久？

M : Long enough to see the sights and get out of there.

男：久到足夠看完景點，然後離開那裡。

W : Oh, I take it you didn't enjoy your visit?

女：喔，所以說你沒有很喜歡你的遊覽？

M : You can say that again.　That joint is so overrated.
Everything costs five times what it does at home.
And the people?　Meh, I hated it.

男：你說的沒錯。那個地方被高估了。每樣東西都比我家鄉那裡
貴五倍。然後人呢？唉，我討厭極了。

Question : How long was the man in Paris?

這位男士在巴黎待了多久？

(A) Two days.　兩天。

(B) One week.　一個禮拜。

(C) It is impossible to say.　很難說。

* Paris〔'pærɪs〕*n.* 巴黎　　enough〔ə'nʌf〕*adv.* 足夠
sights〔saɪts〕*n. pl.* 名勝；風景　　***get out of*** 離開
take it (that) 認為　　visit〔'vɪzɪt〕*n.* 遊覽
You can say that again. 你說的沒錯。
joint〔dʒɔɪnt〕*n.* 地方　　overrate〔'ovə,ret〕*v.* 高估
cost〔kɔst〕*v.* 值…錢　　time〔taɪm〕*n.* 倍
at home 在家鄉　　meh〔mɛ〕*interj.* 嗯
hate〔het〕*v.* 討厭　　impossible〔ɪm'pɑsəbl̩〕*adj.* 不可能的

12. (**A**) M : Wow, Ivy!　You're really good at this.　Do you often
play video games?

男：哇，艾薇！妳真的很厲害。妳經常打電動嗎？

W : Yeah.　My little brother has a Z-Box, so we play from
time to time.

女：是啊。我弟弟有一台 Z-Box，所以我們偶爾會玩。

M：Time to time?! You're like an expert at this game!

男：偶爾?! 妳玩這個遊戲簡直像是個專家！

Question：What does Ivy do with her little brother?

艾薇會跟她的弟弟做什麼？

(A) Play video games. 打電動玩具。

(B) Watch television. 看電視。

(C) Go fishing. 去釣魚。

* *be good at* 擅長　　*video game* 電動玩具
  from time to time 偶爾　　expert〔'ɛkspɜt〕*n.* 專家
  fish〔fɪʃ〕*v.* 釣魚

13. (**B**) M：Would you like to dance?

男：妳想要跳舞嗎？

W：I would, but I'm here with my boyfriend.

女：我想，但我是跟我男朋友來的。

M：Oh, I'm sorry. I thought you were here alone.

男：喔，抱歉。我以為妳是自己來的。

W：No, my boyfriend is in the bathroom, so you better leave before he gets back.

女：不是，我的男朋友在廁所，所以你最好在他回來之前離開。

Question：Why did the woman turn the man down?

為什麼女士拒絕了男士？

(A) She doesn't want to dance. 她不想跳舞。

(B) She has a boyfriend. 她有男朋友了。

(C) She needs to use the bathroom. 她需要上廁所。

* boyfriend〔'bɔɪ,frɛnd〕*n.* 男朋友　　alone〔ə'lon〕*adv.* 獨自
  bathroom〔'bæθ,rum〕*n.* 浴室；廁所
  you better 你最好（= *you had better*）　　*turn down* 拒絕

14. (**A**) Beauty is found everywhere. It is found in the petals of
a rose, and the beautiful feathers of a peacock. Beauty is
in all that is around us, if only you stop to look.
Unfortunately, millions of females across the world do
not realize this simple truth. Their perception of what is
beautiful has been influenced by the mass media. Turn
on your television and…

美的事物到處都有。它可以是玫瑰的花瓣，或是孔雀漂亮的羽
毛。我們被美麗的事物環繞，只要你能停下來看。遺憾的是，
全世界數百萬的女性都不了解這個簡單的事實。她們對美的認
知已經被大衆媒體所影響。打開你的電視然後…

Question：What will the speaker most likely talk about
next?　說話者接下來最有可能說什麼？

(A) The way women are portrayed in the media.
<u>媒體描述的女性。</u>

(B) Finding beauty in everyday places.
在日常的地點尋找美麗的事物。

(C) Make-up and fashion tips for women.
給女性的化妝與時尚的建議。

* beauty〔'bjutɪ〕*n.* 美　　petal〔'pɛtḷ〕*n.* 花瓣
rose〔roz〕*n.* 玫瑰　　feather〔'fɛðɚ〕*n.* 羽毛
peacock〔'pi,kɑk〕*n.* 孔雀　　*if only* 只要
unfortunately〔ʌn'fɔrtʃənɪtlɪ〕*adv.* 遺憾的是
million〔'mɪljən〕*n.* 百萬　　***millions of*** 數百萬的
across the world 在全世界　　realize〔'riə,laɪz〕*v.* 了解
simple〔'sɪmpḷ〕*adj.* 簡單的　　truth〔truθ〕*n.* 事實
perception〔pɚ'sɛpʃən〕*n.* 知覺；感受
influence〔'ɪnfluəns〕*v.* 影響　　mass〔mæs〕*adj.* 大衆的
media〔'midɪə〕*n. pl.* 媒體　　***turn on*** 打開（電源）

way〔we〕*n.* 方式　　portray〔por'tre〕*v.* 描述
everyday〔'ɛvrɪ'de〕*adj.* 目前的
make-up〔'mek,ʌp〕*n.* 化妝
fashion〔'fæʃən〕*n.* 時尚；時裝　　tip〔tɪp〕*n.* 建議

15. (**C**) If you see any criminal activity in Shady Mountain Park,
please do your part as a citizen and tip off the San Jose
police. We can't just turn a blind eye to burglaries or
break-ins anymore. We need to support the efforts of the
San Jose Parks and Recreation Department and the Park
Patrol during the summer to make the park a nice place
to visit for people not only from San Jose, but from
throughout the region.

如果你在 Shady Mountain 公園看到任何犯案行為，請盡你身為
市民的本分，通報聖荷西的警方。我們不能再對竊盜或是入侵住
宅視而不見。在夏季，我們必須支持聖荷西公園與娛樂管理局和
公園巡邏隊所做的努力，使公園成為一個聖荷西及整個地區的人
民，良好的旅遊地點。

Question：What is the problem at Shady Mountain Park?
Shady Mountain 公園有什麼問題？

(A) Pollution. 污染。

(B) Overcrowding. 太過擁擠。

(C) Crime. 犯罪。

* criminal〔'krɪmənl̩〕*adj.* 犯罪的
activity〔æk'tɪvətɪ〕*n.* 活動　　*criminal activity* 犯罪行為
do one's part 盡自己的本分　　citizen〔'sɪtəzn̩〕*n.* 市民
tip off 通報　　San Jose〔,sɑnho'sɛ〕*n.* 聖荷西
blind〔blaɪnd〕*adj.* 盲的；瞎的
turn a blind eye to 假裝沒看到；對～視而不見
burglary〔'bɝglərɪ〕*n.* 竊盜　　break-in〔'brek,ɪn〕*n.* 闖入

support〔 sə'port 〕*v.* 支持　　effort〔'ɛfət 〕*n.* 努力
recreation〔ˌrɛkrɪ'eʃən 〕*n.* 娛樂
department〔 dɪ'partmənt 〕*n.* 部門
patrol〔 pə'trol 〕*n.* 巡邏隊
not only…but (also) 不僅…而且
throughout〔 θru'aut 〕*prep.* 遍及　　region〔'ridʒən 〕*n.* 地區
pollution〔 pə'luʃən 〕*n.* 污染
overcrowd〔ˌovɚ'kraud 〕*v.* 過度擁擠
crime〔 kraɪm 〕*n.* 犯罪

16. (**A**) You have to <u>tip your hat</u> to those people who treat
animals with kindness—the local humane societies, the
pet rescue groups, the responsible owners. Those
individuals who love a dog or a cat or any other creature
are special people.
你必須向那些善待動物的人致敬——當地的人道協會、寵物救援
團體，和負責任的飼主們。那些愛護狗、貓或任何其他動物的
人，都是很特別的人。

Question : What does the man mean by "tip your hat"?
　　　　男士說要「致敬」是什麼意思？

(A) Show respect. <u>表示尊敬。</u>

(B) Give money. 給錢。

(C) Remain quiet. 保持安靜。

* tip〔 tɪp 〕*v.* 輕觸或微舉（帽子）以致敬
　tip one's hat 致敬　　treat〔 trit 〕*v.* 對待
　kindness〔'kaɪndnɪs 〕*n.* 親切；仁慈　　local〔'lokḷ 〕*adj.* 當地的
　humane〔 hju'men 〕*adj.* 人道的；有人情味的人
　society〔 sə'saɪətɪ 〕*n.* 協會；團體　　pet〔 pɛt 〕*n.* 寵物
　rescue〔'rɛskju 〕*n.* 救援　　group〔 grup 〕*n.* 團體
　responsible〔 rɪ'spɑnsəbḷ 〕*adj.* 負責任的

owner〔'onɚ〕*n.* 物主;所有人

individual〔ˌɪndə'vɪdʒʊəl〕*n.* 個人

creature〔'kritʃɚ〕*n.* 動物　special〔'spɛʃəl〕*adj.* 特別的

show〔ʃo〕*v.* 表示　respect〔rɪ'spɛkt〕*n.* 尊敬

remain〔rɪ'men〕*v.* 保持　quiet〔'kwaɪət〕*adj.* 安靜的

17. (**C**) W : Do you buy many magazines?

女:你會買很多雜誌嗎?

M : No.　Why would I?

男:不會。我爲什麼要買?

W : What do you mean?　Don't you like to read and keep up to date with current affairs?

女:你是什麼意思?難道你不喜歡閱讀最新的時事嗎?

M : Yes, I love reading, but I can get all the latest news and gossip on the Internet.　It's much more convenient, and best of all, it's free.

男:是的,我喜歡閱讀,但是我在網路上就可以得知最新的消息和八卦。那樣更加方便,而且最好的是,它是免費的。

Question : Why doesn't the man buy magazines?

爲什麼男士不買雜誌?

(A) It is a waste of paper. 很浪費紙。

(B) He can't afford them. 他買不起。

(C) He can get the same information on the Internet.
他可以在網路上得到同樣的資訊。

* magazine〔ˌmægə'zin〕*n.* 雜誌　mean〔min〕*v.* 意思是

keep up to date with 保持不落於…之後

current〔'kɝənt〕*adj.* 目前的　affair〔ə'fɛr〕*n.* 事情

current affairs 時事　latest〔'letɪst〕*adj.* 最新的

news〔njuz〕*n.* 新聞;消息　gossip〔'gɑsəp〕*n.* 八卦

Internet〔'ɪntə‚nɛt〕*n.* 網際網路
convenient〔kən'vinjənt〕*adj.* 方便的
free〔fri〕*adj.* 免費的
waste〔west〕*n.* 浪費　　afford〔ə'fɔrd〕*v.* 負擔得起
information〔‚ɪnfə'meʃən〕*n.* 資訊

18. (**A**) M：Hi, honey.　I'm home.　Where's Jessica?

男：嗨，親愛的。我回來了。潔西卡在哪裡？

W：Um… I thought you were going to pick her up from soccer practice on your way home from work.

女：嗯…我以為你下班回家途中，會把正在練習足球的她接回來。

M：No.　You were supposed to pick her up on your way home from cooking class.

男：不。應該是妳上完烹飪課後，在回家途中去接她的。

W：I don't have class on Wednesdays, remember?

女：我星期三沒有課，你記得嗎？

M：Oh, my gosh, you're right.　What time is it?　She's probably furious by now.

男：喔，我的天啊，妳說的對。現在幾點了？她現在應該很憤怒。

Question：What does the man imply about Jessica?

關於潔西卡男士暗示什麼？

(A) She is probably angry about having to wait.

<u>她可能會因為要等待而生氣。</u>

(B) She is probably confused by her parents.

她可能因為她爸媽而感到困惑。

(C) She is probably walking home.

她可能正在走路回家。

* honey〔ˈhʌnɪ〕 *n.* 蜂蜜；愛人；親愛的　　***pick sb. up*** 接某人
soccer〔ˈsɑkɚ〕 *n.* 足球　　practice〔ˈpræktɪs〕 *n.* 練習
be supposed to V. 應該…　　cooking〔ˈkʊkɪŋ〕 *n.* 烹飪
on Wednesdays 在每個星期三
remember〔rɪˈmɛmbɚ〕 *v.* 記得
gosh〔ɡɑʃ〕 *interj.* 哎呀！；天啊！
probably〔ˈprɑbəblɪ〕 *adv.* 可能
furious〔ˈfjʊrɪəs〕 *adj.* 憤怒的　　imply〔ɪmˈplaɪ〕 *v.* 暗示
angry〔ˈæŋɡrɪ〕 *adj.* 生氣的
confused〔kənˈfjuzd〕 *adj.* 困惑的

19. (**A**)　M：What does "going Dutch" mean?
　　　男："Going Dutch" 是什麼意思？

　　　W：It means when two people go out somewhere, they
　　　　　split the bill evenly, right?

　　　女：它的意思是，當兩個人出去某個地方，他們會分攤帳單，
　　　　　對吧？

　　　M：How did that get started?

　　　男：這個說法是怎麼來的？

　　　W：I think it has something to do with the Dutch being
　　　　　very tight with their money.

　　　女：我想應該是跟荷蘭人對錢很吝嗇有關吧。

　　　Question：What does "going Dutch" mean?
　　　　　　　　"Going Dutch" 是什麼意思？

　(A) Splitting the bill. 分攤帳單。

　(B) Talking with food in your mouth. 邊吃東西邊說話。

　(C) Leaving the door open all night. 整晚都讓門開著。

* Dutch〔dʌtʃ〕 *adj.* 荷蘭的　 *n.* 荷蘭人　　***go Dutch*** 各付各的
split〔splɪt〕 *v.* 分攤　　bill〔bɪl〕 *n.* 帳單
evenly〔ˈivənlɪ〕 *adv.* 平均地　　***get started*** 開始

have something to do with 和…有關
tight〔taɪt〕*adj.* 吝嗇的
leave〔liv〕*v.* 使處於（某種狀態）

20. (**C**)　W : Do you have your driver's license?

女：你有駕照嗎？

M : No.　I never bothered to get one.

男：沒有。我一直都沒有特地去考一張。

W : But I see you driving your scooter all over town.

女：但我看你在城裡到處騎著你的摩托車。

M : I know, I know.　I'll get around to it.

男：我知道，我知道。我會找時間去考的。

W : You really should.　It's against the law.

女：你眞的應該要去考。這樣是非法的。

Question : Why doesn't the man have a driver's license?

　　　　　爲什麼男士沒有駕照？

(A) He's not old enough.　他年紀不夠大。

(B) He's a bad driver.　他開車技術差。

(C) He's lazy.　<u>他很懶惰。</u>

* driver〔'draɪvɚ〕*n.* 駕駛人　　license〔'laɪsn̩s〕*n.* 執照
　driver's license 駕照　　bother〔'bɑðɚ〕*v.* 麻煩；費心
　scooter〔'skutɚ〕*n.* 摩托車　　**all over** 在…的各處
　town〔taʊn〕*n.* 城鎮
　get around to *sth.* 找時間或機會去做某事
　against〔ə'gɛnst〕*prep.* 違反　　law〔lɔ〕*n.* 法律
　lazy〔'lezɪ〕*adj.* 懶惰的

21. (**C**)　M : Hi, Jody.　What do you know about computers?

男：嗨，茱蒂。妳對電腦有多了解？

W : Not much, Albert. I know how to turn one on and check my e-mail. That's about it. Why, what's your problem?

女：不多，阿爾伯特。我會知道如何開機和檢查我的電子郵件。大概就這樣。為什麼問，你有什麼問題？

M : Oh, I can't get this program to work properly. It keeps freezing up.

男：喔，我沒辦法使這個程式正常運作。它一直當機。

W : You should talk to Meredith. She's a genius when it comes to these things.

女：你應該去找梅勒迪斯談一談。一提到這些事，她是個天才。

Question : What does the woman suggest?

女士給了什麼建議？

(A) Reinstall the program. 重新安裝程式。

(B) Buy a new computer. 買一台新的電腦。

(C) Talk to Meredith. <u>去找梅勒迪斯談一談。</u>

* computer (kəm'pjutɚ) n. 電腦　　***turn on*** 打開（電源）
check (tʃɛk) v. 檢查　　e-mail ('i,mel) n. 電子郵件
That's about it. 大概就這樣。　　get (gɛt) v. 使
program ('progræm) n. 程式　　work (wɜk) v. 運作
properly ('prɑpɚlɪ) adv. 適當地
freeze (friz) v. 結冰；凍結；（螢幕）凍結
freeze up 當機　　genius ('dʒinjəs) n. 天才
when it comes to 一提到　　suggest (səg'dʒɛst) v. 建議
reinstall (,rɪn'stɔl) v. 重新安裝

TEST 23 ▶ 詳解

第一部分：辨識句意（第 1-3 題）

1. (**B**) (A)　　　　　　(B)　　　　　　(C)

Judy's lifelong dream is to visit the Toy Museum in California. 茱蒂一生的夢想就是去參觀加州的玩具博物館。

* lifelong〔'laɪf,lɔŋ〕*adj.* 一生的　　visit〔'vɪzɪt〕*v.* 參觀
toy〔tɔɪ〕*n.* 玩具　　museum〔mju'ziəm〕*n.* 博物館
California〔,kælə'fɔrnjə〕*n.* 加州

2. (**B**) (A)　　　　　　(B)　　　　　　(C)

A typhoon is expected to move down the southeast coast of Taiwan. 有個颱風預計會沿著台灣的東南海岸往下移動。

* typhoon〔taɪ'fun〕*n.* 颱風　　expect〔ɪk'spɛkt〕*v.* 預期
move〔muv〕*v.* 移動　　southeast〔,sauθ'ist〕*adj.* 東南方的
coast〔kost〕*n.* 海岸

3. (**C**) (A)　　　　　　(B)　　　　　　(C)

As Terry packs his bag for school, his MP3 player will be the last thing he packs. 當泰瑞要收拾書包去上學時，他的 MP3 播放器會是他最後收進去的東西。

* pack〔pæk〕*v.* 打包；把…裝入
  bag〔bæg〕*n.* 書包（= *schoolbag*）　　player〔'pleæ〕*n.* 播放器

第二部分：基本問答（第 4-10 題）

4. (**C**) That was one of the best concerts I've seen in ages.
   那是我長久以來看過最棒的演唱會之一了。

   (A) Yes, it was really cold. 是的，那時候非常冷。

   (B) Thankfully the concert hadn't started.
       幸好演唱會還沒開始。

   (C) Really? I wasn't impressed at all.
       <u>眞的嗎？我沒什麼印象。</u>

   * concert〔'kɑnsɜt〕*n.* 演唱會　　ages〔edʒz〕*n. pl.* 長時間
     thankfully〔'θæŋkfəlɪ〕*adv.* 感謝地；幸好
     not…at all 一點也不…　　impress〔ɪm'prɛs〕*v.* 使印象深刻

5. (**B**) Was anyone hurt in the car accident that happened in front of the school?
   在學校前面發生的那場車禍有沒有人受傷？

   (A) It wasn't my fault. 那不是我的錯。

   (B) The driver of the truck suffered a neck injury.
       <u>卡車司機的頸部受傷。</u>

   (C) There is no school today. 今天不用上學。

   * hurt〔hɜt〕*v.* 使受傷　　accident〔'æksədənt〕*n.* 意外
     fault〔fɔlt〕*n.* 過錯　　driver〔'draɪvæ〕*n.* 駕駛人
     truck〔trʌk〕*n.* 卡車　　suffer〔'sʌfæ〕*v.* 遭受
     neck〔nɛk〕*n.* 頸部；脖子　　injury〔'ɪndʒərɪ〕*n.* 傷害
     school〔skul〕*n.* 上學

6. (**C**)　Do you prefer traveling by train or bus?　I find train travel
　　　to be much more enjoyable.

　　　你比較喜歡搭火車還是巴士旅行？我覺得搭火車旅行比較愉快。

　　　(A) Try the YouBike system.　試試 YouBike 系統。

　　　(B) I have an Easy Card.　我有一張悠遊卡。

　　　(C) I'm a bus rider myself.　<u>我個人比較喜歡搭巴士。</u>

　　　* prefer〔prɪˈfɝ〕*v.* 比較喜歡　　　travel〔ˈtrævl〕*v. n.* 旅行
　　　　find〔faɪnd〕*v.* 覺得　　　enjoyable〔ɪnˈdʒɔɪəbl〕*adj.* 令人愉快的
　　　　system〔ˈsɪstəm〕*n.* 系統　　　***Easy Card*** 悠遊卡
　　　　rider〔ˈraɪdɚ〕*n.* 乘客

7. (**C**)　Mom?　Where's my baseball uniform?

　　　媽？我的棒球制服在哪裡？

　　　(A) Leave it alone, Brad.　別管它，布瑞德。

　　　(B) It costs 500NT, Brad.　它要台幣 500 元，布瑞德。

　　　(C) It's in the dryer, Brad.　<u>它在烘乾機裡，布瑞德。</u>

　　　* baseball〔ˈbesˌbɔl〕*n.* 棒球　　　uniform〔ˈjunəˌfɔrm〕*n.* 制服
　　　　leave it alone 別管它；不要打擾它
　　　　cost〔kɔst〕*v.* 值…（錢）　　　dryer〔ˈdraɪɚ〕*n.* 烘乾機

8. (**A**)　Did you backup the files on your hard drive?

　　　你有將檔案備份到你的硬碟嗎？

　　　(A) Yes, I did.　<u>是的，我有。</u>

　　　(B) Yes, I will.　是的，我會。

　　　(C) No, I am.　不，我是。

　　　* backup〔ˈbækˌʌp〕*v.* 將…備份　　　file〔faɪl〕*n.* 檔案
　　　　hard drive 硬碟

9. (**C**)　Don't you think Julie is the prettiest girl on campus?

　　　你不認為茱麗是校園裡最漂亮的女孩嗎？

(A) They sure will. 他們一定會。

(B) He certainly is. 他一定是。

(C) I sure do. I can't take my eyes off her.
   <u>我的確這麼認為。我無法將視線從她身上移開。</u>

* pretty (ˈprɪtɪ) *adj.* 漂亮的　　campus (ˈkæmpəs) *n.* 校園
  sure (ʃur) *adv.* 的確；當然　　certainly (ˈsɝtnlɪ) *adv.* 一定
  can't take** one's **eyes off 無法將視線從…移開

10. (**B**) Have you ever had lunch in the school cafeteria?
   你曾經在學校的自助餐廳裡吃過午餐嗎？

   (A) Where do you want to eat? I'm starving.
      你想去哪裡吃？我快餓死了。

   (B) No, never. <u>不，從來沒有。</u>

   (C) Have you ever tried this? 你曾經試過這個嗎？

   * cafeteria (ˌkæfəˈtɪrɪə) *n.* 自助餐廳　　starve (stɑrv) *v.* 餓死

第三部分：言談理解（第 11-21 題）

11. (**B**) W：Oh, hi, Steve. You're early.
   女：喔，嗨，史蒂夫。你來得真早。

   M：Yes, Ms. Sears. I need to speak with you about my
      book report.

   男：嗯，西爾斯女士。我需要跟妳談談關於我的讀書報告。

   W：Sure. What's going on?
   女：當然可以。怎麼了嗎？

   M：I'm having a hard time understanding what's
      happening in my book. I mean, I read the text, but I
      don't get what's going on.

   男：我很難理解我的書中發生了什麼事。我的意思是，我讀了文
      章，但是我不懂發生了什麼事。

W：Well, Steve.　Shakespeare is not an easy read.　But I have something that may help you.　Hold on a second.

女：嗯，史蒂夫。莎士比亞不容易讀。但是我有某樣東西可能可以幫助你。你等一下。

Question：Who is Ms. Sears?　西爾斯女士是誰？

(A) A chemistry teacher.　一位化學老師。

(B) A professor of literature.　<u>一位文學教授。</u>

(C) A social worker.　一名社工。

* Ms.〔mɪz〕*n.* …女士　　report〔rɪ'port〕*n.* 報告
  book report 讀書報告　　***go on*** 發生
  hard〔hɑrd〕*adj.* 辛苦的　　***have a hard time V-ing*** 很難…
  text〔tɛkst〕*n.* 內文　　get〔gɛt〕*v.* 了解
  Shakespeare〔'ʃek͵spɪr〕*n.* 莎士比亞　　read〔rid〕*n.* 讀物
  second〔'sɛkənd〕*n.* 秒；片刻　　***hold on a second*** 稍等一下
  chemistry〔'kɛmɪstrɪ〕*n.* 化學　　professor〔prə'fɛsɚ〕*n.* 教授
  literature〔'lɪtərətʃɚ〕*n.* 文學　　social〔'soʃəl〕*adj.* 社會的
  worker〔'wɝkɚ〕*n.* 工作者

12. (**C**) M：Who broke the window?

　　　　男：誰打破了窗戶？

　　　　W：Oh, the boys were playing ball in the house again.

　　　　女：喔，男孩們又在家裡玩球了。

　　　　M：How many times have we told them not to play ball in the house?

　　　　男：我們跟他們講了多少次，不要在家裡玩球？

　　　　W：They're going to have to pay to have it fixed this time.　Maybe that will teach them.

　　　　女：這次他們要自己付錢修理。或許那樣他們才能學到教訓。

　　　　Question：Why does the woman want the boys to pay for the window?　為什麼女士要男孩們付窗戶的錢？

(A) To show them respect. 爲了向他們表示尊敬。

(B) To set limits on their ambitions.

爲了限制他們的野心。

(C) To teach them a lesson. 爲了給他們一個教訓。

* break〔brek〕v. 打破　　window〔'wɪndo〕n. 窗戶
time〔taɪm〕n. 次　　pay〔pe〕v. 付錢　　fix〔fɪks〕v. 修理
maybe〔'mebɪ〕adv. 或許　　teach〔titʃ〕v. 教；教訓
show〔ʃo〕v. 向～表示　　respect〔rɪ'spɛkt〕n. 尊敬
set〔sɛt〕v. 設定　　limit〔'lɪmɪt〕n. 限制
set limits on　限制　　ambition〔æm'bɪʃən〕n. 野心
lesson〔'lɛsn̩〕n. 教訓　　**teach sb. a lesson**　教訓某人

13. (**B**) M : How is school going?

男：妳在學校情況如何？

W : Great, but… I'm having a difficult time in English.

女：很棒，但是…我英文課上得很辛苦。

M : Why don't you hire a tutor?

男：妳何不請一位家教？

W : Um… because I can't afford one. I'm just a poor
college student.

女：嗯…因爲我負擔不起。我只是一個貧窮的大學生。

Question : Why doesn't the woman hire a tutor?

女士爲什麼不請一位家教？

(A) She's afraid of speaking. 她害怕開口說。

(B) She can't afford it. 她負擔不起。

(C) She is thinking of dropping out. 她在考慮要休學。

* go〔go〕v. 進展　　difficult〔'dɪfə͵kʌlt〕adj. 困難的；辛苦的
hire〔haɪr〕v. 雇用　　tutor〔'tutɚ, 'tjutɚ〕n. 家教
afford〔ə'ford〕v. 負擔得起　　poor〔pʊr〕adj. 貧窮的
college〔'kɑlɪdʒ〕n. 大學　　afraid〔ə'fred〕adj. 害怕的 < of >
drop out　退學；休學

14. (**A**)　Hundreds of students and teachers spent Friday cleaning up Yellow Pine Park so that it would be a more inviting place to visit.

有數百名學生和老師，週五打掃了黃松公園，以讓它變成一個更吸引人的觀光景點。

Question：What was the main purpose of cleaning up the park?　打掃公園的主要目的是什麼？

(A) To make it more attractive.　要使它更吸引人。
(B) To show community spirit.　要展現社區精神。
(C) To punish the students for poor grades.
　　　為了懲罰成績差的學生。

* ***hundreds of*** 數百的　　spend〔spɛnd〕v. 花（時間）；度過
　clean up 打掃　　pine〔paɪn〕n. 松樹
　inviting〔ɪn'vaɪtɪŋ〕adj. 吸引人的；誘人的
　visit〔'vɪzɪt〕v. 遊覽　　main〔men〕adj. 主要的
　purpose〔'pɝpəs〕n. 目的
　attractive〔ə'træktɪv〕adj. 吸引人的
　show〔ʃo〕v. 展現　　community〔kə'mjunətɪ〕n. 社區
　spirit〔'spɪrɪt〕n. 精神　　punish〔'pʌnɪʃ〕v. 處罰
　poor〔pur〕adj. 差的　　grade〔gred〕n. 成績

15. (**C**)　W：Mr. Silver, I've been with your company for five years, and I've never asked for anything.

女：希爾先生，我在公司已經做了五年，我從來都沒有要求過任何事情。

M：Let me guess.　You want a raise?

男：讓我來猜。妳想要加薪？

W：I think I deserve it.

女：我認為那是我應得的。

Question：What is the relationship between the speakers?
　　　　　說話者之間是什麼關係？

(A) Husband and wife. 夫妻。

(B) Teammates. 隊友。

(C) <u>Employer and employee. 雇主和員工。</u>

* company〔ˈkʌmpənɪ〕 *n.* 公司　　***ask for*** 要求
guess〔gɛs〕 *v.* 猜　　raise〔rez〕 *n.* 加薪
deserve〔dɪˈzɝv〕 *v.* 應得
relationship〔rɪˈleʃənˌʃɪp〕 *n.* 關係
husband〔ˈhʌzbənd〕 *n.* 丈夫　　wife〔waɪf〕 *n.* 妻子
teammate〔ˈtimˌmet〕 *n.* 隊友
employer〔ɪmˈplɔɪɚ〕 *n.* 雇主
employee〔ˌɛmplɔɪˈi〕 *n.* 員工

16. (**B**) Studies suggest that happy people have a lower risk of heart disease and stroke. Among the happiest individuals, the risk was found to be 50 percent lower. While healthier people may tend to be happier people, researchers believe that a positive outlook can positively impact heart health in a number of ways.

研究顯示，快樂的人得心臟病和中風的風險較低。在最快樂的人當中發現，風險低了百分之五十。雖然較健康的人可能比較容易快樂，但研究人員相信，樂觀的看法可能在很多方面，對心臟健康有正面的影響。

Question：What is this talk mainly about?
這段談話主要是關於什麼？

(A) Money. 金錢。

(B) <u>Health. 健康。</u>

(C) Happiness. 快樂。

* study〔ˈstʌdɪ〕 *n.* 研究　　suggest〔səgˈdʒɛst〕 *v.* 顯示
risk〔rɪsk〕 *n.* 風險　　disease〔dɪˈziz〕 *n.* 疾病
heart disease 心臟病　　stroke〔strok〕 *n.* 中風
among〔əˈmʌŋ〕 *prep.* 在…之中

individual〔ˌɪndə'vɪdʒʊəl〕*n.* 個人
percent〔pə'sɛnt〕*n.* 百分之…
while〔hwaɪl〕*conj.* 雖然 (= *though*)
healthy〔'hɛlθɪ〕*adj.* 健康的
tend to 易於；傾向於　　researcher〔rɪ'sɜtʃə〕*n.* 研究人員
positive〔'pɑzətɪv〕*adj.* 正面的；樂觀的
outlook〔'aʊtˌlʊk〕*n.* 看法　　impact〔'ɪmpækt〕*v.* 影響
health〔hɛlθ〕*n.* 健康　　***a number of*** 幾個；許多
way〔we〕*n.* 方式；方面　　talk〔tɔk〕*n.* 談話
mainly〔'menlɪ〕*adv.* 主要地

17. (**B**)　M：Have you ever heard of a singer named Miss Zaza?

　　　　男：妳有聽過一位叫 Miss Zaza 的歌手嗎？

　　　　W：Duh! Of course! She is the biggest pop star in the world.

　　　　女：廢話！當然有！她是全球最知名的流行音樂歌手。

　　　　M：Hmm. That's news to me.

　　　　男：嗯。這件事我還是第一次聽到。

　　　　W：Have you been living in a cave for the last five years?

　　　　女：你最近這五年是住在洞穴裡嗎？

　　　　Question：What does the woman imply?

　　　　　　　　女士在暗示什麼？

　　(A) The man has been living in a cave.

　　　　男士一直住在洞穴裡。

　　(B) The man is out of touch with current events.

　　　　男士不了解時事。

　　(C) The man has poor taste in music.

　　　　男士對音樂的品味很差。

＊ ***hear of*** 聽說　　singer〔'sɪŋə〕*n.* 歌手　　***named***～ 名叫～
　　duh〔də〕*interj.* 哼【用以表示人說的話或做的事很愚蠢】
　　Duh! 廢話！　　***of course*** 當然

big〔bɪg〕*adj.* 偉大的；重要的　　pop〔pɑp〕*n.* 流行音樂
star〔stɑr〕*n.* 明星　　***pop star*** 流行音樂歌手
news〔njuz〕*n.* 新聞　　cave〔kev〕*n.* 洞穴
live in a cave 住在洞穴裡；不知道大家所知道的事
imply〔ɪmˋplaɪ〕*v.* 暗示
out of touch with 不接觸；不知道
current〔ˋkɝənt〕*adj.* 現在的　　event〔ɪˋvɛnt〕*n.* 事件
current events 時事（＝*current affairs*）
taste〔test〕*n.* 品味

18. (**C**) 　M：The light in the bathroom is out again.

　　　　　男：浴室的燈又壞了。

　　　　　W：Didn't you just replace that bulb last week? There
　　　　　　　must be a problem with the wires.

　　　　　女：你不是上禮拜才換掉那個燈泡嗎？一定是電線出了問題。

　　　　　M：I'll call an electrician in the morning.

　　　　　男：我明天早上會打給電工。

　　　　　Question：What is the problem in the bathroom?
　　　　　　　　　　　浴室有什麼問題？

　　　　　(A) The tiles are cracked. 瓷磚裂了。

　　　　　(B) The toilet is clogged. 馬桶塞住了。

　　　　　(C) The light is out. 燈不亮了。

　　　　　* light〔laɪt〕*n.* 燈　　bathroom〔ˋbæθˌrum〕*n.* 浴室；廁所
　　　　　out〔aʊt〕*adj.* （燈）熄滅的　　just〔dʒʌst〕*adv.* 剛剛
　　　　　replace〔rɪˋples〕*v.* 更換　　bulb〔bʌlb〕*n.* 燈泡
　　　　　wire〔waɪr〕*n.* 電線　　electrician〔ɪˌlɛkˋtrɪʃən〕*n.* 電工
　　　　　tile〔taɪl〕*n.* 瓷磚　　cracked〔krækt〕*adj.* 破裂的
　　　　　toilet〔ˋtɔɪlɪt〕*n.* 馬桶　　clog〔klɑg〕*v.* 堵塞

19. (**B**) 　M：Have you noticed that prices are going up on
　　　　　　　everything?

　　　　　男：妳有注意到每樣東西都漲價了嗎？

W : The government needs to step in and do something about it.

女：政府必須要介入，並做點什麼。

M : It's because of their policies that we're in this mess to begin with.

男：起初，就是因爲他們的政策，我們現在才會這麼混亂。

Question : What are the speakers mainly discussing?

說話者主要在討論什麼？

(A) The weather. 天氣。

(B) The economy. 經濟。

(C) The environment. 環境。

* notice〔'notɪs〕*n.* 注意到　price〔praɪs〕*n.* 價格
  go up 上升　government〔'gʌvənmənt〕*n.* 政府
  step in 介入　***because of*** 因爲
  policy〔'paləsɪ〕*n.* 政策　mess〔mɛs〕*n.* 混亂
  to begin with 首先；起初　discuss〔dɪ'skʌs〕*v.* 討論
  weather〔'wɛðə〕*n.* 天氣　economy〔ɪ'kɑnəmɪ〕*n.* 經濟
  environment〔ɪn'vaɪrənmənt〕*n.* 環境

20. (**A**) M : We can watch the football match together tonight.

男：我們今晚可以一起看足球賽。

W : Sorry, but I like volleyball.

女：抱歉，但我喜歡排球。

Question : Why won't the girl watch the football match with the man? 爲什麼女孩不會跟男士看足球賽？

(A) She doesn't like it. 她不喜歡。

(B) She likes football. 她喜歡足球。

(C) She doesn't like volleyball. 她不喜歡排球。

* football〔'fʊt,bɔl〕*n.* 足球　match〔mætʃ〕*n.* 比賽
  volleyball〔'vɑlɪ,bɔl〕*n.* 排球

21. (**C**) Recycling electronics still isn't as easy as it should be, but it's important to get the facts. We now own about 24 electronic devices per household and many of these get replaced regularly. The average cell phone user, for example, gets a new cell phone every 18 months. Fortunately, recycling electronics is becoming more popular, and about 100 million pounds of material is recovered from electronics recycling plants each year.

回收電子產品還是沒有那麼容易，但了解事實是很重要的。我們現在每個家庭至少擁有二十四種電子裝置，而很多都會定期被更換。例如，一般的手機使用者每十八個月會買一支新手機。幸運的是，回收電子產品已經變得更普遍，每年所回收的大約一億磅的材料，是來自電子回收廠。

Question：What is the speaker mainly talking about?
　　　　　說話者主要在談論什麼？

(A) Pollution. 污染。

(B) Technology. 科技。

(C) Recycling. 回收。

* recycle (ri'saɪkḷ) v. 回收
  electronics (ɪ,lɛk'trɑnɪks) n. pl. 電子設備；電子儀器
  get (gɛt) v. 知道；被…；買　　fact (fækt) n. 事實
  own (on) v. 擁有　　electronic (ɪ,lɛk'trɑnɪk) adj. 電子的
  device (dɪ'vaɪs) n. 裝置；設備　　per (pɚ) prep. 每一
  household ('haus,hold) n. 家庭　　replace (rɪ'ples) v. 更換
  regularly ('rɛgjələlɪ) adv. 定期地
  average ('ævərɪdʒ) adj. 一般的　　*cell phone* 手機
  user ('juzɚ) n. 使用者　　*for example* 例如
  fortunately ('fɔrtʃənɪtlɪ) adv. 幸運的是
  popular ('pɑpjələ) adj. 普遍的　　million ('mɪljən) n. 百萬
  pound (paund) n. 磅　　material (mə'tɪrɪəl) n. 材料
  recover (rɪ'kʌvɚ) v. 恢復；重新獲得　　plant (plænt) n. 工廠
  pollution (pə'luʃən) n. 污染
  technology (tɛk'nɑlədʒɪ) n. 科技

 TEST 24 ▶ 詳解

第一部分：辨識句意（第 1-3 題）

1. (**A**) (A)　　　　　(B)　　　　　(C)

Jill woke up from a nightmare in which she was being chased by an angry dog.

吉兒從惡夢中醒來，她夢見自己被一隻生氣的狗追。

* ***wake up*** 醒來　　nightmare〔ˋnaɪt͵mɛr〕 *n.* 惡夢
  chase〔tʃes〕 *v.* 追趕　　angry〔ˋæŋgrɪ〕 *adj.* 生氣的

2. (**B**) (A)　　　　　(B)　　　　　(C)

Larry has just left the pet store and now he's listening to music on his headphones.

賴瑞剛剛離開寵物店，現在他戴上耳機正在聽音樂。

* pet〔pɛt〕 *n.* 寵物　　headphones〔ˋhɛd͵fonz〕 *n. pl.* 耳機

3. (**C**) (A)　　　　　(B)　　　　　(C)

Thomas is sitting at his desk in front of a computer and browsing the Internet.

湯瑪斯正坐在他的書桌前用電腦瀏覽網路。

* browse〔braʊz〕*v.* 瀏覽　　Internet〔ˈɪntəˌnɛt〕*n.* 網際網路

第二部分：基本問答（第 4-10 題）

4. (**A**) I thought the movie was boring. The special effects were so outdated. 我覺得那部電影很無聊。它的特效都過時了。

　(A) I agree. And the ending was so predictable.
　　　我同意。而且結局完全是可預測的。

　(B) Let's sit in the back row. 我們去坐最後一排。

　(C) I'm confused. We watched a movie.
　　　我很困惑。我們看了一部電影。

　* movie〔ˈmuvɪ〕*n.* 電影　　boring〔ˈborɪŋ〕*adj.* 無聊的
　　special〔ˈspɛʃəl〕*adj.* 特殊的　　effect〔ɪˈfɛkt〕*n.* 效果
　　so〔so〕*adv.* 非常　　outdated〔ˌaʊtˈdetɪd〕*adj.* 過時的
　　ending〔ˈɛndɪŋ〕*n.* 結局
　　predictable〔prɪˈdɪktəbḷ〕*adj.* 可預測的
　　row〔ro〕*n.* (一)排
　　back row 最後一排 (↔ front row 第一排)
　　confused〔kənˈfjuzd〕*adj.* 困惑的

5. (**C**) Did you finish your homework? Didn't I say no TV until your homework is finished?

　你功課做完了嗎？我不是說功課沒做完不能看電視嗎？

　(A) Yes, I didn't finish it. 是的，我沒做完。

　(B) No, I'll be home after work. 不，我下班後就會回家。

　(C) Yes, I heard you, and I'm finished with all my homework.
　　　是的，我有聽到妳說的，我功課已經全部做完了。

　* finish〔ˈfɪnɪʃ〕*v.* 做完　　until〔ənˈtɪl〕*prep.* 直到…為止

6. (**C**) Is it safe to ride the Taipei Metro system at night?

　　晚上搭乘台北捷運系統安全嗎？

　　(A) Take the red line to Beitou.　搭紅線去北投。

　　(B) The runner was safe.　跑者是安全的。

　　(C) Generally, yes.　一般說來，是的。

　　* safe〔sef〕adj. 安全的　　ride〔raɪd〕v. 搭乘
　　metro〔'mɛtro〕n. 地下鐵　　system〔'sɪstəm〕n. 系統
　　Taipei Metro system　台北捷運系統　　runner〔'rʌnɚ〕n. 跑者
　　generally〔'dʒɛnərəlɪ〕adv. 通常；一般說來

7. (**A**) You're late again.　What's your excuse this time?

　　你又遲到了。你這次的藉口是什麼？

　　(A) My alarm didn't go off this morning.

　　　　今天早上我的鬧鐘沒響。

　　(B) The water was cold so I went home.

　　　　水很冷，所以我就回家了。

　　(C) They ordered the fish.　他們點了魚。

　　* late〔let〕adj. 遲到的　　again〔ə'gɛn〕adv. 又
　　excuse〔ɪk'skjus〕n. 藉口
　　alarm〔ə'lɑrm〕n. 鬧鐘（= *alarm clock*）
　　go off　（鬧鐘）響　　order〔'ɔrdɚ〕v. 點（餐）

8. (**A**) Is the Internet working or not?　I need to update my blog as soon as possible.

　　網路運作正常嗎？我需要盡快更新我的部落格。

　　(A) The technician is trying to fix it right now.

　　　　現在技術人員現在正試著修理它。

　　(B) I saw it on the Internet.　我在網路上看到它。

　　(C) Check my web page when you have time.

　　　　你有時間的時候看一下我的網頁。

　　* work〔wɝk〕v. 運作　　update〔ʌp'det〕v. 更新
　　blog〔blɑg〕n. 部落格　　**as soon as possible**　盡快

technician〔tɛkˈnɪʃən〕*n.* 技術人員
fix〔fɪks〕*v.* 修理　　***right now*** 現在
check〔tʃɛk〕*v.* 查看　　web page〔ˈwɛbˌpedʒ〕*n.* 網頁

9. (**A**) Excuse me. Do you mind closing the window?
不好意思。你介意把窗戶關上嗎？

(A) Not at all. 一點也不。
(B) Who did it? 誰做的？
(C) You're welcome. 不客氣。

* mind〔maɪnd〕*v.* 介意　　***not at all*** 一點也不

10. (**C**) How was your weekend in the mountains?
你週末在山上過得如何？

(A) This one looks a bit tight. 這個看起來有點緊。
(B) Plump and juicy. 豐滿又多汁。
(C) Much too short. 時間太短了。

* weekend〔ˈwikˈɛnd〕*n.* 週末　　mountain〔ˈmaʊntn̩〕*n.* 山
a bit 有一點　　tight〔taɪt〕*adj.* 緊的
plump〔plʌmp〕*adj.* 豐滿的　　juicy〔ˈdʒusɪ〕*adj.* 多汁的
much too~ 太過~

第三部分：言談理解（第 11-21 題）

11. (**A**) Shopping at farmers' markets is the easiest way to eat locally. You know where the food comes from. After all, the growers are right there and you can ask them. More than one shopper, however, has come home with bags of produce that went uneaten. A bit of planning can keep weekly shopping for produce at a farmers' market fun and make cooking a snap all week long.
在農夫市場購物，是最容易吃到當地食物的方法。你知道食物是從哪裡來的。畢竟，栽培者就在那裡，你可以問他們。然而，不只一位購物者,會帶著許多袋農產品回家,但卻都沒吃。稍微計畫一下,就可以使每週在農夫市場購農產品變得有趣,而且可以讓你一整個禮拜做菜都很輕鬆。

Question： What can you buy at a farmers' market?
你可以在農夫市場買到什麼？

(A) Food. 食物。

(B) Cookware. 烹飪用具。

(C) Farming equipment. 農業設備。

* shop〔ʃɑp〕*v.* 購物　　market〔'mɑrkɪt〕*n.* 市場
  farmers' market 農夫市場　　locally〔'lokəlɪ〕*adv.* 當地地
  after all 畢竟　　grower〔'groɚ〕*n.* 栽培者
  shopper〔'ʃɑpɚ〕*n.* 購物者　　however〔haʊ'ɛvɚ〕*adv.* 然而
  produce〔'prɑdjus〕*n.* 農產品　　go〔go〕*v.* 變得
  uneaten〔ʌn'itn̩〕*adj.* 未吃的　　*a bit of* 一點點的
  plan〔plæn〕*v.* 計畫　　weekly〔'wiklɪ〕*adj.* 每週的
  shop for 購買　　fun〔fʌn〕*adj.* 有趣的
  snap〔snæp〕*n.* 輕鬆的工作　　long〔lɔŋ〕*adv.* 整…
  all week long 一整個禮拜
  cookware〔'kʊk,wɛr〕*n.* 烹飪用具
  farming〔'fɑrmɪŋ〕*adj.* 農業的
  equipment〔ɪ'kwɪpmənt〕*n.* 設備

12. (**C**)　W： Was Jack late for school this morning?
　　　女： 傑克今天早上上學有遲到嗎？

　　　M： I don't know. Ask him.
　　　男： 我不知道。妳去問他。

　　　W： But you're in charge of making sure the kids get off
　　　　　to school in the morning.
　　　女： 但是你負責確認孩子們早上是否有去上學。

　　　M： Yes, but I have no control over what happens once
　　　　　they're out the door. Jack left at his regular time this
　　　　　morning. That's all I know.

男：沒錯，但是一旦他們走出家門，我就無法掌控接下來會發生什麼事。今天早上傑克有按時出門。我只知道這麼多。

Question : What do we know about Jack?

關於傑克，我們知道什麼？

(A) He's never been late to school before.

他以前上學從未遲到過。

(B) He's an early riser. 他是個早起的人。

(C) He makes his own way to school. <u>他自己去上學。</u>

* ***in charge of*** 負責　　***make sure*** 確認
get off 出發；去　　control〔kənˈtrol〕*n.* 控制；掌控
once〔wʌns〕*conj.* 一旦　　***be out the door*** 出門
regular〔ˈrɛgjələ〕*adj.* 固定的　　riser〔ˈraɪzə〕*n.* 起床者
early riser 早起的人　　***make one's way*** 前進；去

13. (**B**) M : Hey, didn't you get my text?

男：嘿，妳沒有收到我的簡訊嗎？

W : No, when did you text me?

女：沒有，你什麼時候傳給我的？

M : Like an hour ago.

男：大概一個小時前。

W : What for?

女：為什麼傳給我？

M : I wanted to ask you a favor.

男：我原本想要請妳幫個忙。

W : What was it?

女：什麼事？

M : Nothing. Forget it.

男：沒什麼。算了吧。

W : Oh, here it is. I somehow missed this. "Hey, would you pick up a six-pack of beer on the way home? Thanks." Oops. Sorry.

女：噢，在這裡。我不知道為什麼沒看見這個。「嘿，妳回家的路上可以買半打啤酒嗎？謝謝。」糟糕。抱歉。

Question：How did the man try to contact the woman?
男士試圖用什麼方式聯絡女士？

(A) Via e-mail. 透過電子郵件。

(B) By text. 用簡訊。

(C) On social media. 用社群媒體。

* get〔gɛt〕v. 收到　　text〔tɛkst〕n. 簡訊　v. 傳簡訊給
  like〔laɪk〕adv. 差不多；幾乎　　favor〔'fevɚ〕n. 恩惠
  ask sb. **a favor** 請某人幫忙　　**forget it** 算了吧
  somehow〔'sʌm,hau〕adv. 不知道為什麼
  miss〔mɪs〕v. 錯過　　**pick up** 買
  six-pack〔'sɪks,pæk〕n. 六罐瓶裝的食物、飲料、啤酒等
  beer〔bɪr〕n. 啤酒　　oops〔ups〕interj. 糟糕；對不起
  contact〔'kɑntækt〕v. 聯絡　　via〔'vaɪə〕prep. 經由
  e-mail〔'i,mel〕n. 電子郵件　　social〔'soʃəl〕adj. 社交的
  media〔'midɪə〕n. pl. 媒體　　**social media** 社群媒體

14. (**A**) I first encountered bird-watching in Taiwan when I lived
in Taipei in 2014. Walk through any park in the city or
bike the trails lining its rivers, and you will inevitably
encounter a gaggle of bird-watchers with tripod-mounted
cameras. They stand on muddy banks and circle around
trees with nests, patiently waiting for a glimpse of a
treasured creature.

我初次在台灣接觸到賞鳥，是 2014 年我住在台北的時候。走在
城市裡的任何公園，或在河邊的小徑騎腳踏車，你一定會遇到把
相機架在三腳架上的一群賞鳥人士。他們站在泥濘的河岸邊，圍
繞著有鳥巢的樹，耐心地等待看一眼這種珍貴的生物。

Question：When did the speaker first encounter bird-
watching? 說話者初次接觸賞鳥是什麼時候？

(A) When he lived in Taipei. 當他住在台北時。

(B) When he lived in Tainan. 當他住在台南時。

(C) When he lived in Taichung. 當他住在台中時。

* encounter〔ɪn'kaʊntə〕v. 遇見　　bird-watching n. 賞鳥
through〔θru〕prep. 穿越　　bike〔baɪk〕v. 騎腳踏車
trail〔trel〕n. 小徑；小路　　line〔laɪn〕v. 沿…排列成行
river〔'rɪvə〕n. 河流
inevitably〔ɪn'ɛvətəblɪ〕adv. 必然地；必定
gaggle〔'gægl〕n. 一群　　bird-watcher n. 賞鳥者
tripod〔'traɪpɑd〕n. 三腳架　　mount〔maʊnt〕v. 架設
camera〔'kæmərə〕n. 照相機　　muddy〔'mʌdɪ〕adj. 泥濘的
bank〔bæŋk〕n. 河岸　　*circle around* 圍繞
nest〔nɛst〕n. 鳥巢　　patiently〔'peʃəntlɪ〕adv. 耐心地
glimpse〔glɪmps〕n. 瞥見；看一眼
treasured〔'trɛʒəd〕adj. 珍貴的
creature〔'kritʃə〕n. 生物；動物

15. (**A**) M：Are you busy?

　　　　男：妳在忙嗎？

　　　　W：Not really.

　　　　女：不會。

　　　　M：Is this a good time for you?

　　　　男：這個時間對妳而言適合嗎？

　　　　W：A good time for what?

　　　　女：適合做什麼？

　　　　M：Would you mind if I asked you a few questions?

　　　　男：妳會介意我問妳一些問題嗎？

　　　　W：Go ahead. Ask me anything.

　　　　女：請便。隨便問吧。

　　　　Question：What will the man probably do next?

　　　　　　　　男士接下來可能會做什麼？

　　　　(A) Ask some questions. 問一些問題。

　　　　(B) Take a nap. 小睡片刻。

　　　　(C) Go shopping. 去逛街購物。

　　* busy〔'bɪzɪ〕adj. 忙碌的
　　　really〔'rɪəlɪ〕adv. 實際上是；其實是

good〔gʊd〕*adj.* 適合的　　***go ahead*** 請便
probably〔'prɑbəblɪ〕*adv.* 可能
nap〔næp〕*n.* 小睡　　***take a nap*** 小睡片刻

16. (**C**) M : Do you think Freddy will be here by six o'clock?
男：妳覺得弗雷迪六點之前會來嗎？

W : I don't know. The traffic is pretty bad.
女：我不知道。現在交通狀況很不好。

M : I hope he didn't take the main highway.
男：希望他沒有走主要公路。

Question : Where is Freddy now? 弗雷迪現在在哪裡？

(A) At home. 在家裡。
(B) At school. 在學校。
(C) In traffic. 在車陣中。

* traffic〔'træfɪk〕*n.* 交通；來往的車輛
pretty〔'prɪtɪ〕*adv.* 相當　　hope〔hop〕*v.* 希望
take〔tek〕*v.* 走（…路）　　main〔men〕*adj.* 主要的
highway〔'haɪ,we〕*n.* 公路

17. (**C**) A young girl sits at her desk, reviewing her homework
assignments for the evening. English: read three
chapters and write a journal response. Math: complete 30
problems, showing all work. Science: do a worksheet,
front and back. French: study vocabulary for tomorrow's
test. It's going to be a long night.
一位年輕女孩坐在書桌前，重新檢查今晚要做的功課。英文：閱
讀三章，並寫一篇心得筆記。數學：完成 30 道題目，列出全部的
計算過程。科學：做一張習題，正反面。法文：研讀明天要考的
字彙。這將是一個很漫長的夜晚。

Question : Which of the following is NOT part of the
girl's homework?
以下何者不是女孩的作業的一部分？

(A) Complete 30 math problems. 完成 30 道數學題目。

(B) Study French vocabulary. 研讀法文字彙。

(C) Read three chapters of history. 讀三章歷史。

* review〔rɪ'vju〕v. 重新檢查；複習
assignment〔ə'saɪnmənt〕n. 作業　　chapter〔'tʃæptɚ〕n. 章
journal〔'dʒɝnl̩〕n. 日記；日誌　　response〔rɪ'spɑns〕n. 回應
journal response　（閱讀）心得筆記　　math〔mæθ〕n. 數學
complete〔kəm'plit〕v. 完成　　problem〔'prɑbləm〕n. 問題
show〔ʃo〕v. 顯示　　work〔wɝk〕n. 做法
science〔'saɪəns〕n. 科學
worksheet〔'wɝk,ʃit〕n.（學生做的）活頁練習題
front〔frʌnt〕n. 正面　　back〔bæk〕n. 反面
French〔frɛntʃ〕n. 法文　　vocabulary〔və'kæbjə,lɛrɪ〕n. 字彙
test〔tɛst〕n. 測驗　　history〔'hɪstrɪ〕n. 歷史

18. (**C**) M：What's the matter? You're walking with a limp.

男：怎麼了？妳走路跛腳。

W：I twisted my ankle during my workout this afternoon.

女：我今天下午運動的時候扭傷了腳踝。

M：Did you go see a doctor?

男：妳有去看醫生嗎？

W：No, it's not that bad. I'll take a painkiller and see how I feel tomorrow.

女：沒有，沒那麼嚴重。我會吃一顆止痛藥，再看看明天覺得如何。

M：Maybe you should stay off your feet for a while.

男：也許妳這陣子應該避免走路。

Question：What does the man suggest? 男士建議什麼？

(A) See a doctor. 看醫生。

(B) Take some medicine. 吃些藥。

(C) Get some rest. 多休息。

* matter〔'mætɚ〕n. 事情　　**What's the matter?** 怎麼了？

limp〔lɪmp〕*n.* 跛腳　　twist〔twɪst〕*v.* 扭傷
ankle〔'æŋkl̩〕*n.* 腳踝　　workout〔'wɜk,aʊt〕*n.* 運動
go see a doctor 去看醫生（= *go and see a doctor*）
bad〔bæd〕*adj.* 嚴重的　　take〔tek〕*v.* 服用
painkiller〔'pen,kɪlɚ〕*n.* 止痛藥　　***stay off*** 避開
a while 一陣子　　suggest〔səg'dʒɛst〕*v.* 建議
medicine〔'mɛdəsn̩〕*n.* 藥　　rest〔rɛst〕*n.* 休息

19. (**C**) W：It was nice of the Petersons to invite us over for dinner.

女：彼得森一家人真好，邀請我們去吃晚餐。

M：Yes, it would be great to see them.　But we need to find a sitter for the kids.

男：對，能夠見到他們真好。但我們會需要找個臨時保姆來照顧孩子們。

W：I'll ask my sister if she has plans this Saturday night.

女：我會去問我姐妹，她這個週六晚上有沒有什麼計畫。

M：If she can't do it, maybe my mother wouldn't mind watching them for a few hours.

男：如果她不行，也許我媽不會介意照顧他們幾個小時。

Question：Who are the speakers?　說話者是什麼身份？

(A) Brother and sister.　兄妹。
(B) Father and daughter.　父女。
(C) Husband and wife.　夫妻。

　* nice〔naɪs〕*adj.* 好的　　***the Petersons*** 彼得森一家人
　　invite〔ɪn'vaɪt〕*v.* 邀請　　over〔'ovɚ〕*adv.* 過去
　　sitter〔'sɪtɚ〕*n.* 臨時保姆（= *babysitter*）
　　watch〔watʃ〕*v.* 照顧　　***a few*** 一些；幾個
　　husband〔'hʌzbənd〕*n.* 丈夫　　wife〔waɪf〕*n.* 妻子

20. (**B**) M：Would you like a bottle of orange juice or a cup of coffee?

男：妳想要一瓶柳橙汁還是一杯咖啡？

W : Neither. I'd like a cup of tea.

女：都不要。我想要一杯茶。

Question : Which is true? 何者是正確的？

(A) The man will have a bottle of orange juice.

男士會拿到一瓶柳橙汁。

(B) The woman won't have a cup of coffee.

女士不會拿到一杯咖啡。

(C) The man will have a cup of tea. 男士會拿到一杯茶。

* bottle〔'batl〕 n. 瓶　　juice〔dʒus〕 n. 果汁
coffee〔'kɔfɪ〕 n. 咖啡　　neither〔'niðɚ〕 pron. 兩者都不
have〔hæv〕 v. 得到；獲得

21. (**A**) W : Hey, Mike. Where have you been?

女：嘿，麥可。你去哪裡了？

M : I was at the gym. I've gained 5kg since I came back home, so I'm trying to get back in shape. What are you doing?

男：我在健身房。自從我回家後，已經胖了 5 公斤，所以我想恢復體型。妳在做什麼？

W : I'm going on a diet because I am a little overweight.

女：我正在節食，因為我有點過重。

Question : What do they both want to do?

他們兩個都想做什麼？

(A) They want to lose weight. 他們想要減重。

(B) They want to gain weight. 他們想要增加體重。

(C) They should take vitamins. 他們應該要吃維他命。

* gym〔dʒɪm〕 n. 健身房　　gain〔gen〕 v. 增加
shape〔ʃep〕 n. 形狀　　***get back in shape*** 恢復體型
go on a diet 節食　　overweight〔'ovɚ'wet〕 adj. 過重的
lose〔luz〕 v. 減少　　weight〔wet〕 n. 體重
vitamin〔'vaɪtəmɪn〕 n. 維他命

TEST 25 ▶ 詳解

第一部分：辨識句意（第 1-3 題）

1. (**C**) (A)　　　　　　(B)　　　　　　(C)

Tina slept through her alarm this morning until her mother came in and yelled at her to wake up.

蒂娜今天早上沒聽到鬧鐘響，一直睡到她媽媽進來大聲叫醒她。

* *sleep through*　不被…吵醒而繼續睡
　　alarm〔ə'lɑrm〕*n.* 鬧鐘（= *alarm clock*）　　yell〔jɛl〕*v.* 大叫
　　wake up　醒來

2. (**B**) (A)　　　　　　(B)　　　　　　(C)

Rod likes Halloween because he can dress up in his costume.　羅德喜歡萬聖節，因為他可以穿上他的服裝。

* Halloween〔ˌhælo'in〕*n.* 萬聖節　　*dress up*　裝扮
　　costume〔'kɑstjum〕*n.* 服裝

3. (**A**) (A)　　　　　　(B)　　　　　　(C)

Jason got hit by a car and was taken to the hospital.

傑森被車撞了，然後被帶去醫院。

* hit〔hɪt〕*v.* 撞　　hospital〔'hɑspɪtḷ〕*n.* 醫院

第二部分：基本問答（第 4-10 題）

4. (**A**) Have you gone to the movie *The Revenant*?

你有去看「神鬼獵人」那部電影嗎？

(A) Yes, I enjoyed it very much. 有，我很喜歡。

(B) No, I've never been there. 沒有，我從未去過那裡。

(C) Yes, I've liked the river for a long time.

是的，我喜歡那條河流很久了。

* movie〔'muvɪ〕*n.* 電影　　***The Revenant*** 神鬼獵人

enjoy〔ɪn'dʒɔɪ〕*v.* 喜歡　　river〔'rɪvɚ〕*n.* 河流

5. (**C**) Are you familiar with Microsoft Word? It's a type of computer software.

你對 Microsoft Word 熟悉嗎？它是一種電腦軟體。

(A) Yes, I've met him before. 是的，我以前見過他。

(B) Yes, he is my friend. 是的，他是我的朋友。

(C) Yes, I use it frequently. 是的，我經常使用它。

* familiar〔fə'mɪljɚ〕*adj.* 熟悉的 < *with* >

type〔taɪp〕*n.* 類型；種類　　software〔'sɔft,wɛr〕*n.* 軟體

frequently〔'frikwəntlɪ〕*adv.* 經常

6. (**C**) Where did Kenny go? He was just here a minute ago.

肯尼去哪裡了？他一分鐘之前還在這裡。

(A) Have you met Kenny? 你見過肯尼了嗎？

(B) I'm in the bathroom. 我在浴室裡。

(C) He left for class. 他去上課了。

* minute〔'mɪnɪt〕*n.* 分鐘

bathroom〔'bæθ,rum〕*n.* 浴室；廁所　　***leave for*** 動身前往

7. (**A**) The meat was so tough that we couldn't cut it. How was the meat? 那塊肉很硬，我們無法切。肉怎麼樣？

   (A) It was too hard. <u>太硬了。</u>

   (B) It was too rare. 太罕見了。

   (C) It was very delicious. 非常美味。

   * meat〔mit〕*n.* 肉　　tough〔tʌf〕*adj.* 堅韌的；堅硬的（= *hard*）
   rare〔rɛr〕*adj.* 罕見的　　delicious〔dɪ'lɪʃəs〕*adj.* 美味的

8. (**B**) I'm scared. The doctor says I'll need surgery to have my tonsils removed.

   我好害怕。醫生說我需要動手術，切除我的扁桃腺。

   (A) I didn't touch it. 我沒有碰它。

   (B) Is that a dangerous procedure? <u>那是一種危險的手術嗎？</u>

   (C) You had better see a doctor. 你最好去看醫生。

   * scared〔skɛrd〕*adj.* 害怕的　　surgery〔'sɝdʒərɪ〕*n.* 手術
   tonsil〔'tɑnsḷ〕*n.* 扁桃腺　　remove〔rɪ'muv〕*v.* 除去；移除
   dangerous〔'dendʒərəs〕*adj.* 危險的
   procedure〔prə'sidʒɚ〕*n.* 程序；手續；手術
   had better 最好

9. (**B**) The girl was frightened. How did the girl feel? 那個女孩受到驚嚇。那個女孩有什麼感覺？

   (A) She was delighted. 她很高興。

   (B) She was afraid. <u>她很害怕。</u>

   (C) She was hungry. 她很餓。

   * frightened〔'fraɪtṇd〕*adj.* 受到驚嚇的；害怕的
   delighted〔dɪ'laɪtɪd〕*adj.* 高興的
   afraid〔ə'fred〕*adj.* 害怕的　　hungry〔'hʌŋgrɪ〕*adj.* 飢餓的

10. (**A**) Is this software free? 這個軟體是免費的嗎？

   (A) No, this is a demo version. You have to pay for the real thing. <u>不是，這是示範版。正版的會需要付費。</u>

(B) No, there are hidden messages. You have to pay attention. 不是,有隱藏的訊息。你必須注意。

(C) Yes, he guards the house. We've never had a problem. 是的,他會守護房子。我們從未有過問題。

* software〔'sɔft͵wɛr〕*n.* 軟體　　free〔fri〕*adj.* 免費的
demo〔'dɛmo〕*n.* 示範　　version〔'vɝʒən〕*n.* 版本
pay for 付~的錢　　***the real thing*** 真貨;正品;正版
hidden〔'hɪdn̩〕*adj.* 隱藏的　　message〔'mɛsɪdʒ〕*n.* 訊息
attention〔ə'tɛnʃən〕*n.* 注意(力)　　***pay attention*** 注意
guard〔gɑrd〕*v.* 守護　　problem〔'prɑbləm〕*n.* 問題

第三部分:言談理解(第 11-21 題)

11. (**C**)　W : Sir, this bill was due yesterday. I'm afraid there's a penalty for the late payment.

女:先生,這帳單昨天就到期了。恐怕會因遲繳而罰款。

M : What!? Today is the 14th. It's due on the 14th.

男:什麼!? 今天是十四日。到期日是十四日啊。

W : Today is the 15th, sir.

女:今天是十五日,先生。

M : Is it? Oh, my goodness!

男:是嗎? 喔,我的天啊!

Question : What is the man's problem?

　　　　這為男士的問題是什麼?

(A) He is late for an appointment. 他約會遲到了。

(B) He is late for work. 他上班遲到了。

(C) He doesn't know what day it is. 他不知道今天星期幾。

bill〔bɪl〕*n.* 帳單　　due〔du〕*adj.* 到期的　　***I'm afraid*** 恐怕
penalty〔'pɛnl̩tɪ〕*n.* 罰款　　late〔let〕*adj.* 遲的
payment〔'pemənt〕*n.* 付款　　***My goodness!*** 我的天啊!
appointment〔ə'pɔɪntmənt〕*n.* 約會;預約

12. (**A**) If you suffer with a health issue or simply want to
improve an area of your health, there are probably
behaviors that you are doing that are standing in your
way. We talk a lot about those things that we should be
doing for health and well-being, but we don't talk as
much about the things we need to stop doing.
如果你有健康問題，或只是想改善健康的某個領域，那可能你現
在的某些行為會阻礙你。我們談論很多該為健康和幸福做的事，
但我們很少談一些我們必須停止做的事。

Question : What does the speaker suggest?
說話者建議什麼？

(A) Behavior is related to well-being. 行為與幸福安康有關。

(B) Addiction is the cause of most health issues.
上癮是大多數健康問題的原因。

(C) Most people are afraid to ask for help.
大多數的人都害怕尋求幫助。

* suffer ('sʌfɚ) v. 受苦；遭受　　health (hɛlθ) n. 健康
issue ('ɪʃu) n. 問題　　improve (ɪm'pruv) v. 改善
area ('ɛrɪə) n. 領域　　probably ('prɑbəblɪ) adv. 可能
behavior (bɪ'hevjɚ) n. 行為　　***stand in*** one's ***way*** 阻礙；妨礙
well-being ('wɛl'biɪŋ) n. 幸福；安康
suggest (səg'dʒɛst) v. 建議
related (rɪ'letɪd) adj. 有關的 < to >
addiction (ə'dɪkʃən) n. 上癮　　cause (kɔz) n. 原因
ask for 要求

13. (**A**) Taiwan tends to have a consistently pleasant year-round
climate. There are no extremes of winter and summer,
only two seasons: wet and dry. Because Taiwan straddles
the equator, sunburn can occur rapidly, even on a cloudy
day.

台灣通常會有令人心情愉快的全年氣候。沒有極端的冬天和夏天，只有兩個季節：雨季和乾季。由於台灣橫跨赤道，即使在陰天，也可能會很快就曬傷。

Question： What is this talk mainly about?

這段談話主要是關於什麼？

(A) Taiwan's weather. 台灣的天氣。

(B) Taiwan's economy. 台灣的經濟。

(C) Taiwan's location. 台灣的位置。

* ***tend to V.*** 傾向於⋯

consistently〔kən'sɪstəntlɪ〕*adv.* 經常；一直

pleasant〔'plɛznt〕*adj.*（天氣）令人心情愉快的；舒服的

year-round *adj.* 全年的　　climate〔'klaɪmɪt〕*n.* 氣候

extremes〔ɪk'strimz〕*n. pl.* 極端的狀態

season〔'sizn〕*n.* 季節　　wet〔wɛt〕*adj.* 濕的；下雨的

dry〔draɪ〕*adj.* 乾燥的　　straddle〔'strædl〕*v.* 橫跨

equator〔ɪ'kwetɚ〕*n.* 赤道　　sunburn〔'sʌn,bɝn〕*n.* 曬傷

occur〔ə'kɝ〕*v.* 發生　　rapidly〔'ræpɪdlɪ〕*adv.* 迅速地

cloudy〔'klaʊdɪ〕*adj.* 多雲的　　weather〔'wɛðɚ〕*n.* 天氣

economy〔ɪ'kɑnəmɪ〕*n.* 經濟　　location〔lo'keʃən〕*n.* 位置

14. (**C**) M： Have you ever eaten at that diner on Brook Street?

男：你有在布魯克街上的那間速食餐廳吃過飯嗎？

W： You mean the one with the big neon sign that says "Eat Here"?

女：你是說有個上面寫著「在這裡吃」的大霓虹燈招牌的那家嗎？

M： Yes, that's it. I can't think of its name.

男：對，就是那個。我想不起它的名字。

W： I don't think it has one. If it did, it would be the Eat Here Diner. Anyway, to answer your question, yes, I have eaten there and the food is outstanding.

女：我覺得它沒有名字。如果有的話，應該會是「在這裡吃速食
　　餐廳」。反正如果要回答你的問題的話，有，我有在那裡吃
　　過，食物很出色。

Question : What are the speakers mainly discussing?
　　　　　說話者主要在討論什麼？

(A) A bar. 一間酒吧。

(B) A city. 一個城市。

(C) A restaurant. 一家餐廳。

* diner〔'daɪnɚ〕 *n.* 餐車式的速食餐廳　　mean〔min〕 *v.* 意思是
  neon〔'niɑn〕 *n.* 霓虹燈　　sign〔saɪn〕 *n.* 招牌
  say〔se〕 *v.* 寫著　　***think of*** 想到
  anyway〔'ɛnɪ,we〕 *adv.* 不管怎樣；無論如何；反正
  outstanding〔'aʊt'stændɪŋ〕 *adj.* 出色的
  mainly〔'menlɪ〕 *adv.* 主要地　　discuss〔dɪ'skʌs〕 *v.* 討論
  bar〔bɑr〕 *n.* 酒吧　　restaurant〔'rɛstərənt〕 *n.* 餐廳

15. (**A**) M : OK, let's start the meeting. We can't wait any longer.
　　　　男：好的，我們開始開會吧。不能再等下去了。

　　　W : But Reggie isn't here yet.
　　　　女：但是雷吉還沒到。

　　　M : I know. We'll have to start without him. It's already
　　　　　ten past two.
　　　　男：我知道。沒有他我們也必須先開始。現在已經兩點十分了。

　　　Question : What time was the meeting most likely
　　　　　　　　supposed to start? 會議原本很可能要幾點開始？

(A) Two o'clock. 兩點。

(B) Two fifteen. 兩點十五分。

(C) Two thirty. 兩點半。

* meeting〔'mitɪŋ〕 *n.* 會議
  not…any longer 不再 (= *no longer*)　　***not yet*** 尚未；還沒

already〔ɔlˈrɛdɪ〕*adv.* 已經　　past〔pæst〕*prep.* 超過
likely〔ˈlaɪklɪ〕*adv.* 可能　　*be supposed to V.* 應該…

16.（ **C** ）M：I hired Tommy to paint the garage this weekend.

男：我雇用了湯米這個週末來油漆車庫。

W：Are you sure that's a good idea? He's only 12.

女：你確定那是個好主意？他才十二歲。

M：Well, he's quite mature for his age and I trust him.

男：嗯，以他的年齡來說他相當成熟，而且我信任他。

W：I understand, but will he do a good job?

女：我了解，但是他能夠把事情做好嗎？

M：I'll be there to make sure he does a good job. It's
time he learned the value of hard work.

男：我會在這裡確認他把事情做好。是時候讓他學會辛苦工作的
價值了。

W：OK, well, I trust you.

女：好吧，嗯，我相信你。

Question：What has Tommy been hired to do?

湯米被雇用去做什麼？

(A) Clean the basement. 打掃地下室。

(B) Wash the car. 洗車

(C) Paint the garage. 油漆車庫。

* hire〔haɪr〕*v.* 雇用　　paint〔pent〕*v.* 油漆
  garage〔gəˈrɑʒ〕*n.* 車庫　　weekend〔ˈwikˈɛnd〕*n.* 週末
  idea〔aɪˈdiə〕*n.* 主意　　well〔wɛl〕*interj.* 嗯
  quite〔kwaɪt〕*adv.* 相當　　mature〔məˈtʃʊr〕*adj.* 成熟的
  trust〔trʌst〕*v.* 信任；相信　　job〔dʒɑb〕*n.* 工作
  do a good job 做得好　　***make sure*** 確認
  「***It's time*** + *S.* + 過去式動詞」表「是…該～的時候了」。
  value〔ˈvælju〕*n.* 價值　　hard〔hɑrd〕*adj.* 辛苦的
  clean〔klin〕*v.* 打掃；清理　　basement〔ˈbesmənt〕*n.* 地下室

17. (**C**)　M : Rumor has it you might drop out at the end of the
　　　　　　　　semester.　I hope it's not true.

　　　　男：謠傳說妳學期末可能會休學。我希望那不是眞的。

　　　　W : Unfortunately, it's very likely to happen.　My mother
　　　　　　has been diagnosed with cancer and I need to be
　　　　　　closer to home.

　　　　女：很遺憾的是，它很有可能會發生。我媽媽被診斷患有癌症，
　　　　　　所以我必須離家裡近一點。

　　　　M : I'm so sorry to hear that.　Is she going to be OK?

　　　　男：聽到這個消息我很遺憾。她會沒事吧？

　　　　W : We don't know yet.

　　　　女：我們還不知道。

　　　　Question : What might happen at the end of the semester?
　　　　　　　　　　學期末可能會發生什麼事？

　　　　(A) The man might transfer to a different school.
　　　　　　男士可能會轉去不同的學校。

　　　　(B) The man might get married.　男士可能會結婚。

　　　　(C) The woman might drop out of school.　女士可能會休學。

　　　　* rumor ('rumɚ) *n.* 謠言　　***rumor has it*** (***that***) 謠傳說
　　　　drop out 退學；休學 (= *drop out of school*)
　　　　end (ɛnd) *n.* 結束；末尾　　semester (sə'mɛstɚ) *n.* 學期
　　　　hope (hop) *v.* 希望
　　　　unfortunately (ʌn'fɔrtʃənɪtlɪ) *adv.* 遺憾地
　　　　diagnose (,daɪəg'noz) *v.* 診斷　　cancer ('kænsɚ) *n.* 癌症
　　　　close (klos) *adj.* 接近的　　sorry ('sɔrɪ) *adj.* 抱歉的；遺憾的
　　　　transfer (træns'fɝ) *v.* 轉學　　different ('dɪfrənt) *adj.* 不同的
　　　　marry ('mærɪ) *v.* 結婚；使結婚　　***get married*** 結婚

18. (**A**)　Election season is upon us and that means that you and
　　　　　your friends are probably discussing the issues and
　　　　　candidates.　Chances are, you'll end up disagreeing with
　　　　　at least some of what your friends believe politically.

選舉季即將到來，這就表示你和你的朋友可能會討論相關的議題和候選人。也許你最後會和你的朋友在政治方面，至少有一些看法會不一致。

Question： What happens during election season?

在選舉季中會發生什麼事？

(A) People express their political opinions.

人們會表達他們的政治觀點。

(B) People make friends with the candidates.

人們會和候選人交朋友。

(C) People agree with each other all the time.

人們會一直同意彼此的看法。

* election〔ɪ'lɛkʃən〕*n.* 選舉

season〔'sizn̩〕*n.* 季節；活動時期；期間

~is upon us ～快到了　mean〔min〕*v.* 意謂著

probably〔'prɑbəblɪ〕*adv.* 可能　issue〔'ɪʃu〕*n.* 議題

candidate〔'kændə,det〕*n.* 候選人　*chances are* 也許

end up + V-ing 最後…　disagree〔,dɪsə'gri〕*v.* 不一致

at least 至少　believe〔bə'liv〕*v.* 相信

politically〔pə'lɪtɪkḷɪ〕*adv.* 政治上

during〔'djurɪŋ〕*prep.* 在…的期間　express〔ɪk'sprɛs〕*v.* 表達

opinion〔ə'pɪnjən〕*n.* 意見；看法

make friends with 和…交朋友

agree〔ə'gri〕*v.* 同意　*all the time* 一直

19. (**B**) W：Here are the files you asked for.

女：這些是你要的檔案。

M：Thanks. I've got another favor to ask, if you don't mind.

男：謝謝。如果妳不介意的話，我還有另一件事要請妳幫忙。

W：Not at all. That's what I'm here for. How can I help?

女：完全不會。那正是我來這裡的原因。我可以幫上什麼忙？

M : These essays need to be corrected and the grades entered into the computer.

男：這些文章需要批改，然後要將成績輸入電腦。

Question : What is the most probable relationship between the speakers?

說話者之間最有可能是什麼關係？

(A) Supervisor and employee. 主管和員工。

(B) Teacher and assistant. 老師和助理。

(C) Brother and sister. 兄妹。

* file〔faɪl〕*n.* 檔案　　favor〔'fevɚ〕*n.* 恩惠
ask *sb.* **a favor** 請某人幫忙　　mind〔maɪnd〕*v.* 介意
not at all 一點也不　　**what…for** 爲什麼 (= *why*)
essay〔'ɛsɪ〕*n.* 論說文；短文
correct〔kə'rɛkt〕*v.* 批改；訂正　　grade〔gred〕*n.* 成績
enter〔'ɛntɚ〕*v.* 輸入　　computer〔kəm'pjutɚ〕*n.* 電腦
probable〔'prɑbəbl̩〕*adj.* 可能的
relationship〔rɪ'leʃənˌʃɪp〕*n.* 關係
between〔bə'twin〕*prep.* 在 (兩者) 之間
supervisor〔'supɚˌvaɪzɚ〕*n.* 主管
employee〔ˌɛmplɔɪ'i〕*n.* 員工　　assistant〔ə'sɪstənt〕*n.* 助理

20. (**B**) W : Excuse me. I think I got off at the wrong stop. Is this Dayton?

女：不好意思。我想我下錯站了。這裡是代頓嗎？

M : No, it's West Dayton. Where are you trying to go?

男：不，這裡是西代頓。妳想要去哪裡？

W : I'm looking for the Dayton Hospital.

女：我正在找代頓醫院。

M : Well, you're in the right place. This is the stop for the hospital. Once you exit the station, turn right. Then follow the signs.

男：嗯，妳來對地方了。這一站可以到醫院。妳一出車站，就右轉。然後就跟著路標走。

W：Thanks.

女：謝謝。

Question：What is the woman looking for?

女士正在找什麼？

(A) Her friend. 她的朋友。

(B) The hospital. 醫院。

(C) A train station. 火車站。

* ***get off*** 下車　　stop〔stɑp〕*n.* 候車站
　west〔wɛst〕*adj.* 西方的　　***look for*** 尋找
　hospital〔'hɑspɪtl〕*n.* 醫院
　right〔raɪt〕*adj.* 對的　*adv.* 向右地
　once〔wʌns〕*conj.* 一旦　　exit〔'ɛgzɪt〕*v.* 離開
　station〔'steʃən〕*n.* 車站　　***turn right*** 右轉
　follow〔'fɑlo〕*v.* 跟隨；遵循　　sign〔saɪn〕*n.* 標誌；告示

21. (**C**) M：How will we go grocery shopping?

男：我們要怎麼去雜貨店購物？

W：I know. I'll ask my dad to drive us.

女：我知道。我會要我爸開車載我們去。

M：That's a good idea. Thanks, Amy.

男：那是個好主意。謝謝，艾咪。

Question：How will they go grocery shopping?

他們要怎麼去雜貨店購物？

(A) They will take a walk. 他們會去散步。

(B) Amy will drive them. 艾咪會開車載他們去。

(C) Amy's dad will drive them. 艾咪的爸爸會載他們去。

* grocery〔'grosərɪ〕*n.* 雜貨店　　shop〔ʃɑp〕*v.* 購物
　drive sb. 開車載某人　　***take a walk*** 散步